The VAT/GST Treatment of Public Bodies

Series on International Taxation

VOLUME 41

Founding Editors

Richard Doernberg, Kees van Raad and Klaus Vogel †

Senior Editor

Professor Dr Kees van Raad,
International Tax Center, University of Leiden

Managing Editors

Professor Ruth Mason,
University of Connecticut School of Law
Professor Dr Ekkehard Reimer,
University of Heidelberg

The titles published in this series are listed at the end of this volume.

The VAT/GST Treatment of Public Bodies

Oskar Henkow

Wolters Kluwer
Law & Business

Published by:
Kluwer Law International
PO Box 316
2400 AH Alphen aan den Rijn
The Netherlands
Website: www.kluwerlaw.com

Sold and distributed in North, Central and South America by:
Aspen Publishers, Inc.
7201 McKinney Circle
Frederick, MD 21704
United States of America
Email: customer.service@aspenpublishers.com

Sold and distributed in all other countries by:
Turpin Distribution Services Ltd
Stratton Business Park
Pegasus Drive, Biggleswade
Bedfordshire SG18 8TQ
United Kingdom
Email: kluwerlaw@turpin-distribution.com

Printed on acid-free paper.

ISBN 978-90-411-4663-2

Printed and Bound by CPI Group (UK) Ltd, Croydon, CR0 4YY.

Table of Contents

List of Abbreviations

AG	Advocate General of the Court of Justice
Bulletin	Bulletin for International Taxation
Court of Justice	Court of Justice of the European Community
EESC	European Economic and Social Committee
EP	European Parliament
EU	European Union
IBFD	International Bureau of Fiscal Documentation
IVM	International VAT Monitor
OJ	Official Journal of the European Union
Prop.	(Swedish) Proposition
RÅ	Regeringsrättens årsbok
SFS	Svensk författningssamling
SOU	Statens Offentliga Utredningar
SN	SkatteNytt
TfS	Tidsskrift for Skatter og Avgifter
TFEU	Treaty on the Functioning of the European Union
UK	United Kingdom
VAT	Value Added Tax
VAT Directive	Council Directive 2006/112/EC of 28 November 2006 on the common system of value added tax, as amended

Preface

This research was financed through a post-doc position (biträdande universitetslektor) at the Department of Business law, School of Economics and Management at Lund University. A research grant that made a trip to New Zealand and Denmark possible was received from the Nordic Tax Research Council.

I would like to thank Associate Professors Henrik Stensgaard and Denis Ramsdahl Jensen and Ph.D. candidate Casper Bjerregaard Eskildsen for their help when I made a research visit to Århus University.

I am also greatly thankful to Associate Professor David White of Victoria University of Wellington for his warm welcome and generous sharing of research results – largely enhancing the quality of my research of the New Zealand GST. Thanks also to his colleagues Vanessa Borg, Nora Munhuu and others at the Centre for Accounting, Governance and Taxation Research at Victoria University of Wellington (VUW) for their friendly welcome of me and assistance during my stay in Wellington, to Marie Parlot and colleagues at the Inland Revenue and Eugen Trombitas and colleagues at PwC, for sharing so kindly with me their views on the topic of this research and the New Zealand GST at large.

Lastly, I am grateful to Professor Ben Terra of Lund University for providing me with comments on a draft of this book during the final stages of its completion.

These individuals have helped to increase the quality of this research. I am solely responsible for the shortcomings.

Oskar Henkow
Lund, October 2012

PART I

Introduction

In this part, the subject of the book is presented and placed in its context. The issues dealt with and questions addressed in the book are set out. There is also a discussion about VAT in relation to public sector activities as well as an assessment of VAT/GST systems in general and the impact of exemptions and exclusions in VAT/GST systems in general.

CHAPTER 1

VAT/GST and the Public Sector: Issues and Problems

§1.01 INTRODUCTION

A substantial part of the economy is controlled by the state – the public sector.[1] In Europe it constitutes around 15% of the economy in terms of employment and around 50% if measured on the basis of total government expenditure as a percentage of GDP.[2] Central and local government is thus, in Europe and in other parts of the world, still an important part of the economy. Actually, the modern capitalist economy is 'a thoroughly mixed system in which public and private sector forces interact in an integral fashion'.[3] This is true even though the trend has increasingly, since the 1980s, been to (perhaps) reduce and (above all) contract out functions of the public sector. The new look on public management has brought about a new situation for public sector bodies.

Around the world, consumption-types of Value Added Taxes (VAT) are raising significant revenues for government. These taxes all have in common that they aim at taxing consumption expenditure indirectly through taxing supplies of goods and services for consideration at all stages in production and distribution. They are general taxes and thereby neutral to how resources are allocated in society. The generality of these taxes implies inclusion of all economic activities, whatever form or body is involved in the provision of goods and services. It also entails a full right to immediately deduct VAT on acquisitions by non-consumers.

Presently, the European VAT system, as most VAT systems, excludes public bodies from the scope of the tax. As a consequence, public bodies are taxed on their inputs as they will be charged VAT on acquisitions made which is not deductible under

1. See further on the public sector, Section §1.03.
2. See Handler, Koebel, Reiss & Schratzenstaller (2005).
3. Musgrave & Musgrave (1989), p. 4.

the EU's (European Union's) VAT system. This creates a number of economic distortions such as a bias to self-supply instead of contracting out, a preference to integrate vertically in the supply chain, a distortion of the tax burden depending on whether the supply is made by a private sector body or a public sector body and so on (see further section §1.02[C]) In addition to the economic distortions, the actual exclusion in EU VAT has given rise to legal uncertainty in the form of interpretational and implementation difficulties in the Member States.

In order to deal with some of the distortions created by the exclusion in EU VAT, some Member States, such as Denmark and Sweden, have enacted VAT compensation schemes and allow a repayment of VAT incurred on acquisitions of public sector bodies.

In other parts of the world a different road is followed. In New Zealand, the ground-breaking decision was taken in the 1980s to include public sector bodies fully within the GST system (so-called full taxation model). Since then the full taxation model has been followed by Australia and (in principle) by Canada.

The European Commission has had the reformation of the treatment of public bodies in European VAT on its agenda since 2000.[4] In its Green paper on the future of VAT from 2010, it also raises the issue on the proper treatment of public bodies.[5] The Commission has also commissioned a study on the treatment and economic impact of exemptions in the public interest, published in 2011.[6] This study recommends that the exclusion is abolished and a full taxation model is introduced.

The overall purpose of the present study is to find a best practice with regard to the treatment of public bodies in a VAT system in general, and in the EU VAT system in particular. The research focuses on VAT systems where exclusion or inclusion of public bodies are currently being applied and how these models function. Particular focus is on the VAT/GST treatment of the income of public bodies and the treatment of input VAT incurred on acquisitions by public bodies.

The book comprises four parts of which this introduction is the first. Part II deals with the first of two basic approaches to the treatment of public bodies in a VAT system; the exclusion model. This model emanates from the EU VAT Directives, thus the EU has the longest experience with it. The EU exclusion model is therefore dealt with in depth.

Part III deals with the second of the basic approaches, namely; inclusion within the scope of the tax. As pointed out above, New Zealand was the first country to apply a full taxation model. The New Zealand GST treatment is also therefore dealt with in detail.

Part IV contains an overall evaluation of the research and discusses what might be considered as 'best practice' in relation to both the exclusion and full tax models. The character of the tax and considerations relating to political philosophy serve as benchmarks in the evaluation.

4. COM(2000) 348 final and COM(2003) 614 final.
5. COM(2010) 695 final.
6. Copenhagen Economics (2011).

The first conclusion of this study is that the VAT system's character should be kept intact and that only direct expenditure for consumption should be included in the tax base. Collective consumption should not form part of the tax base, even if applicable only in transactions between taxpayers. Second, the study concludes that public bodies should be included within the scope of the tax. Third, it is concluded that the link presently required between acquisitions and output transactions in order for the right to deduct input VAT charged on acquisitions should be abolished. Instead, input VAT on acquisitions by a public body should (in principle) be deductible.

In the next section of this chapter, the subject and purpose is discussed. Section §1.03 contains a description and analysis of the extent and meaning of the term public sector.

§1.02 SUBJECT AND PURPOSE

[A] Background to the Exclusion of Public Bodies from the EU VAT System

In the European Union, public sector bodies are excluded from the field of application of the system based on Article 13 of the VAT Directive.[7] To exclude public bodies seems also to be the most common, or even suggested, approach in other jurisdictions' VATs.[8] The reasons stipulated why public bodies are excluded vary.[9] According to Cnossen, the philosophy behind exempting public bodies is that it does not make sense to charge VAT on services funded by budgetary allocation and thereby increasing the public funding.[10] Similarly, if public bodies are taxed, tax is imposed on a purely tax-financed activity. Williams notes that:

> [g]overnmental bodies at the national, regional, and local levels are to be included as taxable persons, in the same way as any other person, if they engage in economic activity. It is appropriate to except from this full rule 'the central lawmaking and executive authority of the State,' as no useful purpose is served in normal situations by such an inclusion. These institutions rarely engage in business activities. By definition, the main activities of the State legislature and the State's central governmental agencies are sovereign activities of the state and not commercial activities. This is also true of the activities of the judiciary in the state courts.'[11]

7. Public bodies are also subject to specific regulations in the TFEU, in particular the competition rules, see Chapter 8. The treatment of public bodies (in the form of State Trading Enterprises) is also dealt with under the GATT agreement, Article XVII. It is recognised that such bodies shall receive equal treatment as regards the application of the rules of GATT, see Koul (2005), Chapter 14.
8. Compare Ebrill et al. (2001). But most commentators consider that public bodies ought to be included, see further Millar (2012).
9. Schenk & Oldman (2007), p. 283.
10. See Cnossen (1998), p. 402.
11. Williams (1996).

De la Feria states that the rationale is of a mixed political and conceptual kind.[12] According to de la Feria, on the one hand, public bodies are involved in a variety of different types of activities which has resulted in the view that the bodies are hard to tax. On the other hand (and more importantly according to de la Feria) there is a perception that the exclusion achieves social and distributional aims as non-taxation increases consumption of merit goods and diminishes the regressivity of consumption-types of VAT.[13]

The rationale behind the exclusion seems to be both practical, in that it is difficult to tax certain public body activities, and social; so-called merit goods should not be taxed and the regressivity of the tax should not be enhanced.[14] As the last-mentioned reason is of an economic kind, it will not be assessed here. Instead, the conceptual difficulties are in focus.

In the following sections, the background to the subject is provided in the form of, first, a description of the character of consumption-type VAT systems (section §1.02[B]) and second, in section §1.02[C] a description of the distortions created by exclusion for public bodies from the field of application of a VAT. Lastly, in section §1.02[D] research issues for this study are presented.

[B] The Character of Consumption-Type VATs

This research is not limited to the European VAT system. The New Zealand GST is also researched. In addition, Norwegian VAT is discussed briefly in relation to the compensation system and the question whether the compensation systems infringe Article 107 TFEU (Treaty on the Functioning of the European Union) on illegal state aid. It is therefore necessary to establish the level of comparability of the EU VAT system with the ones applied in Norway and New Zealand. To that end, the character of the VATs of Norway and New Zealand are, in addition to European VAT, discussed below. Furthermore, in the evaluation in Part IV, the character of the VAT as a tax, serves as a benchmark against which possible treatments of public bodies are measured.

I have discussed the character of *the European VAT system* in some depth previously.[15] The conclusion reached there, which also seems to conform to the generally agreed one, is that European VAT is a general, indirect tax on consumption expenditure, exactly proportionate to the price paid and collected on each transaction at each stage in the production and distribution process.[16] The tax rests on considerations relating to neutrality, neutrality in competition between producers, supplies, imported and locally acquired goods and services and neutrality with regard to taxable persons' VAT burden.[17] The tax is proportional to the price of supplies and charged at each stage of the production and distribution process and allows the amounts paid

12. De la Feria, *Intertax* (2008), p. 148.
13. This view is, as pointed out by de la Feria, also present in Ebrill et al. (2001), p. 65.
14. See further Chapter 2, section §2.01.
15. Henkow (2008), Chapter 3.
16. See Terra & Kajus (2012), Chapter 7.
17. *Ibid.* and Schenk & Oldman (2007) and Henkow *EC Tax Review* (2008).

during the preceding stages of the process to be deducted from the tax payable by a taxable person, with the result that the tax applies, at any given stage, only to the value added at that stage. The final burden of the tax rests ultimately on the consumer.

The *Norwegian VAT*[18] *Act,* does not contain a statement on the character of the tax. It is not explicitly stated in the Act that it is a tax on consumption. It is however clear that the Norwegian VAT system is a consumption-type of VAT.[19] The main provisions of the Norwegian VAT Act are structured as follows.

According to § 1-1, a tax is due on the turnover of goods and services, on the application for private use and upon imports. Turnover is defined in § 1-3 as deliveries of goods for consideration and supplies of services for consideration.

Registered businesses shall, according to § 2-1, calculate and pay VAT on their turnover and on applications for private use (uttak). A business shall register for VAT when business turnover and taxable applications for private use exceed a certain threshold. For certain non-profit organisations the threshold is higher.

Public bodies[20] and those involved in public activities are subject to the tax just like businesses when they are supplying goods and services subject to VAT above the threshold, § 2-1 of the Norwegian VAT act. However, it also follows from the VAT act that the supply of services engaged in as a public authority are exempt from tax.[21]

In addition, state entities are not subject to VAT when they are supplying services to other State entities, subject to the condition that the supplier is not conducting an economic activity. The exemption includes goods that are delivered as a natural element in a supply of services.

Exemptions are not framed as exemptions from the liability to charge output VAT but as exemptions from the scope of the Act. § 3-1of the Norwegian VAT Act specifies that turnover falling under the VAT Act is taxable. The list of exemptions in § 3 is similar to the Swedish and EU lists.

The taxable amount is everything that constitutes the consideration, § 4-1 of the Norwegian VAT Act. The right to deduct input VAT includes VAT on acquisitions used in the registered business, ° 8-1. Excess input VAT is paid back, § 11-5. No right to deduct input VAT exists for VAT on, among other things, restaurant services and business entertainment expenses, § 8-3. A system of adjustment of input VAT relating to capital goods is laid down in § 9-2 et seq. Second hand goods resellers account for VAT on their profit margin, similar to the EU scheme, § 4-5 et seq.

In conclusion, the Norwegian VAT system is a general indirect tax on consumption expenditure, collected at each stage in the production and distribution process, exactly proportionate to the price paid. Exemptions are similar to those of the Swedish VAT system. It is thus in all (here) relevant aspects comparable to the EU VAT system.

18. Lov 2009-06-19-58: Lov om merverdiavgift (Norwegian VAT act).
19. See Gjems-Onstad (2009), pp. 25–30.
20. See § 1-3(1)(k) of the Norwegian VAT act.
21. See § 3-9 of the Norwegian VAT act.

In Chapter 10 *the New Zealand GST Act*, its introduction and the main provisions of the Act are discussed in some detail. Based on the provisions of the Act, it seems to be a general, indirect tax on consumption expenditure and therefore comparable with the European VAT system. That impression is confirmed when case law is consulted. The Supreme Court of New Zealand has stated that:[22]

> GST has been likened to a turnover tax (the outputs are the turnover) but with provision for offsetting deductions (or credits) for the GST content of input costs...[D]iffering from other forms of consumption tax, GST is a multi-stage tax imposed on the value added at every stage of the business activity by which goods or services reach the ultimate consumer. It is a tax on final consumption because it is the sum of the value added by firms at each stage of the supply chain that consumers ultimately purchase and consume. Registered persons producing taxable supplies effectively operate as tax collectors on behalf of the Government and as such are not themselves subject to GST's economic incidence. That is of course consistent with the neutrality and efficiency of the revenue collection rationales that underlie the Act.

Consequently, it is clear both from this quote and the provisions of the New Zealand GST Act that the New Zealand GST shares the characteristics of the European VAT in all relevant aspects studied here.

It is apparent from the above descriptions that the EU, Norwegian and New Zealand VAT systems share a number of characteristics. VAT, as described above, is an all-stage, general indirect tax on consumption expenditure. It is, in all stages up and until the stage where a supply is made to an end consumer, designed to be completely neutral to producers and distributors who can always pass on the tax to the next stage. Effectively it is therefore a tax on consumption expenditure. The level of comparability must therefore be considered to be very high from a tax system design perspective.

[C] Distortions Created by Exemptions and Exclusions

[1] Introduction

The above characterisation of VAT as an all-stage, general indirect tax on consumption expenditure presumes that the producers and distributors are all included in the tax system and able to relieve themselves of the burden of the VAT through the method of deducting VAT charged or charging VAT on the value added. However, all VAT systems have some exclusions of certain producers or distributors and/or certain supplies from the scope of applicability. When a producer or specific supply is excluded, no output VAT is chargeable and, in principle, no input VAT deductible.

22. In *Glenharrow Holdings Ltd v. Commissioner of Inland Revenue* [2008] NZSC 116.

In European VAT, activities of public bodies are excluded from the scope of applicability of the VAT system in so far as the activities are performed under a public law regime and competition is not more than insignificantly distorted.[23]

Exclusions from VAT create distortions. Actually, the distortions created lie at the heart of the creation of the VAT system and are as such nothing new in legal literature on VAT.[24] The distortions created are now, as has been pointed out elsewhere, well understood in economic theory, yet not much research exists on quantification of the economic effects.[25] Below, the distortions are discussed.[26]

[2] Violation of the General Applicability of the Tax

Exemptions and exclusions are in themselves contrary to the very fundaments of a VAT as a general, indirect tax on consumption. They violate the generality of the tax. VAT becomes a factor taken into consideration when a choice is made on what to consume. VAT also becomes a factor in the choice of traders from whom one should acquire goods and services.[27] A VAT, as a general tax, is not intended to impact upon the efficient allocation of resources.[28] Exemptions and exclusions are foreign to the basic design and characteristics of a consumption-type VAT.

[3] Tax Cascading

VAT is a tax on consumption that is intended to be passed on and finally carried by consumers, i.e., individuals consuming goods and services. When producers' and distributors' activities are exempted from VAT, and no input VAT credit is allowed for, their sales will, provided that they can pass on the cost of the VAT,[29] include compensation for non-deductible VAT on acquisitions. When an exempt producer makes supplies to a trader that is liable to account for VAT on its supplies, the VAT charged by the trader liable to VAT will be charged on a VAT element, namely the non-deductible VAT of the exempt producer. VAT will thus be charged on VAT and the VAT cascades through the production and distribution chain.[30]

This creates economic distortions between supplies. The effective VAT rate charged by traders will depend on the magnitude of acquisitions made from exempt suppliers. Also, when exempt supplies are made to end consumers, VAT is effectively charged, but the rate is dependent upon the magnitude of non-deductible VAT in the hands of the exempt supplier. This is not only an economic distortion, where different

23. See further Chapter 2 section §2.03.
24. See for example Terra (1988), Chapter VI.
25. Gendron, *Tax Law Review* (2010).
26. See on this Ebrill et all (2001), Chapter 8, Gendron, *Tax Law Review* (2010), Terra & Kajus (2012), Chapter 7, and de la Feria, *Intertax* (2008), pp. 160–161.
27. Gendron, *Tax Law Review* (2010), p. 12.
28. Any tax affects the efficient allocation of resources. But the VAT is intended to be neutral to the choices made by consumers and producers alike.
29. Which depends on the price elasticity of the supply in question.
30. See for example Gendron, *Tax Law Review* (2010), Ebrill et al. (2001), Chapter 8.

supplies are taxed differently,[31] but it also deviates from the fundamental principle of neutrality of VAT for taxable persons inherent in a VAT system.[32]

[4] Vertical Integration and Self-Supply Bias

Public bodies perform a variety of functions and provide a variety of services to the public, companies and other public bodies. It is not, from an economic perspective, evident that a public body most efficiently performs all these functions. It may well be that they are more efficiently performed by a private entity, i.e., it may be preferable to contract out the performance of certain tasks for which a public body is responsible.[33] Public bodies performing activities under a public law regime are excluded from the scope of EU VAT. As they cannot deduct input VAT incurred, a disincentive is created against contracting out activities to third party suppliers. However, economic evidence is not present that a decision to contract out or self-supply is primarily based on VAT considerations.[34]

Be that as it may, where public bodies are excluded from the scope of VAT, and consequently cannot deduct input VAT incurred, a disincentive is created to contract out public body functions. This disincentive is foreign to the character of the VAT and can, unless justified, legitimately be questioned. This disincentive lies at the heart of this research – the compensation schemes under which VAT is refunded to public bodies are motivated by a need to establish a levelled playing field between self-supplying and contracting out public body functions.[35]

[5] Administration and Compliance Burden

All exemptions and exclusions create the need to define the excluded area and to define the borderline between the taxed and exempt, or excluded, areas. As a consequence, exemptions and exclusions are complicating the administration of, and compliance with, the VAT system. It is doubtful that the benefit of exemptions and exclusions, in

31. See Gottfried & Wiegard (1991), pp. 307–328. The authors' research suggests that these distortions are especially grave with regard to public services.
32. Terra & Kajus (2012), Chapter 7.3.1.
33. There seems to be some evidence in economic literature that contracting out is more economically efficient, especially with regard to certain activities, see Dijkgraaf & Gradus (2003), Wassenaar & Gradus (2004) and Wassenaar, Dijkgraaf & Gradus (2010). De la Feria *Intertax* (2008), considers the self-supply bias is all the more serious since the economic literature (first two articles referred to above) suggests that it may be more efficient to contract out certain activities, at p. 160. However, interestingly the importance of a solution for the VAT bias towards self-supply has not been proved. In the last mentioned article referred to, which contains an assessment of the Dutch scheme of refunds of VAT incurred by municipalities, the authors conclude that the introduction of the compensation fund, five years after its introduction, had not yet caused any significant increase in contracting out municipality activities. Municipalities state that arguments other than budgetary are leading the decision-making process, see p. 632. Proof of that it is the VAT that is the primary factor for an inefficient allocation of resources in this regard is lacking.
34. *Ibid.*
35. See further Chapter 5 to 7.

terms of lowering the cost of certain goods and services for consumers, are outweighing the cost the exclusion or exemption brings about.[36]

[D] Purpose and Method

The public sector can broadly be defined as the part of the economy that is controlled by the state. With regard to a study on the VAT treatment of public bodies, this definition gives rise to the fundamental question of whether this part of the economy should be included or excluded from the VAT system. As can be seen from the description of the effects of exclusion in section §1.02[C], there seems, at first sight, to be a strong case for a full taxation system. One might question however, whether the EU treatment really is as bad as the described distorting effects suggest or whether the New Zealand model really is so perfect that jurisdictions with exclusion models ought simply to replace these existing systems with a New Zealand style system? These are the questions which triggered this research and which form the basis for the critical analysis contained in this book.

The research concerns the two basic options available, exclusion or inclusion of public bodies within the scope of the tax, as appearing in their 'original' form, that of the EU and New Zealand respectively. The purpose of this research is to evaluate the present legal treatment of public bodies in the EU VAT system, the special compensation schemes applied in Sweden and Denmark and the treatment in New Zealand with an overall aim of establishing a best practice in VAT in general and in European VAT in particular.

As this is a legal study of the treatment of public sector bodies in a VAT system, focus is on legal issues arising and these are discussed mainly from a system design point of view.[37] The system design point of view entails the use of benchmarks towards which the legal treatment is evaluated. Above all, the character of consumption-type VATs is used as a benchmark. Inherent in a consumption-type VAT is, first, that it should ultimately tax expenditure for consumption by private individuals, second, that the tax has as broad a coverage as possible and third, that the tax is applied to all stages in the production and distribution process. The general characteristic of the tax implies that all economic activities ought to be taxed as long as they (ultimately) constitute input to consumption as evidenced by expenditure for consumption made by private individuals. The burden and complexity of administration and compliance is an additional benchmark.

The legal issues discussed are selected based on their relevance specifically in relation to the technical and legal treatment of public bodies. For example, the chargeable event is not discussed, as this is not of vital importance when the treatment is discussed from a system design point of view.[38] Focus is on the major issues in this

36. See Gendron, *Tax Law Review* (2010), p. 13.
37. Economic issues are not discussed.
38. This does not mean that no specific issues arise with regard to the chargeable event when public bodies are involved.

context, such as the treatment of public bodies as taxable persons, their right to deduct input VAT on acquisitions and the treatment of the income of public bodies.

The method applied is the traditional method of jurisprudence. The aim, as regards European Union Law, has been to use the methods of interpretation applied by the Court of Justice of the European Union.[39] One of the particular characteristics of interpreting EU law is that all language versions are equally authentic. In this study, the English, German, French, Danish, Swedish, Dutch, Italian and Spanish versions of the most important provisions have been consulted.

The starting point of the analysis is to establish the law as it stands. The legal situation is established in EU VAT, under the Swedish and Danish VAT compensation schemes for central and local government entities, and under the New Zealand GST Act. In addition, the VAT compensation schemes are discussed in relation to the prohibition against state aid in Article 107 TFEU and whether payments of compensation under the schemes constitute illegal state aid.

Also, other jurisdictions use the methods applied in Sweden and Denmark (compensation schemes) and in New Zealand (so-called full taxation models). These jurisdictions' rules are only discussed based on secondary sources and in order to contextualise the treatment from a system design perspective.

The research is of a comparative, legal kind. A comparative legal study has been conducted of the Swedish and Danish compensation systems as well as of New Zealand's GST treatment of public bodies.

Any comparative legal study entails difficulties, above all that interpretation of laws of another jurisdiction influenced by the whole legal culture and tradition of the jurisdiction in question. If a specific law is interpreted in isolation and outside its context, there is a great risk that the interpretation is wrong.[40] It is noticeable that as regards comparing VAT systems, the similarities with regard to purpose, structure and concepts used is very great.[41] Actually, it has turned out to be quite easy to compare technical features of the various VAT systems compared in this study. However, with regard to interpretational issues and the discussion of the law as it stands in above all New Zealand, difficulties have been encountered in the difference in how provisions are interpreted compared to in European VAT (and, in particular, in Sweden). With regard to New Zealand, a common law country, in order to substantiate the correctness of interpretation, the result has been benchmarked against the leading commentary on New Zealand GST.[42] The method of interpretation used for tax laws in New Zealand has also been separately researched.

There is statutory guidance in New Zealand on how a statute shall be interpreted. Section 5(1) of the Interpretation Act 1999 states that the meaning of an enactment must be ascertained from its text and in the light of its purpose.[43] In the past, a literal

39. See Henkow (2008), Chapter 1.5.
40. See Bogdan (1993), Chapter 3.
41. Thuronyi (2003), Chapter 1.2.
42. McKenzie (2008).
43. Prof. Elliffe, in a presentation at Victoria University of Wellington on March 23 2010, made the remark that how an act is interpreted under New Zealand Statutory Law and the Vienna Convention is very similar. According to the Vienna Convention on the Law of Treaties of 1969,

interpretation of tax laws has been predominant in New Zealand's courts. In a literal interpretation, the words of a provision should be given their natural or ordinary meaning. Under this approach, looking at aids outside the statue was inappropriate and revenue statutes were interpreted strictly against the state.[44] However, it now seems to be commonly considered that a purposive approach is dominant also in the courts, and not just in the Interpretation Act.[45]

What is meant by a purposive approach is a matter of debate.[46] It is nevertheless clear that tax legislation should be interpreted in the same way as other statutes.[47]

Even if the exact application of the methods of interpretation used in New Zealand's courts can be discussed, the *Alcan* case seems to be (now) accepted guidance on how to interpret statutory law and tax law in New Zealand.[48] The following can be derived from that judgment.

Words are to be given their ordinary meaning. There must be a strong and sufficient reason before words can be given some other meaning which they are capable of bearing in a particular context. When words are capable of more than one meaning and the object of the legislation is clear, the words must be given such fair, large and liberal construction as will best ensure the attainment of the object of the Act.

Not infrequently, the particular purpose is unclear. In such cases the safest guide to meaning will be found in the actual words of the statute. The question of statutory interpretation should be approached on the premise that the legislature will not have intended absurdity or injustice. Finally, one should always have regard to the total context of the words used and to the purpose of the legislation in order to arrive at the meaning intended. That 'true' meaning must be consonant with the words used, having regard to their context in the Act as a whole and to the purpose of the legislation, to the extent that this is discernible.

§1.03 THE PUBLIC SECTOR

[A] Definitions

To find an all encompassing, generally accepted and workable definition of the public sector suitable for this study is probably an impossible task. If one starts in the dictionaries, the *public sector* is defined in the Oxford Dictionary of Contemporary English as *the part of an economy that is controlled by the state.*[49] In more elaborated

Article 31.1, a treaty shall be interpreted in good faith in accordance with the ordinary meaning to be given to the terms of the treaty in their context and in the light of its object and purpose.

44. White (2005), p. 211 and Alley et al. (2010), pp. 47–49.
45. White (2005), p. 211, Harries et al (2004), p. 65 and Alley et al (2010), p. 47.
46. Harries et al (2004), pp. 65–105.
47. *C of IR v. Alcan New Zealand Ltd* (1994) 3 NZLR 439 at p. 443 McKay J. notes *inter alia* that it would be a mistake to put revenue statutes in some different category from other legislation. All statues are to be interpreted on the same basic approach.
48. *C of IR v. Alcan New Zealand Ltd* (1994) 3 NZLR 439. See White (2005) and Alley et al. (2010), pp. 48–49.
49. The importance of control has also been emphasised in other definitions of public bodies, see IMF (2009).

language, it is probably true to describe the public sector as a part of the state that deals with either the production, delivery or allocation of goods and services by and for the government or its citizens, whether national, regional or local/municipal.[50] Similarly, the Encyclopaedia Britannica defines public administration as the implementation of government policy, often also including responsibility for determining the policies and programmes of governments.

Tilly, who provides a generic definition, starts out with a definition of States as 'coercion-wielding organisations that are distinct from households and kinship groups and exercise clear priority in some respects over all other organisations within substantial territories'.[51] A core sign of clear priority must be the power to tax subordinates. A state has the right to tax those falling within the realms of its sovereignty. A definition, in the same line as Tilly, of what a state is could thus also be found in the power to tax. Those entities that have this power constitute the state.[52]

Barker's definition of the state is more connected to contemporary democratic societies. According to Barker a state is a territorial society organised as a legal association under and in virtue of a constitution. It observes a common law and it enjoys the rights and performs the duties which are guaranteed in the law. This should be contrasted with the earlier notion in Western Europe where the state has been associated with a particular family (the royal family), property (owned by a King, most commonly) and society (i.e., mixed with society and not a legal person in itself). The government, in the broader sense, is the policy-determining branch of this association. In the narrower sense it is the executive, the policy-enforcing organ. The administration is connected herewith. Administration is the collective of persons and bodies who are engaged, under the direction of government, in discharging the public services which must be rendered if the system of law and duties and rights is to be duly 'served'. Where the administration is concerned with the common services of the state, it is central and when it is concerned with the particular services of subdivisions of the state, it is local.

In a similar manner, it can be argued that to uphold the definitions and distinctions between public bodies and other bodies, a distinction must be made between *public* and *private*. The state can, as by Barker, be defined as a territorial society organised as a legal association under and in virtue of a constitution. It observes a common law and it enjoys the rights and performs the duties which are guaranteed in the law. These rights and duties are guaranteed in public law, i.e., public law determines the relationship between the individual and the state.[53] From this the distinction can generally also be obtained, namely, that 'public' refers to the rights and duties performed under the obligations ensued by the state. This is consistent with the

50. As in Wikipedia, visited on 14 sep 2010.
51. Tilly (1992), p. 1.
52. The power to tax is an inherent and omnipresent aspect of government (see Yang *IVM* 2000, referring to the US Supreme Court). It may serve as a definition of government itself.
53. Verkuil (2006).

view put forward in an IMF working paper where it was suggested that ownership and control determines which entities properly belong to the state.[54]

Consequently, how a state is defined is a matter of perspectives, and what constitutes a state seems to change over time and with social and economic preferences. From a historical and global perspective, Tilly's definition is the most compelling. If limited to democratic societies, the definitions and descriptions relying on the Rule of Law and defining what is private and public are also illuminating.

[B] Public Sector Entities

In democratic societies the core administration of a state consists of the government and its ministries, functioning in a vertically integrated hierarchy, parliament and local government.[55] Increasingly also other agencies, authorities and government bodies other than core administrative bodies (below referred to as *agencies*) have appeared to perform the functions of government.[56] Actually, the administrative landscape of the vast majority of European states includes a significant number of autonomous public bodies. These bodies take on a number of forms and operate within a wide range of frameworks depending on the historical, institutional and political peculiarities of each country.[57]

However, there can also be found a number of somewhat common denominators. First, government agencies are usually set up by law, but not necessarily. Sweden is, for example, an exception. Many agencies also have management boards, and the chief executive of an agency is most often a civil servant. Agencies are often subject to hierarchical oversight with one ministry (Sweden again being an exception based on the restrictions of ministry involvement in single cases (ministerstyre)). And ministers are usually responsible before parliament for the performance of agencies operating under their ministry. In terms of how agencies are organised, that varies significantly. Most agencies seem to be audited under a special audit function and publish annual reports and accounts. Finally, a general characteristic is that decisions are possible to appeal, i.e., there is the possibility for judicial review.[58]

To take, in this study, the relevant example of Sweden, it is noted that Sweden has both a great number and a great variety, of agencies, which vary both in size, their operation and management and so forth.[59]

54. IMF (2009). The exclusion in EU VAT seems to me to reflect this distinction between private/public (as reflected in the phrase 'governed by public law') and the concepts of ownership (public bodies) and control (acting as such, i.e., under public law), see further Chapter 1 section §2.03. Compare de la Feria, *Intertax* (2008), footnote 10. She suggests that this is a civil law distinction not clearly discernable in common law countries.
55. OECD (2002).
56. OECD (2002), pp. 9–10.
57. Flinders, Matthew (2004), p. 528.
58. See Martin (2008). See the OECD report for a discussion of the evolution, reasons behind and drivers of change and transfer of government functions to these 'looser' bodies. That may have been established to avoid administrative constraints, empower management and emphasise service delivery.
59. Martin (2008), pp. 68 - 69.

In addition to the above core and wider government, a number of companies are (often) owned by the state. These also sometimes provide public services. Thus, there are numerous forms of public bodies, which vary in size, management, ministerial supervision and involvement, legal form and so forth. Bodies falling under this wider definition of public bodies include all types of bodies, even private law companies. What distinguish these as public bodies may be said to be the involvement of the state in their activities - these bodies being entrusted with activities that the state considers should be performed by an entity that is to some degree controlled by the state.

There is a trend towards contracting out and privatising functions in core sectors such as water, energy, waste management, health and social care.[60] Increasingly, functions traditionally performed by public bodies are performed by private law entities. The VAT consequences of contracting out activities have increased the tensions in the EU VAT treatment of public bodies.

[C] Functions of Public Bodies

Public bodies are involved in very different types of activities. The activities range from core state functions such as making laws, managing the justice system and managing the monetary system and allocating funds between various sectors and to individuals in need, activities of a clear social nature such as running hospitals and schools, managing the water supply to running commercial companies such as telecommunication companies or even producing goods and services, extracting minerals etc. Actually, it seems very hard to draw up a definitive list of the activities public bodies are engaged in. However, that doesn't mean that it is impossible to distinguish certain kinds of activities, or rather functions that public bodies are engaged in. Importantly, the function of a body cannot determine whether it is public or private.[61]

First, Governments provide public goods. Public goods can be defined as a function that is non-rival and non-excludable. When a citizen enjoys such a function, that does not mean that the goods are not available for another citizen (non-rivalry) nor that a citizen is excluded from enjoying the same function (non-excluding).[62] Examples of such public goods that share the above characteristics are the defence, the police force, the justice system, infrastructure in the form of roads etc., and so forth, but also education, land registration services, registration of partnerships/marriages etc. (i.e., where an individual directly receives some 'benefit' from the provision of the function).

In an Ernst & Young study, a different definition is made of public goods and services, namely that these are the goods (and services) supplied by governments

60. I.e. the sectors studied in PSIRU (2004), see the Conclusions on p. 107.
61. See IMF (2009).
62. Musgrave and Musgrave distinguish between the following functions when discussing the major functions of taxes, in a wide sense, in society; the allocation function, the distribution function, the stabilisation function and the coordination of budget functions, see Musgrave & Musgrave (1989), pp. 6–14. It seems that the first two functions correspond to the provision of public goods and services and the redistribution of income and wealth, see Ernst & Young (1998), p. 3.

because of the failure of the market system to supply a socially optimum quantity of them.[63] In the Ernst & Young study two characteristics of public goods are pointed out (of importance in a VAT context); first, public goods are supplied on a collective basis, with no identifiable supply transactions, to individual consumers/buyers and second, it is, due to this, not possible to charge explicit fees to individual consumers - they instead have to be funded by taxes or similar mandatory charges. It seems to me that the definition of public goods in the Ernst & Young study deviates from the traditional definition. Even public goods may take the form of supplies, in the broad meaning of something yielding utility to someone, to individual consumers. Take the example of education - in many countries at least basic education is available to everyone (non-rivalry and non-excluding). Yet, to receive education clearly constitutes supplies to individuals. Even the access to a road may be seen as non-public goods as the usage of one may exclude the possibility of usage of another (from that particular road).[64] The definition provided is based on an analysis that certain services are provided as a consequence of market failure and that a distinction is made towards 'merit goods'. It seems that there is no consensus on which services are properly supplied by government, but rather that it is debated among economists exactly which functions ought to be performed by governments. Even services with a public goods-character may be supplied by others and it may be possible to charge for them, unless one applies a very narrow definition (i.e., only encompassing the defence, justice system, legislator and similar functions).

Be that as it may, certain goods and services are supplied to the collective and are enjoyed by anyone without limiting others access to them, and no exclusive individual benefit can be found. These are usually funded through taxes, as no individual supplies are made that can be identified and charged for. These are referred to in the Ernst & Young study as collective services. In addition, the traditional definition of public goods seems to include services supplied that can be enjoyed individually, but for social reasons the (full) price is not charged. These are defined as 'merit' goods in the Ernst & Young study. Both these types of activities are performed within the sphere of the *allocation* function, and hence are public goods proper under the definition most commonly applied.

Second, Governments *reallocate* funds and income. Redistribution of wealth and income merely involves transfers of income or wealth from one person, or group of persons, to another and transfers of wealth from one stage of a person's life to another (inter-temporal allocation).[65] As pointed out in the Ernst & Young study, and by me in previous research, the pure transfer of wealth does not constitute a production,

63. Ernst & Young (1998), p. 4. Whether the chicken or the egg comes first is an intriguing question yet not decisive. Musgrave & Musgrave also discusses the provision of public goods in a market failure context.
64. Compare the discussion in Musgrave & Musgrave (1989), p. 8.
65. In Ernst & Young (1998), only the transfer between individuals or groups of individuals is discussed, pp. 3–4. However, redistribution of wealth also takes place when individuals pay social security contributions on their salary and receive pensions when retiring. This is referred here to as inter-temporal allocation, following the standard denotation, see for example Attanasio et all. *Journal of Economic Literature* (2010). See also Henkow (2008), Chapter 3.

distribution or consumption activity.[66] Nothing is entering the economic cycle when income and wealth is redistributed. Only the consumption possibilities shift between individuals.

Public bodies do not exclusively engage in the function of reallocating funds. Financial institutions provide services facilitating inter-temporal allocation and whenever a donor gives of her wealth to the needy, allocation occurs – in both cases outside the sphere of the Government. However, it is a characteristic of certain activities of government that they serve the function of allocation.

Third, Governments provide *regulatory* services. There are a number of services performed by public bodies, some more specific to public bodies than others. Services are sometimes provided under a special legal (public law) regime where only public bodies are allowed to perform the services/functions in question. These services form a category of themselves in the Ernst & Young study, referred to as regulatory services.[67] These services, it is argued there, cannot be supplied in the private sector as they are made exclusively in public administration and government functions, such as passports, motor vehicle registration, registration of land, building permits etc. It is furthermore argued in the study, that it is therefore also difficult to apply commercial principles in setting the prices of the services. It seems to me that this category is not as easily defined as one may think at first sight. Also, private entrepreneurs may perform services that have a public administration function. This category seems to depend upon the legal regime applicable, rather than the function in itself.

Lastly, a number of services are performed by public bodies that potentially can also be, and are more and more frequently during the last decades, performed by private sector entities. Examples of such services are supplies of electricity, natural gas, water, telecommunications, commercial production of goods and services, postal services and public transport services.[68] Some of these services may perhaps be seen as public goods in some countries; or at least as merit goods. Yet most of these supplies are made by public bodies since at one point in time it seemed proper (or perhaps profitable) that government engaged in the activity in question. Actually, these activities are very diverse. In Sweden, the state is engaged in running shops for selling alcohol, mining minerals and supplying electricity for example. In New Zealand, the state was, prior to the shift in policy in the 1980s, engaged in a number of more commercial enterprises, such as running an oil refinery. Exactly which activities states are engaged in and what is considered proper to engage in varies over time and depends on political preference.

[D] Conclusions

It is difficult to find an all encompassing and useful definition of the public sector. It is submitted here that a proper definition in an economic context is to view it as the part of the economy that is controlled by the state. The state can furthermore be defined as

66. Ernst & Young (1998), pp. 3–4 and Henkow (2008), Chapter 3.
67. Ernst & Young (1998), p. 5.
68. Compare examples listed in the Ernst & Young (1998), p. 6.

an organisation that is distinct from households and kinship groups and exercises clear priority in some respects over all other organisations within a substantial territory. Public sector bodies, which take a variety of forms, may on the one hand, following the definition, even comprise limited liability companies controlled by the state. Public bodies can on the other hand also be defined as those judicially belonging to the state.

It has proved impossible to define the public sector based on the functions performed by it. Yet, the functions performed are interesting to assess in the light of a consumption-type VAT. Two functions can be distinguished, based on their character and the fact that they do not neatly fit into the VAT system: the function of allocation, in the form of the provision of public goods, and the function of reallocation the redistribution of wealth and income.

The pure redistribution of wealth and income does not fall within the field of application of VAT. Public bodies are involved in such redistribution and there is thus a need to distinguish the consequences for public bodies of the fact that the VAT system does not cover this particular activity. In Chapter 15 this issue is discussed further.

The provision of public goods in the present context can be defined as the provision of collective services. In principle, these services are not provided to specific individuals, or a specific group of individuals and are thus not rendering direct utility to individuals (thereby, instead, resulting in collective consumption). The functions resulting in collective consumption are not reserved for the public sector but also performed by the private sector.[69] This is so as regards regulatory services, merit goods and services and other collective consumption goods.

However, individuals may pay for collective services to be performed when they are receiving a benefit from the fact that the services are provided. One example is a company running a shopping mall that pays a public body for a road to be constructed. Public goods are non-rivalry; all members of the public get to use the road. The road however also renders, specifically to the company, the benefit of smoother access to the mall. The service provided by the public body is a collective service, building a road for everyone to use, but it also yields direct utility to the company in question. In a VAT system, these situations, i.e., when a direct payment is made to a public body with a view to the public body performing certain collective services which will have the additional effect of bringing a specific benefit to a particular person, ought to be distinguished from situations in which no individual benefit is rendered and paid for directly.

With regard to the VAT/GST treatment of public bodies, a distinction could therefore be made between collective services paid for through taxes and subsidies, those funded by fees and dues and those for which some other form of consideration is received. With regard to collective services paid for through taxes or subsides, there is no direct payment for any services provided. In principle therefore, collective services funded through taxes or subsidies should not fall within the scope of VAT. On the other hand, any consideration received which could be linked to the provision of collective services (as in the above example of the road construction) should in

69. Pension funds allocate funds as the state does. Associations may build roads free for anyone to use, and so on.

principle fall within the scope of VAT. Fees and dues are in principle linked to direct services as they are only paid when services are provided. The problem with this distinction is that it is not based on the function or character of the activities performed and services provided but on the means of their funding. There is thus a tension between the differentiation in VAT/GST treatment based on how activities are funded and the fact that the same type of activity could be funded in different ways. The functions, as discussed in this chapter, are not different just because funding differs.

Part II
Exclusion Systems

In this part, the original and most common treatment of public bodies in a VAT system, i.e., exclusion from the scope of the system, is discussed. An in-depth legal analysis of the treatment of public bodies in the EU VAT system is provided. The focus is on the extent of the exclusion from the scope of the system, the treatment of income of public bodies, the deduction of input VAT and other issues.

This part of the book also contains an appraisal of compensation schemes enacted in order to mitigate the preference to self-supply inherent in the exclusion model and the compatibility of such systems with the prohibition against state aid in the TFEU. The compensation schemes applicable in Denmark and Sweden are examined in-depth.

CHAPTER 2

The Exclusion of Public Bodies from the Scope of European VAT

§2.01 INTRODUCTION

European VAT is designed to be a general, indirect tax on consumption expenditure with as broad a base as possible. Despite this, there are several exclusions from the VAT base in the VAT Directive. One of these concerns public bodies. Article 13 of the VAT Directive defines when states, local and regional government are excluded from the scope of European VAT. In addition, several other provisions of the VAT Directive refer to public bodies. These are discussed in the present chapter.[1]

Article 13(1) of the VAT Directive thus regulates situations where a public body is not performing economic activities. Article 9 of the VAT Directive contains the main provision on the scope of the concept of taxable person stating that a taxable person is anyone engaged in economic activities. It is clear from case law,[2] and from how the provision is worded, that a public body must perform an economic activity, thus falling within the scope of Article 9, in order for the exclusion in Article 13 to be actualised. Therefore it must first be ascertained whether a public body's activities constitute economic activities for the purposes of Article 9.[3]

1. Public bodies perform state functions. Consequently, references are made to public bodies in the VAT Directive which do not concern the treatment for VAT purposes of public bodies as such. For example, Article 62(2) defines the chargeable event as the point in time when the tax authorities becomes entitled under the law to claim the tax. These kinds of provisions are not discussed further in this Chapter.
2. See, for example, Case C-288/07 *Isle of Wight Council and others*, pp. 29–31.
3. De la Feria *Intertax* (2008) states that overall two fundamental questions arise; is the transaction taxable or non-taxable, and, if it is taxable, is it exempt or not exempt (at p. 149). As is obvious from my analysis I see it differently. First, it must be determined whether the public body activity is at all an economic activity falling within the scope of the EU VAT system. Second, whether the public body is acting as such must be determined. Third, it must be

It should be noted that not all activities of public bodies are excluded from the scope of VAT. If that were the case the exemption for their activities in Article 132 would not be necessary.[4]

§2.02 PUBLIC BODIES' ACTIVITIES AS NON-ECONOMIC ACTIVITIES

Article 9 of the VAT Directive defines a taxable person as:

> ... any person who, independently, carries out in any place any economic activity whatever the purpose or results of that activity.
>
> Any activity of producers, traders or persons supplying services, including mining and agricultural activities and activities of the professions, shall be regarded as 'economic activity'.
>
> The exploitation of tangible or intangible property for the purposes of obtaining income therefrom on a continuing basis shall in particular be regarded as an economic activity.

The provision has been interpreted very widely so as to include all types of economic activities and activities at all stages of a business – at start-up and rounding-up of a business.[5] The Court has consistently held that (now) the VAT Directive confers a very wide scope on value added tax, comprising all stages of production, distribution and the provision of services and that in accordance with the requirements of the principle that the common system of value added tax should be neutral, the term 'exploitation' refers to all transactions, whatever may be their legal form, by which it is sought to obtain income from the goods in question on a continuing basis.[6] Furthermore, the term 'economic activities' is objective in character, in the sense that the activity is considered per se and without regard to its purpose or results.[7]

In accordance herewith, even transactions forming a part of a carousel fraud have been found to constitute economic activities for the purposes of Article 9.[8] Consequently, all activities entailing transactions by which it is sought to obtain income, which are performed independently,[9] constitute economic activities, as long as an income is received that can be linked to the performance of the activities (something which is discussed in the next section).

---

determined whether the activity potentially distorts competition. Lastly, whether the activity is exempt or taxed finally settles whether output VAT is to be accounted for. The analysis in Copenhagen Economics' study of 2011 seems to concur with the approach advocated here.

4. See Case 107/84 *Commission v. Germany*, point 15, where the Court of Justice stated with reference to the exemption for public postal services that it follows from the rules that even if postal activities are assigned to bodies governed by public law, the exemption and the reference to it contained in (now) Article 13(2) are necessary to exempt the whole of those activities, of which only a part may be regarded as the activities of a public authority in the strict sense.
5. The wide scope of Article 9 has been thoroughly discussed elsewhere, see for example Terra & Kajus (2012), Chapter 9, with reference to the case law of the Court of Justice.
6. Case C-186/89 *van Tiem*, pp. 17–18.
7. See, for example, Case C-267/08 *SPÖ*, p. 17.
8. Case C-354/03 *Optigen and others* and, compare, Case C-285/09 *R*. Yet, the supply of illegal goods does not fall within the scope of VAT, see Case C-158/98 *Coffeshop Sibirië*.
9. Independently' is referring to contracts of employment and similar ties, see Article 10 and, for example, Case C-355/06 *van der Steen*.

In a number of cases, the Court of Justice has dealt with various financial activities and whether they constitute 'economic activities' within the meaning of Article 9(1). It is clear from case law that the mere holding of shares and other equity is not an economic activity. However, when the activity amounts to commercial share dealing, or shares are acquired or held in order to secure a direct or indirect involvement in the management of the companies in which the holdings have been acquired, or where the activity constitutes the permanent and necessary extension of the taxable activity, the activity comes within the scope of VAT.[10] This case law may be difficult to apply for public bodies, yet it is not specific to public bodies but applies to all persons engaged in financial activities. For this reason it is not discussed further here.

In two cases, *Hutchison 3G and others* and *T-Mobile Austria and others*, the Court of Justice has found, contrary to the proposal of AG (Advocate General of the Court of Justice) Kokott, that public bodies' activities of issuing 3G-licences do not constitute an economic activity for the purposes of (now) Article 9 of the VAT Directive.[11] In *Hutchison 3G and others* the United Kingdom allocation of 3G-licences is dealt with and in *T-Mobile Austria and others* the Austrian allocation of 3G-licences is dealt with. The cases were decided on the same day and based on the same reasoning and are therefore dealt with jointly here.

The use of a certain radio-frequency is regulated in EU law by a directive on a common regulatory framework for electronic communication networks and services. The directive has been implemented on the national level in both the UK and Austria and the applicable national law prescribed for authorisation by way of a licence, to use a certain frequency.

The Secretary of the state in the UK (see *Hutchison 3G and others*) and the Telecom-Control-Kommission (*T-Mobile Austria and others*) allocated licences to use certain frequencies (third-generation mobile communications licences, 3G-licences and, in the case of Austria, GSM frequencies as well) by public auction. The undertakings which obtained those licences were those that bid the most money for the frequency lots offered, one of those lots being reserved for a new entrant in the market.

No reference to VAT was made during the auction procedure. The tendering companies, however, sought to recover the sums which they claim to have paid as input VAT (in the UK as a claim for deduction and in Austria as a request to have invoices issued with VAT from the authorities so that VAT could be deducted) under national legislation transposing (now) Article 168 of the VAT Directive. The tendering companies considered that the allocations in question were subject to VAT and that the VAT was included in the amounts paid. In both Austria and the United Kingdom, references were made to the Court of Justice by the national courts where these claims were tried with questions relating to whether VAT should be charged on the transactions in question.

The Court of Justice initially pointed to the wide scope of the common system of VAT and pointed out that it needed to be established whether the allocation of rights to

10. See, for example, Case C-29/08 *AB SKF*, pp. 28–31 and Henkow (2008), Chapter 5.
11. Case C-369/04 *Hutchison 3G and others* and Case C-284/04 *T-Mobile Austria and others*.

use a certain frequency constituted an exploitation of property for the purposes of (now) Article 9. In its assessment of that question, the Court pointed to the fact that the allocation was regulated by EU law and on the national level, the purpose of which was, *inter alia*, ensuring the effective use of the frequency spectrum and the avoidance of harmful interference between radio-based telecommunications systems and other space-based or terrestrial technical systems, and also the efficient management of radio frequencies. For these reasons, the issuing of such authorisations fell exclusively within the competence of the Member State concerned. The Court found that the activity in question constituted a necessary pre-condition for the access of economic operators to the mobile telecommunications market. It could not constitute participation in that market by the competent national authority. Only the operators, who were the holders of the rights granted, operated on the relevant market by exploiting the property in question for the purpose of obtaining income therefrom on a continuing basis.

The Court concluded that in those circumstances, an activity such as that at issue couldn't, by its very nature, be carried out by economic operators. In granting such an authorisation, the competent national authority was not participating in the exploitation of property, consisting in rights to use the radio-frequency spectrum for the purpose of obtaining income therefrom on a continuing basis. By means of that allocation procedure, that authority exclusively carried out the activity of controlling and regulating the use of the electromagnetic spectrum which had been expressly delegated to it. The activity of issuing the licences did therefore not constitute an 'economic activity' within the meaning of Article 9(1) of the VAT Directive.

In *Götz*, the Court of Justice, on its own accord and before answering the questions put by the national court on the interpretation of Article 13, raised the issue whether the activity in question constituted an economic activity falling within the scope of VAT.[12] The activity at issue consisted in gathering, for a given milk marketing year, the objectives of milk producers, in order to allow those who planned to produce at below the threshold applicable to them to sell the delivery reference quantities which they thought they would not use and to allow those who intended, conversely, to exceed that threshold to purchase the corresponding delivery reference quantities without being caught by the additional levy provided for by Regulation No 3950/92. That activity also involved making the offer and the application overlap by fixing a mean price, receiving the delivery reference quantities sold and allocating them to purchasers and receiving and then paying the sums agreed upon for the transfer of those reference quantities.[13]

The Court found that the activity must be treated as a supply of services, as a result of which the offers and the applications of milk producers are compared, thereby allowing a mean price to be set. Consequently, unlike the activity at issue in the case which gave rise to the judgment in *T-Mobile Austria and others*, the activity in question did appear to be capable, as a matter of principle, of being carried out by economic operators.

12. Case C-408/06 *Götz*, pp. 14–23.
13. See Case C-408/06 *Götz*, p. 19.

In conclusion, in European VAT, activities that cannot be engaged in by economic operators, because of the fact that a special legal regime renders economic operators excluded from the activity, and the activity does not in itself entail any exploitation of property for the purpose of making income (such as the activity of regulating and controlling certain frequencies in the electromagnetic spectrum), do not constitute 'economic activities' for the purposes of Article 9 of the VAT Directive.

The standpoint of the Court can, in my view, legitimately be criticised.[14] Regulatory services may, clearly, come within the scope of VAT, as pointed out by AG Kokott in *Hutchison 3G and others* p. 55. Annex I lists public bodies' activities that are always subject to VAT, unless provided on such a small scale as to be negligible. Point 7 of Annex I refers to 'transactions in respect of agricultural products, carried out by agricultural intervention agencies pursuant to Regulations on the common organisation of the market in those products'. It should be added that according to Article 14(2)(a) of the VAT Directive, in addition to the supplies of goods covered by the general rule in Article 14(1), 'the transfer, by order made by or in the name of a public authority or in pursuance of the law, of the ownership of property against payment of compensation' shall also be considered to constitute a supply of goods.

The Court stated that the finding that the issuing was not an economic activity was not called into question by the argument that, having regard to (now) Article 13, it was not inconceivable that a regulatory activity carried out by a body governed by public law may constitute an economic activity, so that that body would have to be considered a taxable person in respect of that activity.[15] Even if such a regulatory activity could be classified as an economic activity, the fact still remains that the application of (now) Article 13 implies a prior finding that the activity considered is of an economic nature.

I fail to see the point of this argument, unless the Court is not only saying that it needs first to be established whether the activity is of an economic character and that the necessity is not affected by whether the activity is a regulatory one or not. Clearly, regulatory services may, in a contextual analysis of the VAT Directive, fall within the scope of VAT.

The question arises of whether there really are any functions that, by their very nature, cannot be performed by an entity other than the state. The Court clearly considers the issuing of the licences at issue to be one such function. But it seems to me that this conclusion was dependent upon, above all, the fact that the activity could not be performed by private entities under applicable regulations. The regulations governing the performance of the activity brought about its non-economic character. The

14. I would have preferred the Advocate General's approach. She concluded that the activities were 'economic activities' falling within the scope of European VAT. The AG instead distinguished the issuing of the licences as an activity engaged in by a public body under a public law regime and not being a 'telecommunication service', which is an activity explicitly included within the scope of VAT by Article 13 and Annex I. She uses the same argument, that the activity simply cannot be undertaken by private companies, but then to motivate her conclusion that Article 13 applies.

15. See Case C-369/04 *Hutchison 3G and others* pp. 41–42 and Case C-284/04 *T-Mobile Austria and others* pp. 47–48.

allocation of frequencies *could* be entrusted a private law entity. The EU legislator and the Member States just considered that it should be entrusted to a state organ. The nature of the activity as non-economic is thus, in the case law of the Court, determined by the legal regime applicable. As a consequence, the position of the Court is contingent upon the status of development of the law and the degree of privatisation of Government activities. If the management and regulation of frequencies in the electromagnetic spectrum were entrusted to one or several economic operators, it seems that the arguments of the Court do not hold ground. The activity as such could be performed as an economic activity.[16]

But the question remains whether there are really any functions that, by their intrinsic nature cannot be performed by an entity other than the state. It seems to be that it is possible, if not advisable, to contract out any function of a state. In the final analysis, all services performed can be performed by persons/entities not being employed by, or part of, the state.[17]

The distinction provided by the Court is furthermore not, in my view, consistent with the general characteristics of the VAT. Public bodies are not consumers and should therefore properly be excluded from the burden of VAT. Here the paradox of VAT comes into play – by including them in the VAT system, public bodies are excluded from the burden of VAT which is clearly the preferred treatment. It is therefore more correct to view public bodies as service providers (taxable persons) than consumers. Lastly, the objective character of 'economic activities' is lost when the classification is dependent upon the public law regime applicable to the activity.

Be that as it may, the Court of Justice has found that the issuing of 3G-licences is not an economic activity for VAT purposes. It needs therefore to be discussed what other activities that should be equally treated.

In the proceedings before the Court of Justice, reference had been made to competition law cases as support for the conclusion that where the powers of a public authority are exercised there is no economic activity. The AG commented on this by pointing out that competition law and the common VAT system are based on differing concepts of economic activity.[18] Under competition law, the exercise of public authority is considered to be the criterion precluding an activity from having relevance for competition purposes. No separate provision is made there, however, for the activities of a state when exercising public authority. In contrast hereto, the AG points out that

16. I note that the line of reasoning in the cases dealt with in this section has been followed by the Court of Justice with regard to the activities of a political party in Case C-267/08 *SPÖ*. In that case the Court states that 'the SPÖ is therefore carrying out a communication exercise in keeping with attainment of its political objectives and which seeks to spread its ideas as a political organisation. More specifically, the SPÖ's activity, particularly through the intermediary of the Landesorganisation, is the development of informed political opinion with a view to participation in the exercise of political power. In carrying out that activity, the SPÖ does not however participate in any market.' The activity was therefore not an economic activity within the meaning of Article 9.
17. With the exclusion, perhaps, of the head of the state, compare the reasoning behind the public sector reform of New Zealand in the 1980s, see Chapter 10 below.
18. See the Opinion of Advocate General Kokott in Case C-369/04 *Hutchison 3G and others* pp. 57–59.

the concept of economic activity in (now) the VAT Directive is wider than its corresponding term under competition law. The exercise of public authority is not initially a factor here. That element is not taken into consideration until a later stage of appraisal, that is to say in the context of the special provision in (now) Article 13. That provision would be virtually superfluous if, by analogy with competition law, there were to be no scope at all for the application of the (now) VAT Directive in the case of acts by public authorities.

Despite these, in my view, convincing arguments for not applying cases on competition law and the concept of economic activities and public bodies in the sphere of VAT, the Court of Justice did just that. After reaching the conclusion that the issuing was not an exploitation of property it adds, with reference to a competition law case,[19] that the fact that the issuing of licences such as those at issue in the main proceedings gives rise to a payment cannot affect the legal status of that activity.

The concept of 'economic activities' in competition law is dealt with in some detail in section §8.04 below. In EU competition law, a distinction must be drawn between a situation where the state acts in the exercise of official authority and that where it carries on economic activities of an industrial or commercial nature by offering goods or services on the market.[20] In order to make the distinction between the two situations, it is necessary to consider the nature of the activities carried on by the public undertaking or body on which the state has conferred special or exclusive rights. It is in this context that the Court in *Cali* stated that the levying of a charge that forms an integral part of the exercise of the official authority cannot affect the legal status of the activity.

The Court in *Hutchison 3G and others* referred to this statement without further explanations. It is hard to read the statement and reference as meaning anything else other than that when determining the scope of what constitutes an economic activity for the purposes of Article 9 in the VAT Directive, no regard shall be had to whether the activity in question is charged for. The fact that it is charged for does not make it an economic activity. However, that statement is hard to reconcile with, above all, *Hong Kong Trade Development Council*,[21] where the Court effectively held that the status of taxable person in (now) Article 9 (the objective liability to tax) cannot be separated from the issue of whether the activity was paid for and therefore comes within the scope of (now) Article 2 (the subjective liability to tax). Consequently, even if the assessment of whether an economic activity is present should be undertaken without regard being had to the fact of whether the activity in question is charged for with fees, consideration being directly linked to supplies made is a pre-condition for the activity to come within the scope of the VAT Directive anyway. The Court's statement is thus only relevant when determining whether the activity is an economic activity at all, and not when determining whether the activity actually falls within the scope of VAT.

19. Case C-343/95 *Cali*.
20. Case C-343/95 *Cali* pp. 16–24.
21. Case 89/81 *Hong Kong Trade Development Council*.

When an activity is of a non-economic nature, the fact that charges are made for the activity does not change its non-economic nature.[22]

The question arises, however, of to what extent competition law case law on the concept of economic activity is relevant when determining the concept in VAT, except for the fact that whether a payment is made is not relevant in either system. It is noted in section §8.04 that the Commission considers case law on Article 9(1) of the VAT Directive to be relevant in competition law based on the principle that competition law and VAT share the aims of elimination of distortions of competition. It seems to me that this is not an argument strong enough for considering competition law case law to be directly applicable in the sphere of VAT. Reference is made to the discussion above and arguments presented by AG Kokott. However, it can definitely not be ruled out that the Court will infer more competition law cases in the sphere of VAT to determine the content of the concept of 'economic activities'. With the reference in *Hutchison 3G and others* the Court has opened up for inferring competition law cases.

§2.03 THE EXCLUSION OF PUBLIC BODIES FROM THE SCOPE OF VAT

[A] Context and Structure of the Exclusion

As noted in section §2.02, the definition of what constitutes economic activities in Article 9 confers a very wide scope on European VAT. Actually, the only explicit exclusion is for employees, i.e., persons acting dependently but then only in an employer-employee relationship.[23] All other persons engaged in any kind of economic activity are taxable persons for the purposes of European VAT, with the exception of public bodies when their activities are covered by Article 13 of the VAT Directive:

> Article 13 reads as follows[24]:
>
> 1. States, regional and local government authorities and other bodies governed by public law shall not be regarded as taxable persons in respect of the activities or transactions in which they engage as public authorities, even where they collect dues, fees, contributions or payments in connection with those activities or transactions.
>
>   However, when they engage in such activities or transactions, they shall be regarded as taxable persons in respect of those activities or transactions where their treatment as non-taxable persons would lead to significant distortions of competition.
>
>   In any event, bodies governed by public law shall be regarded as taxable persons in respect of the activities listed in Annex I, provided that those activities are not carried out on such a small scale as to be negligible.

22. This was also clarified by the Court itself in Case C-408/06 *Götz*, p. 21, where the Court states that it is necessary to determine, in order for an activity to fall within the scope of VAT, whether it is done for consideration, but the fact that an activity is paid for does not per se mean that a given activity is economic.
23. Case C-355/06 *van der Steen*.
24. A linguistic comparison is made in the sections below, in connection to the discussion of the conditions of the provision.

> 2. Member States may regard activities, exempt under Articles 132, 135, 136, 371, 374 to 377, and Article 378(2), Article 379(2), or Articles 380 to 390, engaged in by bodies governed by public law as activities in which those bodies engage as public authorities.

The provision constitutes a limitation of the broad scope of European VAT. It is clear from Articles 14(2)(a) and 25(c) (discussed in section §2.03[E]) that supplies made pursuant to a law and not a contract are also taxable transactions. It also follows from the wording of Article 13 that the activities of public bodies in principle fall within the scope when involved in an activity for consideration ('even where they collect dues, fees, contributions or payments... ') whatever form the consideration may take, but when they are engaged in activities governed by public law they ought not be treated as taxable persons.

Article 13(1) in its first paragraph excludes public bodies when engaged in activities as public bodies from the sphere of taxable persons. In order for Article 13(1) first paragraph to be applicable, it is clear from case law that two cumulative conditions needs to be fulfilled, the body has to be a public body and it has to 'act as such', i.e., engage in activities as a public body.[25] The Court has held that the derogation provided for covers principally activities engaged in by bodies governed by public law acting as public authorities, which, while fully economic in nature, are closely linked to the exercise of rights and powers of public authority. The fact that such bodies are subject to VAT on those activities does not potentially have an anticompetitive effect, inasmuch as they are generally engaged in exclusively, or almost exclusively, by the public sector.[26] Article 13(1) first subparagraph is dealt with in sections §2.04[C] and §2.04[D] below.

Article 13(1) second and third paragraphs reduce the scope of the exclusion in cases where there is a significant distortion of competition (second paragraph) or where the activity as such is presumed to result in distortions of competition (third paragraph). These activities are listed in Annex 1 of the VAT Directive. Even if a public body (performing an economic activity) acts as a public body it shall thus in two situations, covered by the second and third paragraphs of Article 13(1), not be treated as such. The Court of Justice has made important statements on the structure of the provision and the exclusions.[27] A public body may be responsible for carrying on certain activities of an essentially economic nature where those same activities can also be carried on in parallel by private operators, with the result that the treatment of that body as non-taxable person may give rise to distortions of competition.[28] According to the Court, it is that undesirable result that is sought to be avoided by specifying that certain activities (listed in Annex I) are 'in any event', unless they are negligible, subject to VAT.[29] In other words, the activities listed in the Annex are presumed to lead

25. These two criteria were originally formulated in Case C-107/84 *Commission v. Germany*, point 15 and Case C-235/85 *Commission v. Netherlands*.
26. Case C-288/07 *Isle of Wight Council and others*, pp. 31–39.
27. Case C-288/07 *Isle of Wight Council and others*.
28. Case C-288/07 *Isle of Wight Council and others*, p. 33.
29. Case C-288/07 *Isle of Wight Council and others*, p. 34.

to distortions of competition.[30] Furthermore, there may exist on the national level other activities of an essentially economic nature, not listed in Annex I, which are also carried on in parallel by public bodies and private operators.[31] It is precisely to these activities that the second paragraph applies.[32] Consequently, the second and third paragraphs are closely linked and pursue the same objective of limiting the scope of the exclusion provided for in the first paragraph of (now) Article 13(1), subjecting public bodies to VAT in line with the general characteristics of the VAT system.[33] The two paragraphs shall consequently be interpreted as a whole[34] and are dealt with in section §2.04[E].

The phrase 'in any event' consequently indicates, as a clarification, that with regard to certain activities, there is no need to see whether they fall within the exclusion in the first paragraph of Article 13(1) or whether their exclusion would lead to a distortion of competition – they fall within the scope of VAT in any case, provided that they are performed to a more than negligible extent. Since the list of activities in Annex I includes primarily non-public administration activities, the conclusion must be that the exclusion in the first paragraph does not rule out the situation that such activities are covered. The exclusion therefore is quite wide – potentially covering all types of activities engaged in by public bodies with the limitation that they are governed by public law and do not give rise to significant distortion of competition or are listed in Annex I and performed to a more than negligible extent. The AG in *Câmara Municipal do Porto* seems not to agree when he states in point 34 of his opinion that:

> it cannot conversely be inferred from the application of the definition criterion of the nature of the legal regime that any activity, that is to say even a purely commercial one, could be declared an activity engaged in as a public authority by a regime of public law. If that were so, there would be no need for the fourth subparagraph of Article 4(5) under which activities exempt under Article 13 – these are predominantly ones which serve the public good or are in the public interest (such as the renting out of accommodation) – may be considered as activities which bodies engage in as public authorities. The provision of the third subparagraph of Article 4(5) would also otherwise be inconsistent, since it conversely makes certain activities – possibly also those engaged in as public authorities – subject to VAT.

Considering the Court's statements in *Isle of Wight Council and others* the AG's conclusions seem incorrect.

Based on the wording and context, the first purpose of the provision seems to be to exclude all activities of public bodies when performed under a public law regime. Potentially, the provision covers a range of activities performed also by private law entities. It is exactly this situation, and the distortions of competition that may arise, that the second and third paragraph regulates. The second purpose is thus to ensure that public bodies are not treated as non-taxable persons when they potentially (or

30. Case C-288/07 *Isle of Wight Council and others*, p. 35.
31. Case C-288/07 *Isle of Wight Council and others*, p. 36.
32. Case C-288/07 *Isle of Wight Council and others*, p. 37.
33. Case C-288/07 *Isle of Wight Council and others*, p. 38.
34. Case C-288/07 *Isle of Wight Council and others*, p. 39.

actually) compete substantially with private law entities, i.e., to ensure compliance with the principle of neutrality of the tax.[35]

[B] History and Reform Suggestions of the Exclusion of Public Bodies

The preparatory acts of European VAT do not contain any information on the treatment of public bodies.[36] The First Directive was silent upon the treatment of public bodies. The Second Directive contains a statement on the treatment of public bodies in Annex A(2), which explains Article 4 of the Second Directive containing the definition of 'taxable person'. According to the Annex, regional and local government bodies and other public corporate bodies shall not as a general rule be considered as taxable persons in respect of activities which they pursue in their official capacity as official authorities.[37]

Article 4(5) of the Proposal for a Sixth Directive excluded states, regional and local government authorities, and other bodies governed by public law as regards their activities pursued as public authorities from the scope of VAT. However, the second paragraph stated that where they carry out transactions covered by paragraph 1,[38] they shall be considered to be taxable persons in respect of such transactions. Furthermore, the second paragraph, containing a list of activities that ought to be considered as carried out by a taxable person, explicitly referred to activities of broadcasting authorities, and of the agricultural intervention agencies in respect of dealings in agricultural products in pursuance of a Regulation on the common organisation of the market in the relevant product.[39] The Explanatory Memorandum to Article 4 provided the following comment as regards public bodies[40]:

> Lastly, it is provided that legal persons governed by public law must be treated as taxable persons to the extent that they pursue economic activities not inherently those of a public authority, that is to say activities which could be pursued by persons governed by private law without usurping the basic functions and powers of the State, provinces, communes and other public law bodies in general administration, the administration of justice, or national security or defence. A particular result of this definition is that the management of motorways, canals or harbours constitutes a taxable economic activity.

The Commission later published amendments to its original proposal. The second paragraph was amended as follows:[41]

35. Notably, the Court of Justice has not stated what the purpose of the exclusion is. However, the Court has discussed the purpose of the limitations of the exclusion. The suggested purpose is also supported by the history of the provision, see next section.
36. There are no comments on the treatment, neither in the ABC-reports nor the Neumarkt report.
37. See Terra & Kajus, *A Guide to the European VAT Directives (online)*, Part 3.1, Chapter 4.9.1.
38. Paragraph 1 read: 'Taxable person' means any person who independently and regularly carries out in any place transactions pertaining to the occupations specified in paragraph 2, or who occasionally carries out one of the transactions specified in paragraph 3, whatever the purpose or results of such occupations or transactions may be.
39. See the proposal for a Sixth Directive (1973), p. 36.
40. See the proposal for a Sixth Directive (1973), p. 8.
41. See, Commission Amendments to the Sixth Council Directive, p. 35.

> However, where they carry out transactions covered by paragraph 1 which, from the economic point of view, and independently of national legislation, would be likely to be carried out by persons governed by private law, they shall be considered to be taxable persons in respect of such transactions. This provision extends to the activities of broadcasting authorities, and of the agricultural intervention agencies in respect of dealings in agricultural products in pursuance of a Regulation on the common organization of the market in the relevant product.

In its Memorandum to the amendment the Commission gave the following explanation:[42]

> A more precise definition of the circumstances in which bodies governed by public law must be treated as taxable persons has been requested in various quarters. The proposed new text, while referring back to transactions (production, trade, etc.) as defined in paragraph 1 of that Article, specifies that they must be transactions which could be carried out by persons governed by private law:
>
> (a) from the economic point of view
> (b) independent of national legislation.
>
> The first condition is intended to exclude the treatment of the State etc. as a taxable person for economic activities which private firms could not perform without usurping the basic functions and powers of the States and other bodies governed by public law (general administration, the administration of justice, or national security or defence).
>
> The second condition is intended to include the State etc. within the scope of the tax in respect of economic activities which private firms could exercise without usurping the basic functions of the State, but which in fact they cannot exercise because of the existence in national legislation of a provision reserving such exercise to the State.

The text as finally adopted read as follows:

> States, regional and local government authorities and other bodies governed by public law shall not be considered taxable persons in respect of the activities or transactions in which they engage as public authorities, even where they collect dues, fees, contributions or payments in connection with these activities or transactions.
>
> However, when they engage in such activities or transactions, they shall be considered taxable persons in respect of these activities or transactions where treatment as non-taxable persons would lead to significant distortions of competition.
>
> In any case, these bodies shall be considered taxable persons in relation to the activities listed in Annex D, provided they are not carried out on such a small scale as to be negligible.
>
> Member States may consider activities of these bodies which are exempt under Article 13 or 28 as activities which they engage in as public authorities.

In the recast of the Sixth Directive, the wording slightly changed, and the current version in Article 13 of the VAT Directive read as follows (changed words in italics):

42. See Terra & Kajus, *A Guide to the European VAT Directives (online)*, Part 3.1, Chapter 4.9.2.

1. States, regional and local government authorities and other bodies governed by public law shall not be *regarded* as taxable persons in respect of the activities or transactions in which they engage as public authorities, even where they collect dues, fees, contributions or payments in connection with those activities or transactions.

   However, when they engage in such activities or transactions, they shall be *regarded* as taxable persons in respect of those activities or transactions where *their* treatment as non-taxable persons would lead to significant distortions of competition.

   In any *event, bodies* governed by public law shall be *regarded* as taxable persons *in respect of* the activities listed in Annex I, provided *that those activities* are not carried out on such a small scale as to be negligible.
2. Member States may *regard* activities, *exempt under Articles 132, 135, 136, 371, 374 to 377, and Article 378(2), Article 379(2), or Articles 380 to 390, engaged in by bodies governed by public law* as activities in which *those bodies engage* as public authorities.

It is interesting to note from the historical description that in the Second Directive, public bodies engaged in activities acting as such were generally excluded. But in the proposal for a Sixth Directive the exclusion for public bodies did not cover activities that were considered economic activities, thus falling within the scope of VAT. The consequence of this was that in the original proposal, only the basic functions and powers of the state, provinces, communes and other public law bodies in general administration, the administration of justice, or national security or defence were excluded from the scope of VAT. The Council made amendments to this and significantly increased the scope of the exclusion, as can be seen from the text of the adopted provision.[43]

The purpose of the exclusion originally seems to have been to exclude only core public administration by public bodies and include within the scope all economic activities that were, or could potentially, be engaged in by private bodies. The very different structure and wording of the adopted text following the amendments made by the Council indicates that the Council was not pleased with the narrow scope of the exclusion. The Council did not add any clarification in the preamble or elsewhere. This makes it hard to find what the legislator's intentions were. The substantive amendments indicate however that it is different from that which the Commission intended. The only guidance that can be found is the wording and structure of the adopted provision. It was suggested in section §2.03[A] that the purpose of the provision is, first, to exclude all activities of public bodies when performed under a public law regime. Potentially the provision covers a range of activities performed also by private law entities. It is exactly this situation, and the distortions of competition that may arise, that the second and third paragraph regulate. The second purpose is thus to ensure that public bodies are not treated as non-taxable persons when they potentially

43. See AG Mischo in Joined cases 231/87 and 129/88 *Carpaneto Piacentino and others* point 43, referred to in Terra/Kajus, Guide, Chapter 4.9.2.

(or actually) compete substantially with private law entities. The historical assessment supports these conclusions.

The treatment in (now) Article 13 of the VAT Directive has since been commented on by the Commission and the subject of two studies commissioned by the Commission. The Commission, in its First Report on the Common system of VAT states, among other things, the following:[44]

> It is left to the Member States to define the activities engaged in by public bodies 'as public authorities'. It was not possible to produce a Community definition because of the wide divergences between Member States on this point. This situation gives rise to a number of difficulties, albeit limited in extent by the list given in Annex D to the Directive, concerning the activities in respect of which the above bodies are considered taxable persons.
>
> ...
>
> Another source of difficulty lies in the provision contained in the second subparagraph of Article 4(5), by which bodies governed by public law, when they engage in activities or transactions referred to in the first subparagraph, 'shall be considered taxable persons in respect of these activities or transactions where treatment as non-taxable persons would lead to significant distortions of competition.' It is sometimes difficult in practice to determine whether or not that last condition is met.
>
> The Commission considers that this situation is unsatisfactory and that the conditions and limits of liability for tax of bodies governed by public law should be spelt out in more specific terms.
>
> Under German law, for instance, land-registry offices were not considered taxable persons, although some of their duties were the same as those performed by quantity surveyors who, as members of a profession, were liable for VAT. The professional association of quantity surveyors attacked the exemption of land-registry offices. Since the situation could lead to 'significant' distortions of competition, the German authorities made the transactions performed by these offices subject to VAT at the standard rate with effect from 1 January 1982.

In 1998 the Commission published a report commissioned by it and written by Ernst & Young entitled 'A Study of the Methods of Taxation of Public Bodies'. The report is referred to at various places in this research.

More recently the Commission has discussed the treatment of public bodies in the Commission's Green paper 'On the future of VAT Towards a simpler, more robust and efficient VAT system'.[45] The Commission notes that the rules applying to public bodies create differences in the VAT treatment of similar activities depending on the status of the supplier. The evolution in the Member States towards privatisation and the deregulation of activities traditionally reserved for the public sector has increased these differences. Furthermore, where public bodies are exempt or outside the scope of VAT, they have an incentive to limit outsourcing in order to avoid paying VAT that they cannot deduct. VAT thus becomes a factor influencing investment and spending decisions.

44. See COM(83) 426 final, pp. 30–31.
45. COM(2010) 695 final.

In a Commission staff working document accompanying the Green paper, the Commission elaborates on the shortcomings of the present system.[46] The Commission adds to the description of shortcomings related to the neutrality of the tax that because VAT on investment by public bodies cannot be recovered, it is often argued that the present VAT regime works against the need to develop investment in public goods. The Commission also points at the wide discretion for Member States to define notions such as 'public body'. As a result, there is no EU approach to the activities that public bodies engage in as 'public authorities'. Lastly, the Commission points at the complexity of the current legal regime, which recognises three categories of activities. They can be taxed, they can be within the scope of VAT but exempt or they can be outside the scope of VAT. The problem is not restricted to determining the VAT status of the supply; it also makes determining the right of deduction of public bodies more complicated. Lastly, exemptions in the public interest are also not very precisely defined.

In the consultation launched by the Green paper, the question was asked whether the current VAT rules for public authorities were acceptable, particularly in terms of tax neutrality, and if not, why not.

The Commission itself points at a few alternatives. One way forward could be to include all the economic activities of public bodies in the scope of VAT and to draw up a list of those activities to be excluded. An alternative would be to clarify and modernise the conditions under which public bodies can no longer be considered to be outside the scope of VAT. More limited reforms could also be envisaged such as an option to tax for public bodies, along the lines of what has been proposed by the Commission for financial services. Modernisation of the current exemptions and clarification of the rules laid down in Article 13 could also be envisaged. An option would also be to rely on Member States' present capacity to implement national refund schemes outside the VAT system. This solution gives a lot of flexibility to Member States.[47]

The Commission also refers to the study (which was then not yet finalised) by Copenhagen Economics. The study, the Commission states, will go beyond a description of the problems and will also look how economically important the differential VAT treatment is. According to the working paper, based on an assessment of the economic importance of the differences, the study will look at what options exist to reduce VAT distortions and present the pros and cons with a view to achieving a level playing field for VAT. The study is explicitly to consider a full taxation model along the lines of what is currently in force in countries such as New Zealand and Australia.

The study referred to by the Commission in the Green paper written by Copenhagen Economics and KPMG was published in 2011 and is entitled 'VAT in the Public Sector and Exemptions in the Public Interest'. It is referred to throughout this research.

46. SEC(2010) 1455.
47. The Commission also reiterates its initiative in 2003 to remove the VAT exemption applicable to postal services. This proposal is still on the table at the Council.

[C] Definition of a 'Public Body'

Public bodies for the purposes of VAT are referred to in Article 13 of the VAT Directive as 'states, regional and local government authorities and other bodies governed by public law'. The phrase '[b]odies governed by public law' in the first paragraph reads 'offentligrättsliga organ' in the Swedish version, a wording which excludes all state-owned companies and similar which cannot be considered to constitute an organ of the state. The Danish version has a similar wording. The French version refers to 'de droit de public' similar to the Dutch and German which refer to 'öffentlichen Rechts'. It has been pointed out that the English phrase has no particular meaning in British law.[48] The versions are thus not entirely consistent and the expressions used do not necessarily have a meaning under national law. But the wording nevertheless implies that it is the legal regime applicable to the body, whatever form as long as it is public in character, that determines whether it is a public body or not.

The Court of Justice has interpreted the provision on several occasions. It is clear from the case law that the decisive criterion is whether the body is governed by public law or not.[49] Two judgments of the Court of Justice are of particular interest, Case 235/85 *Commission v. Netherlands* and *Recaudadores*.[50]

Commission v. Netherlands concerned the question of whether the official services performed by notaries and bailiffs under statute in the Netherlands were subject to VAT. Notaries and bailiffs are self-employed in the Netherlands but their activities are regulated by statute. The Court of Justice pointed out the wide scope of the definition of taxable persons in (now) Article 9. In view of the wide definition of economic activities, encompassing all the activities of the professions, without any reservations in respect of professions regulated by statute, the activities in question must as such be considered to be economic activities.[51] In view of the neutral character of 'economic activities', the Court continued, the fact that the activities consist in the performance of duties which are conferred and regulated by law in the public interest is irrelevant.[52] This was substantiated by the fact that (now) Article 25(c) specifically states that certain activities carried on in pursuance of the law shall be subject to VAT. An activity carried on by a private individual is not exempted from VAT merely because it consists in carrying out acts falling within the prerogatives of the public authority. The Court of Justice concluded that even if the bailiffs and notaries were exercising the powers of public authority, they were not 'bodies governed by public law' as they were not part of the public administration but pursuing an independent economic activity.

The line of reasoning was followed in *Recaudadores*. That case concerned the activities of Spanish tax collectors – Recaudadores de las Zonas Primera y Segunda (tax collectors of the first and second zones). Under Spanish legislation, the tax collectors for a zone are appointed by the local authority whose taxes they collect and must

48. See Terra & Kajus, *A Guide to the European VAT Directives (online)*, Part 3.1, Chapter 4.9.2.
49. See, for example, *Carpaneto Piacentino and others* point 12.
50. Case C-202/90 *Recaudadores*.
51. *Commission v. Netherlands*, point 9.
52. *Ibid.* point 10.

provide the security fixed by that local authority. In the performance of their functions they are directed by the local authority. They are entitled to remuneration in the form of a collection premium, which is a percentage of the sums recovered without constraint, and a proportion of the supplements added on in the event of enforced recovery. Finally, they set up their own offices and recruit their auxiliary staff themselves.

The Court of Justice merely pointed out that it had already held in *Commission v. Netherlands* that an activity carried on by a private individual is not excluded from the scope of VAT merely because it consists in the performance of acts falling within the prerogatives of the public authority. Consequently, if a commune entrusts the activity of collecting taxes to an independent third party, the exclusion from VAT provided for in (now) Article 13 is not applicable.

It is thus clear from the case law that a public body is only a public body if it is part of the public administration and that the definition excludes private entities from the scope of the exemption. An activity carried on by a private entity is not excluded from the scope of VAT merely because it consists in the performance of acts falling within the prerogatives of the public authority. Irrespective of any activity that may involve a function of the state, if the entity that is performing the activity in question is not governed by public law, the activity is not excluded from the scope of VAT.

In both cases, the Court of Justice stated that a body is only a public body if it is part of the public administration. It should be noted that the concept of public administration is not unambiguous but may also include entities such as limited liability companies controlled by the state, at least if viewed in a general EU law context.

In Case C-188/89 *Foster and others*, the Court of Justice discussed the direct effect of directives in relation to the British Gas Association. The Court noted that it had already held that directives had direct effect vis-à-vis the tax authorities, local or regional authorities, constitutionally independent authorities responsible for the maintenance of public order and safety and public authorities providing public health services.[53] The Court thereafter stated that a body, whatever its legal form, which has been made responsible, pursuant to a measure adopted by the state, for providing a public service under the control of the state and has for that purpose special powers beyond those which result from the normal rules applicable in relations between individuals is included among the bodies against which the provisions of a directive capable of having direct effect may be relied upon.[54]

53. Case C-188/89 *Foster and others*, point 19.
54. Case C-188/89 *Foster and others*, point 20. When a body is classified as such a body, i.e., it is in essence 'the state' for the purpose of (now) Article 288 TFEU, individuals can rely directly on directly applicable provisions of a directive as against those bodies. It seems to follow from this that the body in question can then not rely upon national law in turn, thereby 'avoiding' the obligations it has under the directive in question. For the purposes of EC law, it is part of the state. Interestingly, the Swedish Supreme Administrative Court has, in RÅ 2003 ref 99, considered that it could not rely directly on the VAT Directive against a local authority when the VAT Directive was not correctly implemented. It seems to me that the judgment by the Swedish court is hard to reconcile with the principle of superiority of EC law. The Swedish state has obliged itself to follow EC law when becoming a member of the EU. That obligation extends to

In contrast to *Foster*, in *Recaudadores*, the Court of Justice excluded from the scope of Article 13 of the VAT Directive bodies (the tax collectors) that clearly were responsible for providing public services and were doing so under the control of the state. In addition, according to AG Tesauro's Opinion in the case, the tax collectors enjoyed some rights and prerogatives peculiar to civil servants.[55] Thus, it seems that the tax collectors did have special powers beyond those which result from the normal rules applicable in relations between individuals. Consequently, the tax collectors seemed to be part of the state for the purposes of EU law in general following *Foster*, but they were not considered excluded from the scope of VAT in accordance with Article 13 of the VAT Directive. The exclusion in Article 13 is narrower than the definition of those bodies constituting the state in EU law in general. The reference made by the Court of Justice to public administration is thus referring to a more narrow concept than in EU law in general.

That concept does not cover limited liability companies, even if wholly owned by the state. The only difference between an organ of the state and a wholly owned company of the state is the legal status of the latter. The functions and control of the state may be the same. However, the condition that a body has to be a public body to come within the scope of the exclusion in Article 13(1) is a condition precisely relating to the legal form of the body involved. This conclusion is in line with the narrow approach of the Court in *Recaudadores* and it is consistent with the Swedish version of the Directive. This conclusion is also in line with a strict interpretation of the exclusion from VAT for public bodies.[56]

[D] Activities Engaged in 'As A Public Authority'

Article 13 of the VAT Directive states that states, regional and local government authorities and other bodies governed by public law shall not be regarded as taxable persons in respect of the activities or transactions in which they engage *as public authorities*.[57] The French version reads 'en tant qu'autorités publiques', i.e., approximately 'in so much as [the activities are performed] as a public body'. The German version is consistent herewith, 'im Rahmen der öffentlichen Gewalt obliegen', as are the other versions assessed.

The Court of Justice has consistently held that this criterion means that activities pursued as public authorities within the meaning of (now) Article 13 of the VAT Directive are those engaged in by bodies governed by public law under a special legal

all entities that are classified as 'the state' within the meaning of that agreement (i.e., the Treaty), including local government.

55. See the Opinion in *Recaudadores* point 2.
56. It is a different conclusion than the one reached in my thesis, Henkow (2008), p. 197.
57. Article 2 states that the scope covers taxable persons 'acting as such'. This implies that a taxable person may act in different capacities, both as an economic operator and as a non-economic operator. Similarly, Article 13 only excludes from the scope of VAT public bodies when acting as public bodies (i.e., public bodies acting as such). As I see it this is consistent with the structure of the VAT Directive.

regime applicable to them and do not include activities pursued by them under the same legal conditions as those that apply to private traders.[58]

The definition originates from the judgment in *Carpaneto Piacentino and others*.[59] In that judgment, the Court of Justice considered whether certain activities engaged in by local authorities were excluded from the scope of VAT. The activities were concessions in respect of graves, cemetery vaults and chapels, and selling concessions of surface rights and the sale with full ownership of rights, of land in connection with the subsidised building of homes, the taking out of public ownership and sale of a piece of roadway, water supply, the concession for the operation of the public weighbridge, the sale of wood resulting from the lopping of trees and the sale of fittings for cemetery vaults.[60] The Court of Justice stated that a definition of the condition that the body is acting as a public body cannot be based on the subject-matter or purpose of the activity engaged in.[61] These circumstances are decisive factors in relation to determining the application of Annex I and the exemptions from VAT.[62] Instead, it is the way in which the activities are carried out that determines the scope of the treatment of public bodies as non-taxable persons. The provision excludes activities engaged in by public bodies not as bodies governed by public law but as persons subject to private law. Consequently, the only criterion to distinguish with certainty between these two categories of activity is the legal regime applicable under national law.[63] When public bodies act under the same legal conditions as those that apply to private traders, they cannot be regarded as acting 'as public authorities'.[64]

In *Marktgemeinde Welden*, the relevant activity in the case before the Court was the leasing of immovable property.[65] The municipality constructed a new building and the premises were let by the municipality itself to a brewery which operated them as a restaurant. The municipality applied for the option to tax. However, the municipality did not supply the restaurant equipment, such as the cookers, machines, extractor hoods, furniture and crockery but only the building. Under German Law, that was not considered as leasing of immovable property but an asset management service for which the option was not available. Consequently, the letting was exempt from VAT. The Court of Justice found that the municipality was acting under the same legal conditions as private traders and not as a public authority.[66]

58. See, for example, Case C-408/97 *Commission v. Netherlands* point 35.
59. Joined cases 231/87 and 129/88 *Carpaneto Piacentino and others*. Case C-4/89 *Carpaneto* was substantially similar to this case. The only new issue raised was actually referred back to the national court to decide! See Case C-4/89 *Carpaneto* points 6 and 9.
60. Joined cases 231/87 and 129/88 *Carpaneto Piacentino and others* point 2.
61. Joined cases 231/87 and 129/88 *Carpaneto Piacentino and others* point 13.
62. Joined cases 231/87 and 129/88 *Carpaneto Piacentino and others* point 14.
63. Joined cases 231/87 and 129/88 *Carpaneto Piacentino and others* point 15.
64. Joined cases 231/87 and 129/88 *Carpaneto Piacentino and others* point 16.
65. Case C-247/95 *Marktgemeinde Welden*.
66. With regard to the effects of Article 13(2) in the case, see Chapter §2.03[F] below.

Providing access to roads against payment was the activity dealt with in four infringement proceedings against the Netherlands, Greece, Ireland and France respectively.[67] The Commission claimed that it is only in respect of activities or transactions in which they engage as public authorities that bodies governed by public law are not considered to be taxable persons. The activity of providing access to roads does not come into that category, as it does not fall within the core responsibilities of public authority which can never be delegated to private bodies, bearing in mind that the rule that bodies governed by public law are not taxable persons must be interpreted strictly.[68]

The Court of Justice did not agree. A body may not only be acting as a public authority in respect of activities falling within the definition of public authority in the strict sense of that term, which do not include providing access to roads on payment of a toll. With regard to the activity in question, the Court found with regard to the Netherlands, Greece and Ireland that the Commission had failed to put evidence required to substantiate the alleged failure to fulfil obligations as regards the condition relating to pursuance of an activity as a public authority. With regard to France it was however common ground that some traders providing access to roads were governed by private law. As these were not obliged to charge VAT on their supplies, France was found to have failed to fulfil its requirements under (now) Article 13 in so far as these traders were concerned.

Câmara Municipal do Porto deals with parking charges.[69] The question was whether the City Council was liable for VAT on charges received, and the first question asked by the national court related to whether the City Council was acting as a public body when letting out spaces for parking vehicles.

The Court of Justice commented that the question could not depend on the subject-matter or purpose of the activity.[70] Similarly, whether or not the City Council owned the land or whether that land was part of its public or private property, was not in itself determinative of whether it was carrying on that activity as a public authority. It was instead for the national court to determine whether that activity was being engaged in under a special legal regime applicable to bodies governed by public law or under the same legal conditions as those that apply to private economic operators. The fact, the Court of Justice continues, that the pursuit of the activity involved the use of public powers, such as authorising or restricting parking on a public highway or

67. Case C-408/97 *Commission v. Netherlands*, Case C-260/98 *Commission v. Greece*, Case C-358/97 *Commission v. Ireland* and Case C-276/97 *Commission v. France*.
68. See Case C-408/97 *Commission v. Netherlands* point 22, Case C-260/98 *Commission v. Greece* point 23 and Case C-276/97 *Commission v. France* point 26. It seems to me that the Commission may have read Case C-107/84 *Commission v. Germany* point 15 in which the Court of Justice might be interpreted to have stated that only activities of public authorities in the strict sense are covered by the exclusion in (now) Article 13(1). The suggested infringement seems to test to what extent this statement was true. If viewed in the perspective of legislative history, the answer seems clear – such a strict scope of the exclusion is not supported by the historical development of the exclusion.
69. Case C-446/98 *Câmara Municipal do Porto*.
70. See, also in the following, points 20–22.

penalising by a fine the exceeding of the authorised parking time, showed that the activity was subject to a public law regime.[71]

Consequently, the restriction to activities engaged in as a public authority 'as such' is not a restriction to public administration in the strict sense. It may include activities such as providing access to roads or letting out parking spaces that are not strictly public administration tasks. The decisive issue is whether the legal regime applicable is that of public law or private law. On the one hand, when the activity involves the use of public powers (such as authorising or restricting parking in public roads) the activity is engaged in under a public law regime. On the other hand, when the activity is engaged in under the same legal conditions as those that apply to private traders, it is not engaged in as a public authority. It is clear from *Câmara Municipal do Porto* that an activity is not performed under public law simply because it is part of the public policy.[72]

[E] Limitations of the Exclusion

[1] Introduction

According to the second paragraph of Article 13(1) of the VAT Directive, when public bodies engage in activities or transactions acting as such within the meaning of Article 13(1), they 'shall be regarded as taxable persons in respect of those activities or transactions where their treatment as non-taxable persons would lead to significant distortions of competition'. According to the third paragraph, public bodies shall in any event be considered as taxable persons when they are performing certain activities listed in Annex 1 on a scale that is more than negligible.

The Court has held that both these paragraphs should be interpreted as a whole and that both deal with distortions of competition that can arise when public bodies are excluded from the scope of VAT.[73] Also, the phrase 'in any event' shows that with regard to the activities listed in Annex 1, there is no need to see whether they fall within the exclusion in the first paragraph of Article 13(1) or whether their exclusion would lead to a distortion of competition – they fall within the scope of VAT in any case, provided that they are performed to a more than negligible extent.

The Court of Justice has commented on the limitations on several occasions. From *Götz*, it can be discerned that the limitation in cases of distortions of competition

71. The judgment conforms with the Opinion of the AG who noted in point 42 of the opinion that as an additional indication, it may be relevant whether the parking regulations are intended to manage the space available for parking and aid traffic flows or merely to cover parking, whether a distinction is drawn between car parks in terms of restricted short-stay car parks and unrestricted long-stay car parks or whether long-term car parks are involved, or whether charges are made for them by parking meter, parking ticket or long-term parking permit. Furthermore, it may be significant whether or not the places are guarded and whether exceeding the parking time is punishable by a fine or provision is made merely for an additional payment or a contractual penalty (under civil law).
72. See the reference to public traffic policy in the Opinion in *Câmara Municipal do Porto*, point 31 and the judgment of the Court which does not refer to public traffic policy at all.
73. Case C-288/07 *Isle of Wight*.

is there to 'maintain the fiscal neutrality in respect of VAT'.[74] This is even more clearly formulated in *Halle*, where the Court states that the second paragraph of (now) Article 13 'is intended to ensure compliance with the principle of neutrality of the tax, which precludes, in particular, treating similar supplies of services, which are thus in competition with each other, differently for VAT purposes'.[75] In *Isle of Wight*, where the Court explicitly states that the second and third paragraphs of (now) Article 13(1) must be interpreted as a whole, it also refers to the statement in *Halle*.[76] The purpose of both the second and third paragraphs of Article 13(1) is thus to ensure compliance with the principle of neutrality of the VAT in particular through ensuring that distortions of competition do not arise.[77]

[2] Significant Distortion of Competition

The reference to 'significant distortions of competition' reads in French 'des distorsions de concurrence d'une certaine importance'. The German version refers to 'Grösseren Wettbewerbsverzerrungen'. The language versions seem inconsistent as there seems, at least potentially, to be a difference between a 'significant distortion' and a 'distortion of some importance' or a 'greater distortion of competition'. The question arises whether it is necessary that the distortion has some magnitude or whether it is enough that it is just not insignificant.

The Court of Justice held in *Carpaneto Piacentino*[78] that the provision contains a derogation from the rule of treatment of bodies governed by public law as non-taxable persons in respect of activities or transactions engaged in by them as public authorities where that treatment would lead to significant distortions of competition. Thus, with a view to ensuring the neutrality of the tax, which is the major objective of the European VAT system, that provision envisages the situation in which bodies governed by public law engage, under the special legal regime applicable to them, in activities which may also be engaged in, in competition with them, by private individuals under a regime governed by private law or on the basis of administrative concessions. The Court of Justice also held that the application of the rule regarding significant distortions of competition involves an assessment of economic circumstances.[79]

The concept of significant distortion of competition was also discussed in *Câmara Municipal do Porto*.[80] Advocate General Alber noted that bodies governed by public law are subject to VAT where their treatment as non-taxable persons would give them an advantage leading to significant distortions of competition and adversely affecting competitors.[81] Member States are free to choose any other wording or to lay down a

74. See Case C-408/06 *Götz*, p. 42.
75. Case C-430/04 *Halle*, p. 24.
76. See Case C-288/07 *Isle of Wight*, p. 43.
77. See, for a different view, de la Feria, *Intertax* (2008), p. 151. She suggests that the objective is to introduce an element of flexibility into the rigidity of the main rule.
78. Joined Cases 231/87 and 129/88 *Carpaneto Piacentino and others* point 22.
79. *Carpaneto Piacentino*, point 32.
80. Case C-446/98 *Câmara Municipal do Porto*.
81. *Câmara Municipal do Porto*. point 48 of the Opinion.

general, quantitative limit unrelated to a specific case – corresponding, for example, to the special scheme for small undertakings with a fixed amount of annual turnover – in order to make bodies governed by public law taxable where their treatment as non-taxable persons could lead to significant distortions of competition as envisaged in the directive.[82] The underlying aim of European VAT is to harmonise the area and ensure the neutrality of VAT.[83] The national court must, according to the AG, determine whether a competitive market exists for these activities or transactions, that is to say, whether these services are also offered by private persons. In the case of the letting of areas for the parking of vehicles, the national court will have to determine whether the provision of parking spaces at parking meters and the letting of car park spaces form one single market or two different markets. In that respect, it may be important whether uniform prices apply or whether price differences exist between parking meters and parking ticket machines and car parks. In addition, the national court will have to determine whether the car park market is split in terms of short-term and long-term parking or whether it forms a single market for competition purposes.[84]

The Court of Justice referred to its case law and noted that Member States are free to choose, from the various methods of achieving the results defined by the second and third paragraphs, that of entrusting an administrative body with the task of specifying the situations in which an activity carried on by a body governed by public law may be regarded as bringing about significant distortions of competition or as being negligible and of applying those criteria to individual cases, provided that its decisions on application may be reviewed by the national courts. Consequently, the Court did not elaborate on what criteria were relevant but essentially left it to the national authorities to decide on the method to be applied when determining the existence of a distortion of competition.

Similarly, in *Halle*, the Court left it to the national court to find out whether competition was significantly distorted because of an exemption for the municipality's provision of crematorium services and, if so, the operation of the crematorium would be taxable.[85]

In contrast hereto, in *Götz*, the Court of Justice discussed relevant criteria in determining whether a distortion of competition was present. The Court discussed the relevant geographical market, which was determined based on EU law, with relation to whether a significant distortion of competition was at hand.[86] The Court of Justice discussed actual trade in milk and the services provided by milk-quota sales points, their geographical division and the presence of any private traders supplying similar services. The Court concluded that the milk-quota sales points were not faced with private operators providing services which were in competition with the public services. There was therefore no distortion of competition.[87]

82. *Câmara Municipal do Porto*. point 50 of the Opinion.
83. *Câmara Municipal do Porto*. point 54 of the Opinion.
84. *Câmara Municipal do Porto*. point 58 of the Opinion.
85. Case C-430/04 *Halle*, p. 26.
86. Case C-408/06 *Götz*. See also section §2.03 [E][3]
87. *Götz* points 44–46.

In *Salix*, the issue was raised of whether the second paragraph of Article 13(1) was applicable not only when a distortion of competition arose to the detriment of private competitors but also when a distortion of competition arose to the detriment of public bodies, and whether, in such circumstances, they should be treated as non-taxable persons based on Article 13(1) first and fourth paragraphs.[88] The Court concluded that the provision was applicable also in these situations and gave four reasons for its conclusions. First, the wording of the provision did not exclude the situation that competition could be distorted to the detriment of public bodies. Second, the second paragraph should be broadly construed as it restores the general rule of Article 9. Third, there was nothing in the objective of the second paragraph that suggested that public bodies should suffer from distortions of competition. Lastly, to apply the second paragraph also better ensured the neutrality of the tax with regard to the right to deduct input VAT.

As can be seen, a definition of what method or criteria should be applied when determining the existence of a significant distortion of competition is at large lacking. The Court in essence has left it to the Member State to determine exactly what method to be used.[89] It is not strange that the Court's case law focuses on the aim of the provision which should be achieved by the Member States in their implementation.[90] Member States are free to choose how they want to implement the provisions of the VAT Directive, as long as the aim pursued is fulfilled. Sometimes the aim pursued by the provision to be implemented can only be fulfilled in a certain way. The discretion of the Member State is then reduced. In the context of implementing the provision in question, the Court has gone further than providing general guidance on the aims to be achieved with the provision. The Court has provided guidance on how the material issue before the national court should be solved (in *Götz* and *Carpaneto*). The Court must thus in these cases have considered that the aim could only be fulfilled in a certain way. Anyway, defining more precisely exactly when a distortion of competition arises seems hard to realise. Whether a distortion of competition arises is a factual question rather than a legal question. The only legal question concerns the method to be used, including relevant factors to be considered in the application of that method. Here, the Court has provided guidance when it states that it is a question of economic appraisal, i.e., an economic method shall be used. As regards factors relevant, the Court has also provided guidance, albeit limited, in above all *Götz*.

Furthermore, it is clear that the Court views distortions of competition as a concept that is connected to fiscal neutrality. According to the Court, the principle of fiscal neutrality includes the principle of elimination of distortions of competition.[91] When fiscal neutrality is distorted, distortions of competition also arise. It therefore

88. Case C-102/08 *Salix*. The case is discussed in more detail in the next section.
89. Henkow (2008), p. 199. De la Feria has considered that these judgment focus on the scope of discretion of Member States rather than on defining the concept of significant distortion of competition itself. She has also suggested that the case law focuses more on the aim than on the means whereby the aim is achieved, see De la Feria *Intertax* (2008), p. 151.
90. Compare Case C-102/08 *Salix* and the answer to the national court's first question.
91. See Case C-363/05 *JP Morgan*, p. 47. See, regarding the principle of fiscal neutrality in VAT, Terra & Kajus (2012), Chapter 2.5.

first needs to be determined whether the products and services provided by the public body and the private entrepreneur that are allegedly in competition with each other meet the criteria of being similar.[92]

[3] Mandatory Exclusions

According to the third paragraph of Article 13(1) of the VAT Directive, bodies governed by public law shall be regarded as taxable persons in respect of the activities listed in Annex I, provided that those activities are not carried out on such a small scale as to be negligible. Annex I lists the following activities:

(1) telecommunications services;
(2) supply of water, gas, electricity and thermal energy;
(3) transport of goods;
(4) port and airport services;
(5) passenger transport;
(6) supply of new goods manufactured for sale;
(7) transactions in respect of agricultural products, carried out by agricultural intervention agencies pursuant to Regulations on the common organisation of the market in those products;
(8) organisation of trade fairs and exhibitions;
(9) warehousing;
(10) activities of commercial publicity bodies;
(11) activities of travel agents;
(12) running of staff shops, cooperatives and industrial canteens and similar institutions;
(13) activities carried out by radio and television bodies in so far as these are not exempt pursuant to Article 132(1)(q).

In both the English and French versions of the provision, 'such a small scale as to be negligible', refers to a negligible scale. The German version refers to a scale that 'nicht unbedeutend ist', and in Swedish 'försumbart liten skala'. The language versions dealt with thus seems more or less consistent.

The wording of the provision implies that it is not necessary, with regard to the listed activities, to know whether they are engaged in by a public body acting as such, or whether there is a significant distortion of competition should the activities fall outside the scope. In any case, the listed activities fall within the scope of VAT. It also seems clear from the wording that it is a requirement that, in order for Annex I-activities to be performed as a taxable person, they have to be performed to a more than negligible extent. However, the case law shows that this is not a correct conclusion.

92. See Case C-363/05 *JP Morgan*, p. 46.

In *Carpaneto Piacentino and others* the Court of Justice was asked whether the provision in question required the Member States to transpose into their tax legislation the criterion of the non-negligible scale of activities as a condition for treating bodies governed by public law as taxable persons in respect of the activities listed in the Annex, and whether they must lay down for that purpose a threshold below which such bodies are treated as non-taxable persons.[93]

The Court noted that, contrary to the case with regard to determining the scope of the exclusion in (now) the first paragraph of Article 13(1), the subject-matter and purpose of the activity is of importance with regard to the mandatory exclusions.[94] The Court of Justice furthermore observed that the provision in question makes the rule that public bodies are not to be regarded as taxable persons subject to a limitation which must be added to those resulting from the condition laid down in the first paragraph, namely that the activities must be engaged in as public authorities, and from the derogation laid down in the second paragraph in cases where treatment as non-taxable persons would lead to significant distortions of competition. The third paragraph thus seeks to ensure that certain categories of economic activity, the importance of which derives from their subject-matter, are not freed from VAT[95] on the ground that they are carried out by bodies governed by public law as public authorities. However, the obligation to treat bodies governed by public law as taxable persons in respect of the activities listed in the Annex is imposed on the Member States only in so far as the activities in question are not negligible in scale. Having regard to the structure of the provision in question, the Court of Justice continues, it must be interpreted as meaning that the Member States are free to exclude from the scope of such compulsory treatment the activities listed in the Annex in so far as they are carried out on a negligible scale, but are not required to do so.

In *Câmara Municipal do Porto*, the Court of Justice confirmed its finding, stating that the provision gives Member States the option of taking account of the negligible scale of activities or transactions engaged in by bodies governed by public law, in order to exclude them from being taxable persons for VAT, solely with respect to the activities set out in (now) Annex I.[96]

The wording of the third paragraph and the structure of the provision seems to impose an obligation upon the Member States to first, exclude public bodies from the scope of VAT and second to impose limitations on that exclusion when (a) the public body is not acting as such, (b) where there is a significant distortion of competition and (c) where Annex I-activities are performed and not to a negligible scale. However, as the Court of Justice has interpreted the provision, Annex I-activities are liable to VAT provided that the Member States determine so, even if they are performed only to a negligible extent. Whether an activity is performed only to a negligible extent is still of

93. Joined Cases 231/87 and 129/88 *Carpaneto Piacentino and others* p. 25.
94. Joined Cases 231/87 and 129/88 *Carpaneto Piacentino and others* point 14.
95. The English translation of the case is wrong in point 26. The Italian original has been used to rectify the mistake.
96. *Câmara Municipal do Porto* point 27.

importance, since the Member States are obliged to treat public bodies as taxable persons if an Annex I-activity is performed to a more than negligible extent.[97]

Notably, it has not been clarified what is negligible. From the wording of the provision it seems that the negligibility refers to the magnitude of the activity as such. It seems highly possible that the (optional) requirement of negligibility is aimed at being a simplification. Public bodies are generally excluded from the scope and they often engage in exempt activities. If they are then fully excluded from the scope of VAT (based on the third subparagraph, see below), they do not have to account for VAT as soon as they perform an Annex I-activity to a very limited extent. The limitation of the provision as regards the scale of the activity seems then, considering Article 13 as a whole, likely to deal with cases where the treatment as a non-taxable person would result in non-neutrality. This reasoning conforms with how the Court of Justice interpreted the provision in *Isle of Wight*.[98] Article 13 constitutes an exclusion from the scope of VAT and the limitations of that exclusion to guarantee the neutrality of the tax. An Annex I-activity cannot therefore be considered to be negligible if it is performed in competition with others, thus encroaching upon the neutrality of VAT.

Annex I has to date been dealt with in two cases before the Court of Justice. In *Götz*, the Court of Justice tried whether a milk-quota sales point, set up by a German Land in correspondence with a regulation on the common organisation of the market in milk, fell within the scope of points 7 (thus having the status as an agricultural intervention agency) or 12 (having the status of a staff shop) of (now) Annex I.[99] The Court of Justice found that the milk-quota sales point established by the Landesanstalt intervened in the milk sector pursuant to a regulation on the common organisation of the market; it was clear that that activity related not to milk, but to delivery of reference quantities. It did not therefore concern agricultural products within the meaning of point 7. Furthermore, the task of the milk-quota sales point differed significantly from that of an agricultural intervention agency, which was characterised by the purchase and resale of the agricultural products themselves, as may be undertaken by any economic operator. The logic of the automatic liability to VAT inherent in the Annex in question thus excluded from its scope the activity of allocating milk quotas among the producers as the centralisation of the different offers of those producers was not the result of an operator purchasing and reselling agricultural products on the market.

It was furthermore possible to ascertain from a linguistic comparison of point 12 that the term 'staff shop' referred to entities responsible for selling various products and goods to the staff of the undertakings or authorities to which they were attached. That was not the task of the sales point at issue, as that point was responsible for contributing to the balancing out of delivery reference quantities, with a view to limiting them, in the best interests of each producer.

---

97. Compare de la Feria *Intertax* (2008), pp. 152–153 who seems to be surprised by the Court's interpretation and finds that the first condition in the third paragraph, that the activity is an Annex 1 activity, is the essential criterion.
98. Case C-288/07 *Isle of Wight* p. 75.
99. Case C-408/06 *Götz*.

In *Zweckverband*, the company Zweckverband ensured the supply of drinking water and disposal of sewage on behalf of a number of towns and municipalities in the district of Torgau-Westelbien.[100] Accordingly, the activities of the Zweckverband included, *inter alia*, the collection, piping, treatment and supply of drinking water to its customers, that is to say the owners of buildings connected to the water supply network. In that context, it laid mains connections at the request of its customers, for which it received a single fee corresponding to the cost of that work. The connection remained the property of the Zweckverband.

The Court was asked whether laying a mains connection formed part of the supply of water referred to in point 2 of (now) Annex I. The Court of Justice replied that the supply of water is characterised by making water available to the public and that that supply was carried out by means of fixed networks intended to provide a service to the public. Moreover, laying a mains connection consisted in the installation, by the Zweckverband, of piping permitting the connection of a building's water system to the fixed water supply network. It was common ground that, if that connection was not made, it was impossible to make water available to the owner or occupier of the building. Accordingly, that connection was essential for making the water available.

The Court held that, since, first, the objective of the third subparagraph of (now) Article 13, was to ensure that the categories of economic activity of a certain importance that were listed in (now) Annex I, which include the supply of water, are not exempted from VAT on the ground that the service was rendered by a public body, second, the supply of water is characterised by making water available to the public and, finally, a mains connection is essential for making it available, that connection formed part of the supply of water referred to in point 2 of the Annex.

In *Hutchison 3G* and *T-Mobile Austria*, the Court held that the issuing of licences for using a certain frequency in the electromagnetic spectrum was not an economic activity within the meaning of Article 9. It was therefore not relevant to consider, *inter alia*, whether the issuing was covered by Annex D point 1 'Telecommunications' of the Sixth Directive, which was a question put to it by the referring courts. (The wording has changed in the recast. Annex 1 point (1) of the VAT Directive refers to 'Telecommunications services'.) But Advocate General Kokott carefully considered this issue in her opinions in the cases.[101]

The Advocate General initially points out that the sectors listed in (now) Annex I essentially relate to economic transactions that often are or have been engaged in by the state in the exercise of its public authority just because of their significance to the public interest, but which can also be provided by private sector undertakings. Some of the economic sectors stated have now been liberalised. Private undertakings are here actually in competition with former monopoly suppliers, some of which have been privatised and some of which are still state-owned. At the time that the Sixth VAT Directive was adopted in 1977 it clearly took such a development into account.

Starting with the wording of the provision, the Advocate General notes that it does not provide any clarification as to whether the issuing of the licences in question

100. Case C-442/05 *Zweckverband*.

101. See pp. 78 and 80–96 of the Opinion in Case C-369/04 *Hutchison 3G*.

falls under the provision. If a historical approach is taken, it could conceivably be argued that the award of mobile communications licences to private undertakings could not be covered by the term 'telecommunications' because licences of that kind did not exist on the date that the Directive was adopted in 1977. At that time, the state administrative postal authorities were providing telecommunications services under their own direct management. The Community legislature probably did not therefore originally intend to adopt legislation in relation to telecommunications licences. The provisions of (now) the VAT Directive should however also be interpreted systematically, with particular reference to its objective.

The definition of telecommunications services in the 10th indent of Article 9(2)(e) of the Sixth Directive might initially play a part in such a systematic approach. In that indent, a definition of telecommunication services could be found within the context of defining the place of supply of services. The language versions of this provision are not consistent. Particular significance is therefore to be attached to the meaning and purpose of the provision. The Advocate General finds that this legislation was intended to ensure that telecommunications services provided from outside the Community to customers in the Community were taxed in the Community. This recital only relates to telecommunications services in the narrower sense as the licences are always awarded by the appropriate national authorities.

In the proceedings, reference had also been made to the definition of 'telecommunications services' contained in Article 2(4) of Council Directive 90/387/EEC of 28 June 1990 on the establishment of the internal market for telecommunications services through the implementation of open network. According to that definition, the award of UMTS licences did not constitute a telecommunications service. The Advocate General pointed to the different wordings, *telecommunications services* in the internal market directive and *telecommunication* in the Sixth VAT Directive (N.B. changed to *telecommunications services* in the recast). She considered that the latter term could be construed as a wider description of that sector of activity, including activities other than telecommunications services in the narrower sense.

What was decisive, in the eyes of the Advocate General was, however, the spirit and purpose of the relevant provision. The supplies listed in the Annex are those supplies that are, or could be, typically offered by private sector undertakings as well. There is thus a presumption of a material effect on competition in general. The purpose of the legislation is to put the state in the same position in these circumstances as a private sector taxable person.

Equating the state with private sector taxable persons is only appropriate in relation to telecommunications services in the narrower sense as both supplies can now also be offered by private sector undertakings. As things stand at present, however, the initial award of licences to use defined parts of the spectrum is a task that is reserved to the state. Even if the award of licences might possibly in certain circumstances have to compete with the resale of licences by private concerns, it is not appropriate to equate the state in general with private sector taxable persons in that sphere of activity.

[F] Treatment as a Public Body When Exempt Supplies are Made

According to Article 13(2), Member States may regard activities, exempt under Articles 132, 135, 136, 371, 374–377, and Article 378(2), Article 379(2), or Articles 380–390, engaged in by bodies governed by public law as activities in which those bodies engage as public authorities.

The provision gives Member States the option to treat a public body that is acting as a taxable person making exempt supplies as a non-taxable person. The treatment as non-taxable person vis-à-vis taxable person but exempt does not result in the same consequences in all situations. With regard to the right to deduct input VAT, whether the acquirer is a taxable person or non-taxable person is of importance, though the distinction is of less importance after the amendment to the VAT Directive that at large equates the status of non-taxable person with that of a taxable person with regard to the right to deduct input VAT on the purchase of goods forming part of the business assets.[102] In addition, in the case of a public body purchasing investment goods, the rules on adjustments of deduction are not available, were the public body to become a taxable person starting an economic activity.[103] When goods are acquired from another Member State within the EU, the intra-Community acquisition should not be accounted for by non-taxable persons, unless a specific threshold has been exceeded.[104] If a taxable person acquires the goods, the intra-Community acquisition is taxed independently of whether the threshold is exceeded or not. Lastly, Articles 43 and 44 may entail an obligation to account for VAT on the acquisition of services from another country under the reverse charge mechanism. Consequently, being a taxable person and making exempt supplies and being a non-taxable person does not have exactly the same result.[105]

Article 4(5) fourth subparagraph of the Sixth VAT Directive referred to activities exempt under Article 13 or 28 of the Sixth VAT Directive. The provisions of Article 13 of the Sixth Directive are found in, *inter alia*, Articles 132, 135 and 136 of the VAT Directive. The provisions of Article 28 can be found in, *inter alia*, Articles 371, 374 and 376 of the VAT Directive. Consequently, Articles 375, 377 and 380–390 have been added to the provision in the recast of the Sixth VAT Directive into the VAT Directive.

The Commission commented on the provision in its proposal for a Recast Directive under the heading 'Accuracy of references'.[106] According to the Commission, in order to make the references as precise as possible, they have been limited to cover only the relevant parts of the provision referred to. It can also be seen when the new references are studied and compared with the old ones that the parts of Articles 13 and 28 that are not referred to are not relevant in the present context. Under the heading 'Maintenance of the status quo' the Commission also comments on certain changes

102. See further Chapter 4.
103. See Case C-378/02 *Waterschap Zeeuws Vlaanderen*.
104. See Article 2(1)(b)(i) and Article 3 of the VAT Directive.
105. See also Terra & Kajus, *A Guide to the European VAT Directives (online)*, Part 3.1, Chapter 3.8.2.4.
106. COM(2004) 246 final, p. 20.

made necessary to keep the status quo.[107] One example provided is the stand still clause in (now) Article 176 and an adaptation where the relevant point in time, for new Member States, is the date of accession – something which is actually a codification of case law.[108] It seems to me that the changes made in the context of (now) Article 13(2) also fall into this category of necessary changes to maintain the status quo. Articles 375, 377 and 380–390 originate in the Acts of accession of Member States joining the EU after the Sixth VAT Directive came into force and concern the right to retain exemptions already present in their domestic VAT acts when joining the EU. Article 371 of the VAT Directive already allows the continued exemption of certain activities listed in (now) Annex X, Part B for Member States which at the time when the Sixth VAT Directive came into force already exempted these activities. The change made in the recast is to allow also those Member States later joining the EU the same treatment, but only as regards certain activities listed in Annex X, Part B.

In *Marktgemeinde Welden*[109] the national court raised the question of whether (now) Article 13(2) allows Member States to treat tax-exempted activities, in respect of which it is possible to opt to be taxed, of bodies governed by public law as activities which they engage in as public authorities, although they pursue them under the same legal conditions and in the same way as private traders. The Commission claimed, first of all, that conferring the status of taxable person on bodies governed by public law or conferring that status on them and exempting them from VAT has the same result. In addition it stated that (now) Article 13(2), as a provision derogating from the basic system, should be strictly interpreted and apply to activities exempted only in so far as the exemptions expressly associate them with bodies governed by public law. Therefore, Member States were not authorised to exclude bodies governed by public law from treatment as taxable persons in respect of activities, such as the letting of buildings, which do not satisfy the requirement set out in (now) Article 13(1).[110]

The Court of Justice noted that it appeared from the case file that the letting activity of the public authority in question was carried out under the same legal conditions as those to which private traders are subject. Consequently, (now) Article 13(1) could not be used to deny the municipality the status of taxable person.[111]

However, (now) Article 13(2) gives Member States the option of regarding activities exempt from VAT as activities of a public authority and hence of excluding bodies governed by public law from treatment as taxable persons in respect of those activities. Since the provision does not draw any distinction between those activities, Member States are authorised to exclude, from treatment as taxable persons, bodies governed by public law which carry out exempted activities, even if they are performed in a similar manner to those of a private trader. If the activity of the public body is, by virtue of (now) Article 13(2) to be considered to have been carried out as a non-taxable person, it is for the national court to determine whether there would arise any

107. COM(2004) 246 final, p. 21.
108. Case C-409/99 *Metropol Treuhand*.
109. Case C-247/95 *Marktgemeinde Welden*.
110. Case C-247/95 *Marktgemeinde Welden*, pp. 14–16.
111. Case C-247/95 *Marktgemeinde Welden*, p. 18.

distortions of competition within the meaning of Article 13(1) second subparagraph, by treating the public body as a non-taxable person.

In *Câmara Municipal do Porto*, the Court of Justice followed its reasoning in *Marktgemeinde Welden*. The Court found that (now) Article 13(2) is not intended to limit the benefit of treatment as a non-taxable person for VAT under the first paragraph of Article 13(1), but on the contrary permits Member States to extend that treatment to certain activities pursued by bodies governed by public law which, although not activities engaged in by those bodies as public authorities, may nevertheless be considered as such under (now) Article 13(2). Where those activities are thus treated as activities engaged in by bodies governed by public law acting as public authorities, they must also, in order to be non-taxable under the first paragraph of (now) Article 13(1), satisfy the conditions in the second paragraph of that provision.

The letting of spaces for the parking of vehicles is excluded from the activities exempted under Article 13B(b) of the Sixth Directive by point 2 of that provision, with the consequence that such an activity cannot be treated under (now) Article 13(2) as an activity engaged in by a body acting as a public authority, if it does not in itself satisfy that condition.

In *Salix*, the Court of Justice was asked whether a Member State must have an express legal provision stating that public bodies are non-taxable persons when performing exempt activities for (now) Article 13(2) to be applicable.[112] The Court pointed to the fact that (now) Article 13(2) was a derogation from the main rule in Article 9 and that it should be strictly construed. Member States were free to apply it, yet if they chose to do so, they must make a specific election to that effect. They may however choose the legal technique they regard as appropriate. Member States must however lay down an express provision in order to be able to rely on the option provided for in (now) Article 13(2), according to which specific activities of bodies governed by public law that are exempt are considered as activities of public authorities.

Neither from the history of the provision nor from the case law of the Court is it clear what the purpose of Article 13(2) is. I submit that the sole purpose of the provision is simplification. By treating a public body as falling outside the scope of VAT also with regard to activities that are exempt, and not subject to VAT anyway, the need to register etc. is (to some extent) avoided. Consistent with the suggested purpose, the second subparagraph of Article 13(1) is also according to *Marktgemeinde Welden* applicable to public bodies considered as non-taxable persons based on Article 13(2). Thus, Article 13(2) is not intended to affect the substantive scope of the exclusion from VAT but simply to provide the possibility to simplify the administration of a public body.

Terra and Kajus argue that the Court should have limited the reach of Article 13(2) to activities exempt under Article 132.[113] They point to the fact that unequal treatment may occur between different Member States when public bodies engaged in activities exempt under Article 135 may be treated as non-taxable persons.

112. Case C-102/08 *Salix*.
113. Terra & Kajus, *A Guide to the European VAT Directives (online)*, Part 3.1, Chapter 3.8.2.4.

Complexities arise when Article 135 is made applicable; above all due to the fact that certain transactions may be subject to tax anyway, following the possibility to opt to tax in Article 137. Consider, for example, the situation where a public body leases out immovable property and is considered as a public body based on Article 13(2). The public authority then seeks to opt for taxation. It seems that in that case, once the public body opts to be taxed, the public body should no longer be considered to be making exempt supplies and should not be treated as a non-taxable person. However, as the Court ruled in *Marktgemeinde Welden*, the option is not to be applicable in this case, something which obviously distorts the system and creates effects which are not simplifying the system at all.[114]

114. For a different view on how to read Article 13(2), see de la Feria *Intertax* (2008) She seems to consider that Article 13(2) extends the scope of the exclusion in Article 13(1). Terra & Kajus, *ibid.*, Jimenez *Intertax* (2008) and KPMG in Copenhagen Economics' (2011) – all seem to read the provision as a simplification without the effects read into it by de la Feria.

CHAPTER 3

The Treatment of the Income of a Public Body

§3.01 INTRODUCTION

A characteristic of public bodies' activities is that they are often hard to measure. Activities such as redistributing wealth and providing public goods are normally not directly, but indirectly, paid for through taxes. The output produced by public bodies is thus often not paid for in prices in the same way as what is typically the case in the private sector.[1] Article 2 of the VAT Directive subjects the supply of services and goods for consideration by a taxable person acting as such to VAT.[2] The Court of Justice has consistently held that in order for a supply to come within the scope of VAT, it has to be 'for consideration' i.e., there has to be a direct link between payments made and the supply performed.

Consistent with the basic characteristics of the European VAT system, Article 73 lays down as a main rule that the taxable amount is everything that constitutes the consideration obtained from the customer or a third party. It is clear from the case law of the Court of Justice that the taxable amount is the subjective value, i.e., everything actually received from the customer and that it cannot be a fictitious amount, objectively assessed. That would be contrary to the fundamental characteristics of the European VAT system as a neutral tax on consumption, exactly proportionate to the price paid. However, Article 73 of the VAT Directive extends the basis of assessment to include, in addition to the price paid, 'subsidies directly linked to the price' within the taxable amount. Considering the way public body activities are funded, this extension is of particular importance.

1. It has been reported that some Member States take into account the nature of the consideration when determining whether Article 13 covers a public body's activity, see, Jiménez, *Intertax* (2008).
2. In addition, intra-Community acquisitions of goods and imports of goods from outside the EU are subject to VAT. These taxable transactions are not dealt with here.

In the following sections, after discussing the direct link requirement (in section §2.03[B]) and subsidiaries directly linked to the price (in section §2.03[C]), a few cases are discussed where the Court of Justice has found that a transaction could not be taxed since it did not lead to consumption (section §2.03[C]). Lastly, fees and taxes and mandatory charges are discussed, followed by conclusions.

§3.02 DIRECT LINK

Article 2 of the VAT Directive has been considered to contain a requirement, inherent in the wording of the provision, for there being a service or goods supplied on the one hand and consideration paid on the other. There has to be a direct link between the supply made and the consideration received (in cash or kind).[3] If there is no link whatsoever between a payment and activities performed, the payment does not fall within the scope of VAT. Consequently, when damages are paid, which are not linked to supplies of anything but paid as compensation for loss, or when a part of the profit of a company is distributed as dividends, or when donations, gifts and concessions are provided, what is paid does not constitute consideration within the meaning of the VAT Directive, as it is not linked to any supply. In the following paragraphs, the most important cases are discussed and conclusions made.

In *Aardappelenbewaarplaats*[4] the Court of Justice dealt with a cooperative that ran a potatoes storage facility for its members. The Court of Justice was asked (essentially) whether a potato-storage service, for which no explicit charge was made, the only consideration being the unspecified reduction in the value of the shares, could be considered to be made for 'consideration' within the meaning of European VAT and therefore fall within the scope of VAT. The Court of Justice stated that European VAT contained a requirement of a direct link between any service provided and consideration paid which does not occur in a case where the consideration consists of an unascertained reduction in the value of the shares possessed by the members of the cooperative. Such a loss of value may not be regarded as a payment received by the cooperative providing the services.

Apple & Pear Development Council[5] concerns an English-Welsh council established under a government legal act. The activities of the Council were to promote the production and marketing of apples and pears in England and Wales including conducting research into these aspects. Every apple and pear grower of a certain size in England and Wales was obliged to register with the Council. The registrants were charged a mandatory annual charge (to meet the expenses of the council) calculated based on the hectares of land planted with apple or pear trees or a specific amount in respect of every 50 apple or pear trees planted on a grower's land. It was clear from the documents before the Court of Justice that the Council was considered to be a taxable person.

---

3. See cases dealt with just below and, generally, Terra & Kajus, *A Guide to the European VAT Directives (online)*, Part 3.1, Chapter 2.7.
4. Case C-154/80 *Aardappelenbewaarplaats.*
5. Case C-102/86 *Apple & Pear Development Council.*

The Court of Justice noted that the Development Council's functions related to the common interests of the growers. In so far as the Council was a provider of services, the benefits deriving from those services accrued to the whole industry. If individual apple and pear growers received benefits, they derived them indirectly from those accruing generally to the industry as a whole. Moreover, no relationship existed between the level of the benefits which individual growers obtained from the services provided by the Development Council and the amount of mandatory charges which they were obliged to pay. The Court of Justice therefore concluded that there was no direct link between the services provided by the Council and the mandatory charges.

It shall also be noted that the Court of Justice in *Tolsma*[6] considered that the money paid to a street musician was not directly linked to services performed. The Court of Justice stated that there has to be contractual relationship between the parties involved in order for the presumed consideration to constitute 'consideration' within the meaning of European VAT.[7]

In *Kennermer Golf*[8], the Court of Justice dealt with annual subscription fees to a golf and country club. The question arose whether the fees should be seen as directly linked to services performed, despite the fact that some members may not use the facilities at all. The Court of Justice stated that the fact that the annual subscription fee was a fixed sum which could not be related to each personal use of the golf course did not alter the fact that there was reciprocal performance between the members of a sports association and the association itself. The services provided by the association were constituted by the making available to its members, on a permanent basis, of sports facilities and the associated advantages, and not by particular services provided at the members' request. There was therefore a direct link between the annual subscription fees paid by members of a sports association and the services which it provided.

In *RCI*[9], the Court of Justice dealt with payments made in connection with timeshare usage rights. RCI's business consisted in facilitating and organising the exchange of timeshare usage rights held by its members in holiday accommodation outside that Member State. RCI operated a week-for-week timeshare usage rights exchange scheme known as 'RCI Weeks'. Membership of the RCI Weeks scheme entitled a member to deposit holiday usage rights in respect of his timeshare property into a pool of timeshare accommodation ('the Weeks Pool') and to have made available to him the holiday usage rights deposited by other members into the Weeks Pool. The depositing of holiday usage rights into the Weeks Pool did not entail the transfer to RCI Europe of rights in the property to which the usage rights deposited related.

RCI Weeks members paid an enrolment fee, which covered a period from one to five years, and annual subscription fees. In addition, an exchange fee was payable on the date of the request for an exchange. The question arose before the Court of Justice

6. Case C-16/93 *Tolsma*.
7. See Terra & Kajus, *A Guide to the European VAT Directives (online)*, Part 3.1, Chapter 2.7. The contract does not have to be legally enforceable though, but can be 'binding in honour only', see Case C-498/99 *Town & County Factors*.
8. Case C-174/00 *Kennermer Golf*.
9. Case C-37/08 RCI.

of the proper treatment of those fees and, in particular, whether they constituted consideration for services rendered.

The Court of Justice found[10] that although it is true that a closer examination of RCI Europe's business model shows that in return for payment of the enrolment fee, a member initially received only access to the RCI Weeks exchange scheme, it was also true that, for the owner of timeshare usage rights, membership of such a scheme would be pointless if he had no intention of exchanging his rights for those of other members.

If there was no intention to exchange timeshare usage rights through the market created by RCI Europe, the enrolment and annual subscription fees would lack any point. The service provided by RCI consisted of RCI undertaking to supply in the future the service required at the request of one of its members. Furthermore, the owner of a right who was registered with the RCI Weeks scheme and regularly paid annual subscription fees had the opportunity of exchanging his right for that of another owner and paying merely the exchange fee. The enrolment and subscription fees were in fact paid by members in return for a service provided, or to be provided, by RCI in order to facilitate the exchange of its members' timeshare usage rights, rather than rental through a third party agency. The enrolment and annual subscription fees must therefore be regarded as constituting consideration for participation in a system originally conceived to enable each member of RCI to exchange his timeshare usage right. The service supplied by RCI consisted in facilitating the exchange and the enrolment, and annual subscription fees represented the consideration paid by members for that service.

Case C-246/08 *Commission v. Finland* concerns public legal aid offices and legal aid services provided in legal proceedings in return for a part contribution paid by the recipient. The Commission complaint concerned the fact that Finland did not levy VAT on legal aid services when they were provided by public offices in legal proceedings in return for a part contribution from the recipient of the service. The Commission considered that these provisions of services constituted economic activities and that there was a direct link between the remuneration paid and the services provided. It is clear from the case that payments for legal services were to be paid by the recipient of the services where his disposable income exceeded the limit set for entitlement to free legal aid but did not exceed the ceiling barring all entitlement to legal aid.

The Court of Justice noted first that the legal aid services in question were not provided by the public offices free of charge and thus without any consideration, since the recipients of those services were required to make a payment to the public offices. However, it was established that the payment concerned was only a part payment, ranging from 20% to 75% of the fees payable for legal advice.

Although this part payment represented a portion of the fees, its amount was not calculated solely on the basis of those fees, but also depended upon the recipient's income and assets. Thus, it was the level of the latter – and not, for example, the number of hours worked by the public offices or the complexity of the case concerned

10. Case C-37/08 *RCI* pp. 28–35.

– which determined the portion of the fees for which the recipient remained responsible. It followed that the part payment made to the public offices by recipients of legal aid services depended only in part on the actual value of the services provided – the more modest the recipient's income and assets, the less strong the link with that value will be.

Furthermore, according to data provided by the Finnish Government, the part payments made in 2007 by recipients of legal aid services provided by the public offices amounted to EUR 1.9 million, whilst the gross operating costs of those offices were EUR 24.5 million. Even if that data also included legal aid services provided other than in court proceedings, such a difference suggested that the part payment borne by recipients must be regarded more as a fee, receipt of which did not, per se, mean that a given activity was economic in nature, than as consideration in the strict sense.

The Court of Justice therefore found that there was no direct link as required in its case law between the fees paid by the recipient of the services and the legal aid services provided.

As is clear from case law, the requirement of a direct link between supplies and the consideration is very strict. It is not enough that a connection exists between certain activities performed and funding by a presumed recipient of services, but the payment has to be directly linked to specific services. Furthermore, there is a requirement of a contractual relationship between the parties and that the consideration is actually linked to the value of the services provided. Finally, if there is uncertainty as regards whether there is a direct link there seems, based on the Court's judgment in *Tolsma*, to be a preference towards the conclusion that no direct link exists.[11] As a consequence, consumption bundled up with pure transfers of wealth, or concealed in a transfer that may be seen as either a pure transfer of wealth or a production activity, is not taxed.

[A] Subsidies Directly Linked to the Price

Article 73 of the VAT Directive includes in the taxable amount 'subsidies directly linked to the price'. In relation to the treatment of public bodies, this inclusion is clearly of great interest. One of the activities of public bodies is the reallocation of means, i.e., redistribution. That is achieved in part by transferring, sometimes as subsidies, wealth to particular persons. Whether these subsidies are included within the scope of VAT is obviously of great importance with regard to the treatment of public bodies. The content of the extension of the taxable amount to 'subsidies directly linked to the price' is dealt with below.

The distinction between subsidies directly linked to the price and those that are not seems, if one considers only the text of the directive, to be quite difficult. The

11. In AG Geelhoed's opinion, expressed in his Opinion in Case C-184/00 *Office des Produits Wallons*, p. 12, the payment is in truth quite independent of the enjoyment of the musical performance, a similarly strict view of the economic reality.

Commission, in its First Report on the Common system of VAT made the following comments:[12]

> While it is relatively easy to decide straight away that subsidies are 'directly linked to the price' when their amount is determined either by reference to the selling price of the goods or services supplied, or in relation to the quantities sold, or again in relation to the cost of goods or services supplied to the public free of charge, it is extremely difficult to decide in the case of other types of subsidy such as deficit subsidies or operating subsidies, which are paid with the aim of improving a firm's economic position and which are granted without specific reference to any price. The absence of any substantial difference between these two types of subsidy (those 'directly linked to the price are usually also aimed at improving a firm's position), together with the fact that a Member State can convert a subsidy of the first type into a subsidy of the second type, illustrate the fragility of a distinction based on purely formal criteria (the manner in which the subsidy is granted) and thus the inadequacy of the Directive in this respect.

The uncertainty in how the provision should be interpreted has been clarified, at least to some extent, in *Office des Produits Wallon*.[13] Before dealing with that case, it should be made clear that the fact of whether a particular transfer of money is *called* a subsidy, or something else, does not matter as far as defining whether it constitutes 'a subsidy directly linked to the price' or not. In *Keeping Newcastle Warm*, the Court of Justice dealt with a grant scheme established by regulation concerning services related to energy savings (energy advice).[14] A local authority paid the grant, after application by the customer, directly to the network installer carrying out the services under a standard-form agreement. The network installer was obliged to carry out the work for the price stated and, if he did so, was entitled to be paid that price by the other party, and to receive the grant. If the network installer carried out the work and the local authority did not approve the grant application then the applicant for the grant had to pay the network installer the full price of the work. The question arose before the Court of Justice of whether VAT was due on the grant paid. Actually, the national court particularly asked the Court of Justice whether the grant was 'a subsidy directly linked to the price' within the meaning of (now) Article 73. The Court of Justice was very brief in its judgment, merely stating that the grant in question 'may constitute a subsidy'. In any event, the taxable amount is everything which makes up the consideration and it is clear that the sums paid to the network installer was received in consideration for services supplied to certain categories of recipient. As consideration, it formed part of the taxable amount.

Office des Produits Wallons (OPW) was engaged in advertising and selling Walloon products. It also published a magazine. It received a subsidy from the Walloon Region with which it had concluded a framework agreement. Under the framework agreement, OPW was responsible for four types of activity, namely the publication of

12. First Report (COM(83) 426 final) from the Commission to the Council on the application of the common system of value added tax, submitted in accordance with Article 34 of the Sixth Council Directive (77/388/EEC) of 17 May 1977.
13. Case C-184/00 *Office des Produits Wallon*.
14. Case C-353/00 *Keeping Newcastle Warm*.

a catalogue, the publication of a magazine, the running of local offices and participation in local events. Under the framework agreement, OPW 'shall draw up its budgets on the basis of the previous year's subsidy'. The framework agreement also provided that 'permitted expenditure shall include in particular the remuneration of staff, the cost of renting and fitting out premises if necessary, the cost of obtaining necessary equipment and supplies, purchases of goods and services and any other costs, direct or indirect, relating to the activity of OPW, concerned by this agreement'.

The Court of Justice noted first that (now) Article 73 deals with situations where three parties are involved: the authority which grants the subsidy, the body which benefits from it and the purchaser of the goods or services delivered or supplied by the subsidised body. Thus, transactions covered by the provision are not those carried out for the benefit of the authority granting the subsidy.

Second, the Court of Justice stated that operating subsidies covering a part of running costs, which this case concerned, nearly always affect the cost price of the goods and services supplied by the subsidised body. In so far as it offers specific goods or services, that body can normally do so at prices which it would be unable to offer if it was obliged at the same time both to pass on its costs and make a profit.

However, the mere fact that a subsidy may affect the price is not enough to make that subsidy taxable. For the subsidy to be directly linked to the price it is also necessary that it be paid specifically to the subsidised body to enable it to provide particular goods or services. The price of the goods or services must, in principle, be determined not later than the time of the triggering event. Furthermore, the undertaking to pay the subsidy made by the person who grants it has, as its corollary, the right of the beneficiary to receive it. That link between the subsidy and the price must appear unequivocally following a case-by-case analysis of the circumstances underlying the payment of that consideration. On the other hand, it is not necessary for the price of the goods or services - or a part of the price - to be ascertained. It is sufficient for it to be ascertainable.

The Court of Justice left it to the national court to establish the existence of a direct link between the subsidy and the goods or services at issue. In that establishment, it was necessary to verify that the purchasers of the goods or services benefited from the subsidy granted to the beneficiary. The price payable by the purchaser must be fixed in such a way that it diminished in proportion to the subsidy granted to the seller or supplier of the goods or services, which therefore constituted an element in determining the price demanded by the latter. Consequently, the referring court must verify whether each activity gave rise to a specific and identifiable payment, or whether the subsidy was paid globally in order to cover the whole of OPW's running costs. In any event, it was only the part of the subsidy identifiable as being the consideration for a taxable supply that may, in appropriate cases, be subject to VAT.

A number of important conclusions can be drawn from the case. First, a subsidy within the meaning of the provision is granted by an authority, i.e., not all transfer payments are targeted, but only those which are made by an authority. The Court of Justice here followed the Advocate General in *Keeping Newcastle Warm*, who stated that a subsidy is ordinarily understood to mean a sum paid from public funds, usually in the general interest. This was also, the AG pointed out, the way the Court of Justice seemed to use the word 'subsidy'.[15] Consequently, the word 'subsidy' is restricted to payments made out of public funds.

In this context, it deserves reference to AG Stix-Hackl again, and her opinion in *Keeping Newcastle Warm*.[16] She pointed to the fact that:

> a subsidy from public funds may, however, take the most diverse forms. It could, for example, comprise a global subsidy to cover general operating costs, in which case no parties other than the donor and the recipient of the subsidy are affected in any way, or only indirectly. Or it could comprise a subsidy granted by the donor to the recipient to enable a third party to obtain a specific service (or to obtain it more cheaply). As a rule, there can only be a taxable transaction where the subsidy is of the latter type, that is to say one granted in the context of a tripartite relationship. The reason for this is that subsidies from public funds are made in the furtherance of the public interest, not to procure goods or services for the State. In order for there to be a supply, and therefore a taxable transaction for the purposes of Article 2 of the Sixth Directive, the beneficiary of the supply must be a third party.

Second, the wording of Article 73, 'and subsidies directly linked to the price', implies that it is an extension of the scope of the taxable amount to also include subsidies. However, the Court of Justice requires there to be an almost direct link between the subsidies paid and supplies made, i.e., it applies almost the same test as when it determines the existence of a subjective value under the first part of Article 73. This interpretation seems to be shared with AG Stix-Hackl, who has stated, with reference to *Office des Produits Wallons*, that the direct link required in the case law of the Court must also be present between a subsidy and a supply in order for the subsidy to be subject to VAT.[17]

The subsidy must be paid specifically to the subsidised body to enable it to provide particular goods or services. It must also follow a contractual obligation to pay it. This is also shown by the fact that the link to the reduction of the price must be set so that it diminishes in proportion to the subsidy paid.

Third, the Court of Justice states that it is not necessary for the price of the goods or services - or a part of the price - to be ascertained. It is sufficient for it to be ascertainable. This seems to be with *First National Bank of Chicago* in mind, even though the Court of Justice does not refer to that case in its judgment.[18] In that case, the Court of Justice came to the conclusion that it possessed no obstacle to include within the scope of European VAT consideration for services where the consideration was difficult to establish on a transaction basis. However, in that case the overall value added was correctly measured yet not possible to determine on a transaction basis. In addition, the case concerned primarily the calculation of the deductible proportion. In *OPW*, the gross value added is determined by the application of the apparent extension

15. See Case C-384/95 *Landboden-Agrardienste* where the Court of Justice refers to subsidies, in point 20, with the words 'that a payment made by a public authority in the common interest'.
16. Case C-353/00 *Keeping Newcastle Warm*, pp. 39–40 of the Opinion.
17. Opinion in Case C-353/00 *Keeping Newcastle Warm*, p. 46.
18. Case C-172/96 *First National Bank of Chicago*. It is referred to by AG Geelhoed who seems to be making the same point as the Court in his Opinion, see point 15.

of the taxable amount to subsidies. The first case concerns the measurement of the subjective value on a transaction basis and the second concerns determining the scope of the taxable amount. In the case of subsidies, the problem of ascertaining the exact part of the price paid through a subsidy thus concerns the issue of whether the taxable amount should be what is actually paid (the subjective value) or some other amount (objectively ascertainable).

The Court of Justice states that it is not necessary for the subsidy to correspond exactly to the diminution in the price of the goods supplied, it being sufficient if the relationship between the diminution in price and the subsidy is significant. Thus it is not a strict 'direct link' requirement but an 'almost' direct link requirement, or, in the words of AG Geelhoed 'a less close link' than in the case of a payment.[19] This is of profound importance because it means that the extension of the taxable amount to subsidies indeed extends the scope of VAT to include not only the subjective value paid but also, in these cases, an objective value estimated based on whether a change in price is 'significant'. It also means that the apparent extension is a real extension to subsidies that are similar to a subjective consideration yet cannot be measurable exactly.

Lastly, a comment deserves to be made with regard to the statements in the First Report of the Commission quoted above. The Commission there considered it inadequate that Member States can dispose over the forms in which a subsidy is granted. However, that situation remains and with the knowledge of when a 'subsidy' is taxed, Member States can take into account and adjust their subsides so that they entail the preferred VAT treatment (taxed or not taxed). I submit that this is not, however, an inadequacy of the Directive. Rather, it is inherent in any transfer of wealth from state resources that it can be made either as a payment or as a pure transfer of wealth. Such transfers can also influence competition between those that have to account for output VAT and those that are not liable to account for output VAT. The Commission has raised this as a matter of importance before the Court of Justice in *OPW*.[20] The Court of Justice did not comment on it but AG Geelhoed did.[21] In his opinion it is a general characteristic of subsidies paid to traders that they influence competition. In order to prevent them from having undesirable effects on competition, the Treaty contains a prohibition against state aid under the supervision of the Commission. Why then, in addition, should certain types of subsidy be liable to VAT? Also, the effect of taxing subsidies is of limited effect as they may promptly be increased by the state to compensate for the VAT element. This is in my view an important point. The effects on competition that the granting of subsidies entail is not a flaw of the VAT system, but inherent in the granting of the subsidy.

19. Case C-184/00 *Office des Produits Wallons*, Opinion p. 33.
20. Case C-184/00 *Office des Produits Wallons*, Opinion of AG Geelhoed, p. 16.
21. *Ibid.*

§3.03 CASES WHERE NO CONSUMPTION WAS PRESENT

The Court of Justice has, in my opinion, limited the scope of the VAT system due to the fact that no consumption was present in the activities performed for consideration.

In *Mohr*, the Court of Justice dealt with Mr Mohr, who received a grant under a Community regulation for the discontinuation of his milk production. The Court of Justice found that no benefit was provided, either to the Community, or to the national authorities paying the grant. There was therefore not any consumption present in the case and Mr Mohr was therefore not liable to account for output VAT on the grant.[22]

In *Landboden Agraardienst*, a potato grower received compensation for reducing his annual potato production by 20%. Similarly to Mohr, the Court of Justice found that European VAT taxes consumption and that the farmer did not supply a service to any identifiable consumer. Thus no consumption was present and the compensation fell outside the scope of VAT.[23]

In conclusion, in those cases it is to me quite clear that a link exists between the services supplied and the consideration received. The compensation and grant were only paid if the receiver acted in a particular way - cease or reduce production. Especially when considering that Article 25(b) of Directive 2006/112/EC states that a service may consist of an obligation to refrain from an act, this must be considered to constitute a service per se. The Court however limited the reach of the European VAT system to transactions that entail consumption.[24]

§3.04 SUPPLIES MADE UNDER LAW AND MANDATORY CHARGES

The taxable transactions subject to VAT are defined in the VAT Directive.[25] Of particular importance in relation to the activities of public bodies are how transfers of goods and supplies of services are to be treated when made in pursuance of the law or otherwise in connection with public administration. Interestingly, the VAT Directive contains provisions on this particular subject.

According to Article 14(1), a supply of goods is the transfer of the right to dispose of property as owner. In addition hereto, Article 14(2)(a) states that the transfer, by order made by or in the name of a public authority or in pursuance of the law, of the ownership of property against payment of compensation is also (in addition to the supplies defined in Article 14(1)) to be regarded as a supply of goods. Furthermore, according to Article 24(1), a supply of services is any transaction which does not constitute a supply of goods. Article 25(c) states that a supply of service may consist, *inter alia*, in the performance of services in pursuance of an order made by or in the name of a public authority or in pursuance of the law:

22. Case C-215/94 *Mohr*.
23. Case C-384/95 *Landboden-Agrardienste*.
24. See also Henkow (2008) Chapter 3.
25. Articles 14 to 30 of the VAT Directive.

Terra and Kajus make the following observations, with regard to Article 14(2)(a).[26]

> One may argue that the broad definition of Article 14(1) clearly covers the transfers in question. However, from the first sentence of Article 14(2), i.e. 'in addition ... shall be regarded ... ' it follows that the transfers by order of a public authority are not included in the general definition of Article 14(1). The various authentic languages use a different terminology than is used in Article 2(1)(a), rather than for example referring to 'consideration', 'mod vederlag', 'à titre onéreux' or 'gegen Entgelt', the terms 'compensation', 'erstatningsydelse', 'paiment d'une indemnité' are used. It seems to us that without an assimilation of the transfers in question to supplies of goods, it would be possible to argue that no 'economic activity' or taxable transaction has taken place. One of the perverse effects of such reasoning would be that public authorities would prefer to rely on transfers against payment of compensation, rather than on transfers against payment of a consideration.

I agree with the analysis. The scope of taxable transactions is extended to include certain transactions performed, not for consideration but for compensation. One can therefore also draw the conclusion that in the normal course of events, compensation does not fall within the scope of VAT – something which is hard to reconcile with the general character of the VAT.[27] The Court's judgment in Case C-246/08 *Commission v. Finland* confirms this conclusion. Having the character of a 'fee' rather than 'consideration', payment made for legal advice was not held to fall within the scope of the VAT Directive.

The difference in terminology (compensation rather than consideration) seems also to be linked to the character of these transactions. It is clear from the provisions that also in cases where there is no option for a person, but he is obliged under law to sell property, that constitutes a taxable transaction for VAT purposes. Even confiscated goods are supplied for VAT purposes. The link between the actual delivery and payment seems clear. However, it is not a contractual link but a legal obligation.

The scope of VAT thus, by explicit extension, also includes public administrative tasks, in so far they are performed pursuant to the law. This is a significant and important extension of the general rules defining the taxable transactions. This implies that public administration activities which entail some kind of compensation being paid should constitute taxable transactions for the purposes of EU VAT. Mandatory charges may thus fall within the scope of VAT, provided they pass the direct link test. But the extension says nothing on whether it is the same 'direct link' test that is applicable as with regard to taxable transactions supplied 'for consideration'. However, in the light of the judgment in *Commission v. Finland*, it seems that the same test ought to be applied, at least if the judgment is considered to be applicable *mutatis mutandis*.

Article 25(c) of the VAT Directive makes clear that the fact that a particular supply is not made pursuant to a contract but in accordance with a legal rule does not mean that it is not a taxable transaction. However, in order for those transactions to fall

26. Terra & Kajus, *A Guide to the European VAT Directives (online)*, Part 3.1, Chapter 4.3.1.
27. In comparison with the New Zealand's GST definition of the consideration as anything paid, even for the inducement of a supply, compensation seems also to be included. I would, from a system design point of view, have preferred the New Zealand approach.

within the scope of VAT, the additional condition must be met that the transaction in question is directly linked to consideration paid.

The Court of Justice has dealt with mandatory charges under law in *Apple & Pear* and *Commission v. Finland*.[28] In *Apple & Pear* there was a legal rule stating that a certain activity must be paid for. Rather there was a supply of services made but the issue was whether the payment could be linked to supplies made. Article 25(c) was not discussed by the Court. Neither in *Commission v. Finland* was Article 25(c) argued. *Commission v. Finland* confirms the position of *Apple & Pear*. The consideration has to relate to services performed. When the consideration is dependent (also) upon factors totally unrelated to the actual remuneration for the services performed, the link is not sufficiently direct and the consideration falls outside the scope of VAT.

Consequently, an evaluation is needed in all cases of whether the charge made under law is directly linked to services received by an identifiable consumer or recipient. It is clear that the supply is in itself a taxable transaction even if made under law. In order for there to be a direct link in European VAT, the amount of the remuneration must relate to the value of the services performed, and not some other factor. Taxes, but also in principle dues and fees, cannot therefore be said to be directly linked to services received. There is no direct link between the amount of taxes, (and principally also dues and fees) payable and services received from public authorities and institutions. On the other hand, when a fee is calculated based on what is provided, such as a fee payable per visit to a doctor (payable regardless of the income of the patient), then there is a direct link present.

§3.05 CONCLUSIONS

In European VAT, the requirement of a direct link between supplies and the consideration is strict and excludes all transfers not made for specific services or goods that entail benefits for specific individuals, i.e., excluding benefits rendered to society at large where the benefit is not identifiable on an individual basis. It seems that if there is uncertainty as regards whether the link is really direct, there is a preference towards the conclusion that no direct link exists.

As a consequence, consumption bundled up with pure transfers of wealth, or concealed in a transfer that may be seen as either a pure transfer of wealth or a production activity, is not taxed. In addition, a transfer for a production activity is only taxed when the production activity yields specific benefits, and not when the benefit cannot be measured on an individual basis, such as in the case of the provision of public goods.

It is notable that the taxable amount is extended to cover also subsidies paid by a public body which are almost directly linked to supplies made. The extension to subsidies entails an extension of the scope of VAT to include not only the subjective value paid but also, in these cases, an estimate of the objective value based on whether a change in price is 'significant'.

28. Case 102/86 *Apple & Pear* and Case C-246/08 *Commission v. Finland.*

Taxes, but also in principle dues and fees, are therefore typically not directly linked to supplies. There is no direct link between the amount of taxes, (and principally also dues and fees) payable and services received from public authorities and institutions. These are calculated based on criteria other than the value of services received. Finally, the effect that non-taxation of subsidies may have on competition is in principle, as argued by AG Geelhoed, not a flaw of the VAT system but inherent in the granting of a subsidy. If subsidies are taxed, the level of the subsidy could be increased and the increase covered by the payment of additional taxes. However, when a VAT system is operated in a state where the granter of the subsidy is not the same person as the one receiving the income from the VAT (federal systems, communes and state systems), competition at local level is distorted.

CHAPTER 4

Deduction of Input VAT and Other Issues

§4.01 DEDUCTION OF INPUT VAT: GENERAL ISSUES

VAT is a tax on consumption and the right to deduct VAT charged on supplies of goods and services made to a taxable person is indispensable to the system's function. In accordance herewith, the Court of Justice has continuously held that the deduction mechanism is intended to relieve the trader entirely of the burden of the VAT payable or paid in the course of all his economic activities. The common system of VAT consequently ensures neutrality of taxation of all economic activities, provided that those activities are themselves subject in principle to VAT. The right to deduct VAT, as an integral part of the VAT scheme, is a fundamental principle underlying the common system of VAT and in principle may not be limited. It follows that a taxable person may deduct the VAT levied on goods and services acquired for the exercise of his taxable activities.[1]

A pre-condition for the right to deduct is thus that the 'trader' is engaged in an economic activity that is in principle subject to VAT. The application of the VAT rules to supply of goods and services transactions, including the rules on the right to deduct, is dependent on whether the person carrying out the transaction is a taxable person.[2]

Furthermore, the right to deduct is in principle linked to the collection of output VAT.[3] Under the main provision on the right to deduct VAT in the VAT Directive, Article 168, VAT is deductible in so far as goods and services acquired which carry the burden of VAT are used for the purposes of the taxed transactions of the taxable person. The Court has consistently held that the existence of a direct and immediate

1. See, for example, Case C-277/09 *RBS Deutschland Holding*, pp. 38–40 and cases referred to there.
2. Case C-378/02 *Waterschap Zeeuws Vlaanderen*, p. 29. NB. Article 169(b) and (c) deviate from this and grant the right to deduct VAT also for VAT linked to exempt transactions.
3. Case C-184/04 *Uudenkaupungin kaupunki* p. 24 and Case C-277/09 *RBS Deutschland Holding* pp. 35–36.

link between a particular input transaction and a particular output transaction or transactions giving rise to entitlement to deduct is, in principle, necessary before the taxable person is entitled to deduct input VAT and in order to determine the extent of such entitlement. The right to deduct VAT charged on the acquisition of input goods or services presupposes that the expenditure incurred in acquiring them was a component of the cost of the output transactions that gave rise to the right to deduct.[4]

Consequently, where goods or services acquired by a taxable person are used for purposes of transactions that are exempt or do not fall within the scope of VAT, no output tax can be collected or input tax deducted.[5] A non-taxable person, such as a public body acting as such falling within the exclusion of Article 13(1), cannot deduct input VAT incurred. When a public body is both a non-taxable person and a taxable person, input VAT needs to be first allocated to either the activities as non-taxable person or taxable person respectively, and if not possible, a proportion is deductible equivalent to the part of acquisitions that is pertaining to the activities falling within the scope of VAT.[6]

It would, in my opinion, be preferable from a system design perspective to grant the right to deduct input VAT to all traders in so far as the VAT on the acquisition is not exclusively linked to exempt output.[7] However, in European VAT a more limited approach – a requirement of a direct and immediate link with taxed output – has been adopted. It seems evident that problems will arise. There is a tension between the basic principles underlying the VAT system, the fact that the deduction system is intended to relieve the trader entirely of the burden of VAT, and the requirement of a direct and immediate link with taxed output transactions. And problems have certainly appeared.[8] In particular with regard to financial investment activities and handling shares held in subsidiaries, the case law of the Court of Justice is complicated.[9] The case law is however not unique to public bodies, private bodies also have to deal with how to handle input VAT pertaining to financial investments.

Below, one judgment in particular, *Securenta*, is discussed as it has implications on how a public body should deal with input VAT pertaining both to activities which fall outside the scope of VAT based on Article 13(1) and activities which falls inside the scope of VAT.[10]

Securenta's activities involved acquiring, managing and selling real estate, securities, financial holdings and investments of all types. Securenta acquired the

4. See, for example, Case C-29/08 *AB SKF* p. 57 and case law referred to there.
5. See, for example, Case C-29/08 *AB SKF* p. 59, Case C-437/06 *Securenta* and Article 168a and Case C-435/05 *Investrand* and Case C-4/94 *BLP*.
6. Case C-437/06 *Securenta* and Article 168a.
7. Acquisitions linked to consumption are handled within the VAT system through a system of self-supplies, see Articles 16 and 26.
8. The latest case of more significance, where the Court, it could be argued, is granting a right to deduct input VAT even when an acquisition is made that could be clearly linked to exempt output transactions, is Case C-29/08 *AB SKF*.
9. See, for example, Case C-437/06 *Investrand*, Case C-4/94 *BLP*, Case C-29/08 *AB SKF*, Case C-80/95 *Harnas & Helm* and Henkow (2008), Chapter 5.
10. Case C-437/06 *Securenta*.

capital necessary for this by means of the issue of shares and atypical silent partnerships. While offering shares for public subscription, it admitted a multitude of silent partners. The persons thus associated provided capital which the company reinvested.

The Court of Justice was asked how, in the case of a taxpayer who carries out both economic and non-economic activities, the right to deduct input VAT paid is to be determined. The Court found that it was apparent from the information supplied by the national court that Securenta carried out three types of activity: (i) non-economic activities, which do not fall within the scope of the Sixth Directive; (ii) economic activities, which as such fall within the scope of that directive but are exempt from VAT; and (iii) taxed economic activities. The question therefore was, in that context, whether – and, if so, to what extent – such a taxable person had the right to deduct input VAT relating to expenditure which was not attributable to specific output transactions.

It was not disputed in the case that the expenditure connected with supplies of services carried out in the context of the issue of shares and financial holdings was not solely attributable to downstream economic activities carried out by Securenta and was not therefore among the elements which, alone, go to make up the cost of the transactions relating to those activities. If, however, that had been the case, the Court recognised that the supplies of services concerned would have had a direct and immediate link with the taxpayer's economic activities and that a right of deduction would have arisen (following case law on the matter). However, it was apparent from the documents before the Court that the costs incurred by Securenta for the financial transactions at issue were, at least in part, for the performance of non-economic activities.

The Court of Justice concluded that to the extent that input VAT relating to expenditure incurred by a taxpayer was connected with activities which, in view of their non-economic nature, did not fall within the scope of the Sixth Directive, it could not give rise to a right to deduct.

The national court also asked whether, on the assumption that deduction of input VAT was allowed only to the extent that the expenditure incurred by the taxpayer was attributable to economic activities, how the apportionment of the input tax between economic activity and non-economic activity should be carried out. The Court replied that the provisions of (now) the VAT Directive did not include rules relating to the methods or criteria which the Member States are required to apply when adopting provisions permitting the apportionment of input VAT paid according to whether the relevant expenditure relates to economic activities or to non-economic activities. (N.B. after the introduction of Article 168a by Directive 2009/162/EU, it can be claimed that the Directive does entail rules on how to apportion input VAT in situations of acquisitions for economic as well as non-economic activities, see further below.) In those circumstances it was for the Member States to establish methods and criteria appropriate to that aim and consistent with the principles underlying the common system of VAT.

The conclusion must be drawn from *Securenta* that when a public body performs both activities falling within the scope of VAT, i.e., it acts as a taxable person, and activities falling outside the scope of VAT, due to the fact that the activities are covered by Article 13(1), a deductible proportion must be calculated for input VAT not directly and immediately linked to any specific activity.

Consequently, a public body has to consider whether the input VAT is directly and immediately linked:

(1) to activities falling within the scope of VAT; and
  (a) if so, whether the input VAT is directly and immediately linked to taxed or exempt output; or
  (b) if not, how to calculate a deductible proportion, Articles 173–175.
(2) with activities falling both outside and inside the scope (Article 13(1) is applicable to some of its activities and/or some activities are not of an economic nature according to the case law of the Court of Justice of the EU), and if so:
  (a) a deductible proportion needs to be determined based on national legislation complying with the principles of the EU VAT system (presumably based on the use of acquisitions or turnover); and
  (b) another deductible proportion needs to be calculated based on Articles 173–175 if the activities falling inside the scope of VAT are both taxed and exempt.
(3) to activities falling outside the scope of VAT only, in which case:
  (a) in principle no right to deduct exists;
  (b) but the case law of the Court on whether the acquisitions also constitute part of the overhead of the activities performed as a taxable person needs to be taken into account.

It seems to me that it cannot be easy to comply with these rules in a consistent manner in all Member States.

§4.02 ADJUSTMENT OF INPUT VAT

According to Article 184 of the VAT Directive, the initial deduction must be adjusted if it was higher or lower than to which the taxable person was entitled. In the case of capital goods, the adjustment shall be spread over a period of 5 years (in the case of capital goods other than immovable property) or up to 20 years (in the case of immovable property), Article 187.

The provisions are highly relevant for public bodies. Consider the situation where a public body acts as a non-taxable person acquiring certain capital goods. It then starts up an activity, using the assets in question, which it performs as a taxable person. Can it then claim adjustments and ask for a repayment of the input VAT during the adjustment period (5–20 years depending on time of acquisition and type of capital good)? That was the question before the Court in *Waterschap Zeeuws Vlaanderen* (WZV).[11]

11. Case C-378/02.

WZV was a body governed by public law responsible for the public management of water. In carrying out that activity, WZV acted as a public authority and was therefore not a taxable person following (now) Article 13(1). WZV arranged for the construction of a sewage treatment plant and paid VAT on its acquisition. WZV thus acquired the plant in order to perform its task of public management of water in the territory covered by it and, in that context, acted as a public authority.

Four years later, WZV established a foundation for the promotion of the environment in Dutch Flanders ('the foundation'), to which it sold the plant exclusive of VAT. On the day of the sale, WZV was granted a lease of the plant by the foundation for a term of nine years and two days. WZV and the foundation submitted a joint request to opt for VAT to apply in respect of the sale and letting of the plant in accordance with national rules implementing (now) Article 137 of the VAT Directive. WZV thereafter claimed repayment of VAT paid on the construction of the plant based on national rules implementing the capital adjustment rules in Articles 184 et seq. of the VAT Directive. The national court referred to the Court of Justice the question of whether a body governed by public law which purchases capital goods as a public authority and subsequently sells those goods as a taxable person may, in respect of that sale, be entitled to an adjustment.

The Court of Justice in its reply relied on Case C-97/90 *Lennartz* which concerned essentially the same question, but in the case of a private individual acquiring capital goods later used by him as a taxable person. Only a person who is a taxable person, and who is acting as such at the time of the purchase of goods, has a right to deduct in respect of those goods and may deduct the VAT due or paid in respect of those goods if he uses them for the purposes of his taxable transactions. A non-taxable person does not have a right to deduct the VAT he may have paid on the purchase of goods. That person's activities – its supplies of goods or services – do not fall within the scope of the VAT. In *Lennartz*, the Court held that a taxable person is not entitled to adjustments where he had acquired the goods in question in his capacity of private individual. The Court of Justice found that the same must be true of a body governed by public law which acts as a public authority at the time when it purchases capital goods. The public body did not at that time act as a taxable person and consequently it did not have any right to deduct the VAT paid by it in respect of those goods. The fact that that body subsequently acted as a taxable person, cannot result in the deductibility of VAT. A public body cannot be equated to a taxable person carrying out some taxable activities and other exempt activities. The capacity in which the person acts is the decisive factor and that is assessed at the time of acquisition of the goods concerned.

WZV had submitted that the impossibility of deducting the input VAT paid creates a significant distortion of competition which, in its view, justified application of the exception laid down in the second subparagraph of (now) Article 13(1). The Court replied that any distortion of competition stems more from the exercise by the body governed by public law of the right to opt for taxation in respect of the sale and letting of the immovable property concerned than from application of the rule that bodies governed by public law are not regarded as taxable persons in respect of the transactions in which they engage as public authorities. It is inherent in the existence of exceptions to the VAT system that they will interfere to some extent with the application of the principles of neutrality and of equality of treatment.

Consequently, when a public body purchases capital goods in its capacity as a public authority it can never recover any VAT paid on the acquisition under the adjustment rules. It is a pre-condition for the adjustment rules to apply that the capital goods have been acquired by a taxable person acting as such.

In addition to the adjustment rules, the quite recently introduced Article 168a should be considered. According to Article 168a(1), when immovable property[12] forms part of the business assets and is used privately or 'for purposes other than those of his business' VAT on expenditure related to the property shall be deductible only up to the proportion of the property's use for purposes of the taxable person's business. It is clear from the recital to the Directive introducing the provision, and from the Commission's proposal, that the provision is motivated by a more effective application of the principle whereby the deduction arises only in so far as the goods and services concerned are used for the transactions giving rise to the right of deduction.[13] The provision is a reaction against the Court's case law and principles laid down in *Lennartz,* where property used both for private purposes and business purposes (mixed use) could be allocated to the business, with the result that all input VAT was deductible and VAT was chargeable on the use of the property for private purposes.

It seems clear from the legislative history that the provision was not originally aimed at public bodies. The provision as enacted is however clearly broad enough to be also applicable as regards acquisitions of assets by public bodies acting as such. *WZV* also confirms that public bodies should be equated with other persons as regards the principles on adjustments of VAT. There are no reasons to deviate from that as regards the application of Article 168a and it must therefore be concluded that the provision applies to the acquisition of a business asset by a public body that, at least partially, acts as such.

Consequently, when a public body acquires immovable property, any later change in use of the asset must be taken into account in an adjustment of VAT. The principles of this adjustment scheme are the same as for other adjustments, yet it is left to the Member States to enact and formulate these adjustment rules. I note the increased complexities that arise. When a public body acquires immovable property, even when acting as a public body, it must keep track of the use of the immovable property it acquires and adjust input VAT when the use is changed.

§4.03 SUBSIDIES AND THE CALCULATION OF THE DEDUCTIBLE PROPORTION

According to Article 173 of the VAT Directive, when VAT pertains both to transactions in respect of which VAT is deductible and transaction in respect of which it is not, only such proportion as is attributable to the former transactions is deductible. The main

12. According to Article 168a(2) Member States may also apply these rules on expenditure related to other goods forming part of the business assets.
13. Directive 2009/162/EU, recitals 9-12 and COM(2007) 677 final, p. 4.

rule for calculating the deductible proportion, or pro-rata, is found in Article 174 which states that the deductible proportion shall be determined through a fraction comparing the turnover of transactions in respect of which VAT is deductible and non-deductible.

The turnover method is a simplification. The most correct result is reached by tracing how acquisitions are used, and allowing deduction in so far as an acquisition is used for taxed activities. However, a method is needed to determine when an acquisition is used for taxed activities and no allocation can be exact.[14]

Article 174 second subparagraph states that certain amounts shall be excluded from the calculation of the deductible proportion, namely certain amounts attributable to supplies of capital goods and certain incidental transactions. The purpose of the rules on calculation of the deductible proportion is to ensure a neutral taxation, so that all input VAT pertaining to taxed activities is deductible, and VAT is not deductible as regards acquisitions pertaining to exempt activities.[15]

Article 174(1) last paragraph states that Member States may include in the calculation of the deductible proportion the amount of subsidies, other than those directly linked to the price as referred to in Article 73.[16] In so far as Member States have made use of this option, the provision is of importance as regards the treatment of public bodies for VAT purposes. Many public bodies are involved in the redistribution of funds between various entities in the economy. Public bodies both receive and distribute subsidies that do not fall within the scope of the taxable amount. It should be pointed out that the possibility to limit the right to deduction in respect of the receipt of subsidies is limited to situations where a taxable person performs both taxed and exempt activities (mixed activities).[17]

When the right to deduct input VAT is reduced due to the receipt of subsidies, how funds are redistributed will influence the VAT treatment. But how funds are redistributed has nothing to do with VAT as a tax on consumption. Rather, the provision creates VAT costs for producers and their production activities - even if their output is taxed.[18] The provision therefore is fundamentally inconsistent with the principles underlying the common VAT system.[19]

§4.04 EXEMPTIONS

The VAT Directive contains a number of exemptions referring to public authorities. Article 132(1) exempts, *inter alia*:[20]

14. See Henkow (2008), p. 299.
15. Compare Case C-306/94 *Régie* and Henkow (2008), p. 304.
16. The provision has been discussed in the Court of Justice's case law, above all in Case C-204/03 *Commission v. Spain*.
17. Case C-204/03 *Commission v. Spain* p. 25.
18. Also the Commission has pointed to these effects in its First report.
19. Terra & Kajus, *A Guide to the European VAT Directives (online)*, Part 3.1, Chapter 10.3.2.1 seem to fully share this view. They also point to the fact that unequal treatment is created between mixed taxable persons and fully taxable persons, the latter always have a full right to deduct VAT whereas the former may have a limited right due to subsidies received.
20. The letters refers to the letters of the provision. The full text of the letters is not reproduced.

(a) certain services supplied by the public postal services,
(b) hospital care performed by bodies governed by public law,
...
(g) certain welfare and social security work by bodies governed by public law,
(h) services linked to the protection of children by bodies governed by public law,
(i) education services supplied by bodies governed by public law,
...
(n) certain cultural services supplied by bodies governed by public law and
...
(q) certain activities of public radio and television bodies.[21]

Public postal services referred to in Article 132(1)(a) have been defined in case law, foremost in *TNT Post UK*.[22] According to that judgment, the exemptions provided for in (now) Article 132 of the VAT Directive are intended to encourage certain activities in the public interest. That general objective takes the form, in the postal sector, of the more specific objective of offering postal services which meet the essential needs of the population at a reduced cost. This is the same object, in essence, as that of the directive harmonising the internal market of postal services, Directive 97/67, to offer a universal postal service. The Court, based on this, finds that public postal services providers must be regarded as operators, whether they are public or private, who undertake to supply postal services which meet the essential needs of the population and therefore, in practice, to provide all or part of the universal postal service in a Member State, as defined in Article 3 of Directive 97/67.

Public radio and television bodies referred to in Article 132(1)(q) have not been defined in case law.

In all but letters (a) and (q) a reference is made to 'bodies governed by public law'. The question arises of how this expression should be interpreted and whether it has the same meaning as in Article 13, where a reference is also made to 'bodies governed by public law'. It is clear that in a contextual interpretation, considering the VAT Directive as a whole, the same expression should have the same meaning, wherever it appears, unless the specific context of the provision in question does not allow such an interpretation. In the present case, both provisions have the effect of excluding from the scope of VAT certain activities by public bodies. This link is also recognised in Article 13(2) and is clear from the case law of the Court under which both provisions are exemptions from the general rule that all economic activities fall within the scope and that all supplies are taxed respectively. It must therefore be concluded that the expression must have the same meaning within both provisions. What constitutes a public body has been discussed in section §2.03[C] and the discussion is

21. See also Annex X which concerns the possibility to continue to tax or exempt certain supplies. Annex X Part A(2) refers to public radio and television, Part B(3) public postal services and B(8) supplies of water by bodies governed by public law. Article 387(a) provides that Malta under certain circumstances may apply an exemption for the supply of water by a body governed by public law.
22. Case C-357/07 *TNT Post UK*.

thus equally relevant here. Notably, I have not found a case dealing with the exemption that addresses the interpretation of what constitutes 'bodies governed by public law' within the meaning of (now) Article 132. The link between the two provisions has though been recognised by the Court of Justice.[23]

In the scheme of the VAT Directive, before determining whether the exemptions from VAT are applicable, the transaction as such must fall within the scope of VAT. Thus, if the activity in question is performed by a public body acting as such, it does not fall within the scope of VAT under Article 13, and whether the exemptions are applicable, is not of importance. In both Articles 13 and 132 the activities of public bodies are regulated. The services exempt under Article 132(1) seems to be those that do not necessarily involve the use of public powers going beyond those usable in commercial relationships.

The limitation of the exemptions to 'bodies governed by public law' potentially distorts competition, since the exemption is limited to certain bodies, and not exclusively the activity that should be exempt.[24] This is recognised in the provision. For example, in letter (b), the exemption extends to activities 'under social conditions comparable with those applicable to bodies governed by public law, by hospitals, centres for medical treatment or diagnosis and other duly recognised establishments of a similar nature'. The exemption in letter (g) applies to certain services, 'including those supplied by old people's homes, by bodies governed by public law or by other bodies recognised by the Member State concerned as being devoted to social wellbeing'. Letter (i) includes education services supplied 'by other organisations recognised by the Member State concerned as having similar objects'. Article 133(d) and the last paragraph also explicitly state that Member States may limit the scope of letter (n) when the exemption is 'likely to cause distortion of competition to the disadvantage of commercial enterprises subject to VAT'. The Court of Justice has also recognised the principle of fiscal neutrality in this context and Member States ought not to treat similar organisations, which are thus in competition with each other, differently for VAT purposes.[25] In addition, Article 134 states that the supply of goods or services shall not be granted exemption, as provided for in points (b), (g), (h), (i), (l), (m) and (n) of Article 132(1), when: (a) the supply is not essential to the transactions exempted; and (b) where the basic purpose of the supply is to obtain additional income for the body in question through transactions which are in direct competition with those of commercial enterprises subject to VAT.

Consequently, the Community legislator has gone to some length in trying to create neutrality between different economic operators and public bodies, and other organisations enjoying an exemption. The method varies between the various exemptions in Article 132(1). Yet, the overall purpose seems to be to create neutrality between different persons supplying the same kind of services. The only two exemptions

23. In Case 107/84 *Commission v. Germany*.
24. Compare the case law on the exemptions in Article 135(1)(b) to (f) where the status of the provider of the services is of no importance, see Henkow, 2008, Chapter 4. See, also in regard to Article 132(1) and the principle of fiscal neutrality, Case C-216/97 *Gregg & Gregg*, points 19 and 20.
25. See Case C-141/00 *Kügler*, Case C-45/01 *Dornier* and Case C-498/03 *Kingcrest*.

containing no limitations are for public postal services and public radio and television bodies (letters (a) and (q)). Apparently the Union legislator did not consider that distortions might arise as regards these two exemptions or it simply did not care if distortions would arise. The exemptions do not, however, reveal anything on treatment of public bodies as such viewed from a system design point of view.

§4.05 OTHER PROVISIONS

In addition to the provisions discussed above in Chapter 2, the VAT Directive contains other provisions specifically dealing with the treatment of public bodies. Article 199(3)(b) provides Member States with the possibility to regard a non-taxable body governed by public law as a taxable person, for the purpose of accounting for VAT as an acquirer in certain situations. Article 387(a) of the VAT Directive also provides that Malta, under certain circumstances, may apply an exemption for the supply of water by a body governed by public law. Article 152 exempts gold sold to central banks, i.e., the status of the recipient as a specific type of public body, and the type of goods sold, result in exemption from VAT. Article 148 exempts certain services and the supply of fighting ships, a good that is presumably (exclusively) sold to states (and the Ministry of Defence).[26] Article 151(1) also concerns supplies to various organs of the state, diplomats, supplies intended for armed forces of a Member State being a party to the North Atlantic Treaty, supplies to international bodies, etc.

These exemptions are of a practical nature and very specific. They seem to be present to simplify treatment and to deal with the problems inherent in the fact that public bodies are excluded from the scope of VAT by Article 13.

§4.06 CONCLUSIONS ON THE EU EXEMPTION SYSTEM

In the EU exemption system several questions need to be addressed when a public body is to determine whether it is excluded from the scope of VAT or not. First, it needs to be determined whether the activity of the public body is an economic activity at all for VAT purposes. When the activity cannot be performed on the market, it does in principle not fall within the scope of VAT. Second, it needs to be determined whether the body is governed by public law or private law. Only the legal regime applicable under national law can determine which applies. Exclusions are not made in EU VAT for public administration tasks performed by private law entities. Third, it needs to be determined whether the activity in question is governed by public law or private law. Consequently, a public body is only excluded from the field of application of the EU VAT system when, either the activity as such is not economic in nature, or it is governed by public law, under the national law applicable.

Two limitations apply to the latter exclusion in order to ensure that distortions of competition will not arise – in order to respect the principle of fiscal neutrality in respect of VAT. First, a number of listed activities are not covered by the exclusion (and

26. See also Yang *IVM* (2005).

Member States may consider that this limitation is not applicable when activities are carried out on a negligible scale). Second, a test must always be made whether competition will be distorted if the public body is treated as such.

As noted by others, Member States have certain discretion to determine the scope of the exclusion due to the fact that the status of 'public body acting as such' is determined with reference to national law.[27] Importantly, this discretion does not extend to determining when the exclusion does not apply due to the fact that distortions of competition arise. That question, which is a finding of facts subject to review of national courts, is not left to Member States' discretion.[28]

The reference to Member States' national law implies that differences exist between the Member States. This has also been confirmed by the Copenhagen Economics' study, there is unequal treatment between different Member States.

27. Compare de la Feria, *Intertax* (2008).
28. See, for a somewhat different view, de la Feria, *Intertax* (2008).

CHAPTER 5
VAT Compensation Schemes in Denmark

§5.01 INTRODUCTION

Denmark was the first of the Nordic countries to introduce compensation schemes for public authorities. In fact, the Danish system served as an inspiration for the Swedish system. Later, however, changes made in the Swedish system served as inspiration of changes made in the Danish system. These countries' compensation systems have thus evolved somewhat jointly. The schemes have not been the subject of any more in-depth study in Denmark.

In this chapter, the Danish state compensation schemes (section §5.02) and municipality compensation schemes (section §5.03) are dealt with in some detail. Conclusions are made in section §5.04.

§5.02 THE STATE COMPENSATION SCHEME

According to the Danish constitution, all appropriations and taxes have to be based on a law enacted by parliament.[1] The state's budget is fixed each year in (foremost) the Finance Act (Finansloven). The financial position, including with regard to the treatment of VAT on acquisitions that is not deductible based on the Danish VAT Act (see further below), of authorities belonging to the state is thus regulated in the Finance Act.

Each year, the Finansministeriet publishes a Budgetvejledning, in which the Finanslov and administration of the financial accounts of the state is explained. In addition, the financial acts are further defined in Finansministeriet's Økonomisk

1. §46 in *Grundloven*, the Danish Constitution.

Administrative Vejledning (ØAV), Economic Administrative Guide, which is published electronically.[2]

According to the Budgetvejledning[3], Danish VAT on purchases that is not deductible according to the Danish VAT Act, is treated as follows. Appropriations to cover for expenses for capital goods and maintenance thereof (anlægsudgifter) as well as appropriations to so-called self-owing departments, are paid without compensation for non-deductible VAT. The same applies for subsidies to those institutions that are using the funds for purchases of goods and services and are using a financial accounting plan including accounts for non-deductible VAT. In these cases, expenses for non-deductible VAT are booked in the account for refundable VAT expenses. Consequently, VAT that is non-deductible under the VAT Act is fully compensated for as a refundable expense. However, when the VAT pertains to passenger cars, no VAT compensation can be claimed and when the VAT pertains to expenses for accommodation or refreshments, 25% is refundable.

In other situations, i.e., in principle with regard to non-self-owing departments and authorities, costs are booked inclusive of any VAT element. Thus, appropriations must be calculated to also incorporate the VAT element.

In certain cases, special laws or provisions are applicable. One example is the special rules applicable for institutions under the Undervisningsministeriet (Ministry of Education), which can be found in a Bekendtgørelse issued by the Ministry of Education.[4] Under these, a department involved in teaching is compensated for VAT costs (i.e., non-deductible VAT) arising with regard to acquisitions for their activities.

The Danish legislator obviously considers that certain expenditure is so closely linked to private consumption (passenger cars, and accommodation and refreshments) that they are excluded from the scheme or compensation paid is limited. 'Self-owing' departments are able to calculate their costs without taking into account VAT. VAT on investments in capital goods (anlægsudgifter) is always refunded. With regard to non-self owing departments, they are paid appropriations including compensation for non-deductible VAT. The disincentives to contract out inherent in such a system have, as far as I could find, not been discussed in official government documents.

§5.03 COMMUNES' COMPENSATION SCHEMES

[A] Background and History

In Denmark, a refunding mechanism for VAT paid on acquisitions of goods and services by communes[5] has been in place since 1984. It was then introduced as part of

2. See www.oes.dk/oeav.
3. In the 2011 edition, Chapter 2.4.7.
4. BEK nr 1168 af 08/12/2008 *Bekendtgørelse om momskompensation til institutioner for erhvervsrettet uddannelse, institutioner for almengymnasiale uddannelser og almen voksenuddannelse, erhvervsakademier, professionshøjskoler m.fl.*.
5. In Denmark, two kinds of communes were present, the amtskommun and the kommuns. In the reform of in 2006 the amtskommun were abolished and instead regions were created. All are here simply referred to as 'communes'.

a general reform of the financial relationship between the communes and the state.[6] It is noted in the Proposal to the 1984 law that the overall purpose of the law was to make sure that internal production within a commune was not rendered beneficial in comparison to purchasing production from external, private producers that had to pay VAT.[7] Before 1984, in order to achieve such neutrality, communes were required to charge VAT on certain services supplied for their own use (internal supplies). In 1984, the system was changed and VAT on acquisitions from private entrepreneurs was made refundable. The reason for this shift was that a system with refunds of VAT expenditure on purchases was perceived as more administratively simple and more efficient, since the communes in the new system did not have to add VAT to their calculations.[8] In addition, the old system did not handle all distortions as the taxed area (the internal supplies which were taxed) was too narrow. Voices were also raised to increase the taxed area.

Consequently, under the 1984 law, neutrality was achieved through a repayment of VAT on acquisitions made by the commune. When an acquisition was booked in the financial accounts, the value was booked exclusive of VAT and the VAT element was booked in a specific account. This account was used as a basis for an application of a refund of the VAT. Herewith, it is stated in the 1984 Proposal, the economic preference to produce services within communes as compared with acquiring services from external suppliers was no longer in place.

In addition to the compensation scheme for VAT expenditure on acquisitions, a system of compensation for 'hidden' VAT was also introduced in the 1984 law. Furthermore, VAT paid indirectly, hidden in the prices of external entrepreneurs' exempt supplies because of the lack of deductibility of VAT on acquisitions made by the entrepreneur, was also compensated.[9] The compensation was calculated based on a certain percentage of specified types of acquisitions of goods and services, where the supplier could not deduct VAT. The extent of the refund was thus based on the category of the supply, drawn up in a list (the so-called positivliste) which also contained the refund percentages which varied dependent upon which category the acquisition pertained to.

The system established in 1984 was intended to be completely based on self-financing and neutral as regards the impact on the state's finances.[10] The communes thus paid in to the system an amount that ought to cover the VAT compensation paid under the system. Payments into the system were calculated based on each commune's part of the gross tax basis (beskatningsgrundlag) for the communes.[11]

6. See Forslag til Lov om udligning af visse kommunale og amtskommunale udgifter til merværdiafgift og om Det kommunale Momsfond, LFF 1983–1984.2.117. See also Betænkning nr 1437 from the Indenrigs- og Sundhedsminsteriets Finansieringsudvalg 'Et nyt udligningssystem', pp. 196 et seq. where the 1984 law is described.
7. Betænkning nr 1437 from the Indenrigs- og Sundhedsminsteriets Finansieringsudvalg 'Et nyt udligningssystem' p. 197.
8. See 1984 proposal.
9. See further in Chapter 6 on the Swedish compensation schemes which contain a similar system.
10. See 1984 proposal.
11. See Betænkning pp. 197–198.

Payments into the system were thus not directly related to compensation paid from the system for VAT on acquisitions by the commune.

However, it is apparent that an increase of payments to the system was compensated for with an increase of other financial contributions from the state to the communes.[12] Thus, the system was co-financed by the state, through subsidies paid when communes had difficulties paying their share and when the cost of the system increased so that payments into the system were not covering payments from the system.

In a Report on a new equalisation system generally for communes, criticism of the system found in the 1984 law is presented.[13] First, some communes raised objections to the actual effects of the system as they had to pay in more to the system if they contracted out more, than if they self-supplied.

Second, the basis for payment into the system was criticised for not fulfilling its purpose, as it entailed a reallocation of resources between the communes. Communes with a number of citizens above the average contributed more to the system. In addition, if such a commune already had made its major investments (infrastructure is in place etc.), it would in practice pay for other communes' compensation of VAT on their investments.[14]

Third, in the case of an imbalance in the commune's financial position, a deficit may be covered by a compensation paid by the state. If this were the case, any additional cost for the compensation system, that the commune should pay, would in reality be paid by the state. As a consequence, the state would finance in full the VAT element of an increase in expenses above a balanced financial position. The system thus entailed that an increase in the expenses for refunds of the system was paid for by the state resulting in an increase in the state's compensations paid to the communes.

[B] The 2007 Competition Equalisation Law

The present compensation scheme, which can be found in the Competition Equalisation Law, the CEL, was enacted as a part of an agreement between the government and certain parties on a reform of the financial position of the communes in general.[15] It is apparent from the Proposal that the aim to be achieved with the new law was to abolish the system with payments into the system directly by communes and introduce a system whereby the financing of the system was (fully) made through the yearly

12. Betænkning p. 200.
13. See, Betænkning pp. 200–202.
14. These reallocation problems have also occurred under the Swedish system with VAT accounts, see Chapter 6, and are reported to have occurred also in the Finnish system, see Chapter 7 and Betænkning p. 203.
15. See *Forslag til Lov om konkurrencemæssig ligestilling mellem kommuners og regioners egenproduktion og køb af ydelser hos externe leverandører i relation til udgifter til merværdiafgift m.v. samt om momsfondet*, from 29 March 2006 (from the minister of the Indenrigs- og Sundhedsministeriet), 2005/1 LSF 192.

financial regulations between the state and the communes, the block grant (bloktilskuddet).[16] Block grants were consequently reduced when the new law came into force, to compensate the state for taking over the financial responsibility of the system and keep the reform neutral to the state's financial position. In addition, it is stated in the Proposal that the magnitude of compensation paid should be taken into account when future compensation is paid to the communes.

The overall purpose of the reform seems to be simplification of the flows of payments between the communes and the state related to the compensation system. It is clearly pointed out that the communes themselves, and not the state, shall bear the burden of any increase in the costs of the system in the future.

The first section of the CEL states that VAT paid on acquisitions of goods and services by communes is refundable. It is not immediately apparent from the provisions of the CEL that VAT deductible as input VAT under the ordinary system is not also refundable. The wording, 'udgifter... til betalning af afgift ... ' (expenditure ... for the payment of tax ...) does not clearly indicate the scope of the right to deduct. However, as is clear from the second paragraph of the section, the Indenrigs- og sundhedsministeren (the Ministry of Interior and Health) determines the scope of the right to deduct. It is furthermore clear from the Bekendtgørelse § 1 (see further below) that only VAT that cannot be deducted as input VAT based on the VAT Act is refunded.

According to the second paragraph of the first section of the CEL, the Ministry of Interior and Health may provide that VAT on certain acquisitions is not refunded.[17] Consequently, the Ministry of Interior and Health determines the scope of the right to compensation and also the administration of it.[18]

Such rules have been enacted in a Bekendtgørelse.[19] The scope of the right to a refund is determined in that Bekendtgørelse with reference to amounts that have been correctly charged to certain accounts in the financial accounts of the communes. Explicitly excluded is VAT on the costs for busses, ferries, railways and homes for the elderly as well as subsidies (tilskud) paid to transport companies (trafikselskaber) involved in travel through busses, ferries and railways, and common homes for the elderly.[20] The compensation includes costs for purchase of goods, excluding purchases of land itself or buildings, costs for services of external entrepreneurs or craftsmen (Entreprenør- og håndværkerydelser) and other acquisitions of services.[21]

16. *Ibid.*
17. The Law also covers payment of the lønsumsafgift (a tax on the sum of wages in VAT exempt businesses) that is also refunded in certain circumstances and to a certain extent. In addition, certain provisions, that have now been repealed deal with what is called Momsfondet. This research concerns VAT and not other taxes or systems. Neither the lønsumsafgift nor the Momsfondet is discussed here.
18. Compare, Skat, Momsvejledningen 2010-2 (Gældende fra den 20. juli 2010), section D.7 Offentlige institutioners leverancer § 9.
19. See BEK nr 28 af 06/01/2011 Gældene, offentliggörelsedato 19-01-2011, Indenrigs- og SUndedsministeriet.
20. See § 1, 1 (d) in the Bekentgørelse. The Danish terms are *Busdrift, Færgedrift, Jernbanedrift* and *ældreboliger*.
21. See § 1, 1 a) to c) of the Bekentgørelse.

It is clear from the Proposal to the law that the exclusions are made in order to achieve neutrality of competition between private entities and communes engaged in the activity.[22] This could be achieved either by providing for compensation for VAT costs arising at external providers that cannot deduct input VAT (see below on VAT paid indirectly) or through exclusion from the compensation system of certain activities where there is competition. The latter forms the basis for exclusions of payments to companies involved in running busses, ferries and railways. Public transport is exempt from VAT in Denmark, which is allowed for under Article 371 and Annex X B of the VAT Directive. Transport companies are therefore not able to deduct VAT on their acquisitions.

Explicitly excluded from the scope is, furthermore, VAT on the hire of real estate, relating to own leases of immovable property (Egne huslejeindtægter).[23]

As can be seen, the compensation scheme is not applicable to a number of activities that are exempt from VAT in order to avoid distortions between private entities engaged in the activities and public bodies engaged in the same activities. However, not all VAT exempt activities are excluded from the compensation scheme. VAT that is not deductible under the Danish VAT Act due to the fact that it relates to exempt supplies of, for example, education and health care, is still compensated for under the Compensation scheme. Certainly, the same considerations that yielded the exclusion of public transport activities from the compensation scheme could be present with regard to these activities, in so far as private entities are making exempt supplies in competition with public bodies. There seems to have been some kind of evaluation made of where (most) problems would arise, were the compensation system to be made applicable.

As in the 1984 system, the 2007 system entails a compensation scheme for 'hidden' VAT. VAT that is paid indirectly by communes through payments or subsidies is compensated for.[24] The amount compensated is based on the amount booked in the financial accounts multiplied by a percentage of the applicable VAT rate, regulated in an Annex to the Bekentgørelse (the Possitivliste). According to the Annex, the percentages reflect the VAT element of expenses for the acquisitions listed. It is however hard to see this clearly from the numbers in the Annex, as the percentages also take into consideration a specific tax paid based on the sum of salaries (lønsummeavgift). Thus the percentages are both compensation for VAT and for the lønsummeavgift.

The positivliste is detailed and lists, among other things, payments made to certain schools, museums, and for dental care provided through the commune, hospitals, services related to the handicapped and the treatment of addicts.

Section 2 of the CEL provides that VAT repaid should be repaid through the refusionsordningen. Sections 2 and 3 provide that the Indenrigs- og sundhedsministeren has a certain margin of discretion with regard to the administration of the system. According to the Proposal for the Law, the rights granted to the Ministry should be

22. See 'Bemærkninger til lovforslagets enkelte bestemmelser, Til §§ 1 og 2'.
23. See § 4 of the Bekentgørelse.
24. See § 1, 2) of the Bekentgørelse.

strictly construed, so that the actual right of compensation is not limited through administrative rules.[25]

Section 4 of the CEL provides that the state shall pay amounts to cover for communes' payment of VAT. As noted above, the general block grant was reduced to cover for the state's cost of funding the system.

Excluded from the scope of the right to a refund, in accordance with § 5 of the Bekentgørelse, is VAT paid on purchases of goods and services financed through contributions or subsidies (bidrag og tilskud) received by the commune from public bodies or private individuals.[26] Subsidies received from private law entities are however not included in the exclusion.[27]

VAT refunded shall be repaid if a plant (anlæg) is sold within five years.[28] This provision presumably refers to plants as in capital goods. However, the terminology is far from clear in Danish. It is not the same as is used in the Danish VAT Act with regard to capital goods that are subject to adjustments if usage is changed within a period of five years (with regard to capital goods which are not immovable property) or 10 years (with regard to immovable property).

§5.04 COMMENTS AND CONCLUSIONS

The Danish Communes' compensation scheme is quite complex. However, the fact that it is linked to accounting perhaps makes it a bit easier to apply in practice. When an amount is booked in a certain account, it is refundable.

The compensation schemes do not compensate for all VAT incurred in relation to the activities of a public body that is not deductible under the Danish VAT Act. Important exclusions are made to increase neutrality in competition when the same services are provided by private entities which cannot deduct VAT on acquisitions. But a commune or state is allowed to have a refund of input VAT in certain situations when it makes exempt supplies for VAT purposes. The guarantee for neutrality in competition is not complete.

When external suppliers supply exempt services to a commune, compensation is in many cases granted for the hidden VAT cost incurred by the commune. The level of detail of the *positivliste* determining the level of compensation is remarkable. It is claimed to grant refunds based on the typical VAT cost arising but how the refund percentages are calculated has not been displayed.

Even if these calculations are very precise, since they are just calculations they can never exactly reflect the VAT element in each transaction. The system can thus never result in complete neutrality in competition, yet the aim of the system to equate contracting out with self-supplies may still in practice be achieved if the system is perceived as correct and the preference to self-supply is eliminated.

25. See the Proposal under the commentary to §§1 and 2.
26. See § 5 of the Bekentgørelse.
27. See further, Letter to Viborg Kommune, J.nr. 2008-4504 of the Sundhedsministeriet of 8 January 2009.
28. See § 6 of the Bekentgørelse.

CHAPTER 6
VAT Compensation Schemes in Sweden

§6.01 INTRODUCTION

In this chapter, the special measures in national law, which operate alongside the Swedish VAT Act,[1] to deal with VAT on acquisitions made by state entities and local authorities are discussed.

In section §6.02 the treatment of state entities is dealt with and in section §6.03 the compensation schemes for communes are discussed.

§6.02 THE TREATMENT OF STATE ENTITIES

[A] Introduction

In Sweden, a special scheme concerning VAT paid on acquisitions is applicable for state entities. State entities have the right to compensation for (some) VAT paid on acquisitions that is not deductible or refundable under the Swedish VAT Act.

According to Chapter 8 section 8 of the Swedish VAT Act, the state does not have the right to deduct input VAT. This is different from the position under European VAT, see Articles 168–172 of the VAT Directive. A state entity has the right to deduct input VAT if it is engaged in an (economic) activity that entailed such a right – the VAT Directive does not contain a general exclusion of such a right as regards state entities.[2]

1. Mervärdesskattelagen, SFS 1994:200.
2. According to Chapter 1 section 16 of the Swedish VAT Act, the state does not encompass commercial state organs. These are Statens Järnvägar, Luftfartsverket, Sjöfartsverket and Svenska Kraftnät. The concept of 'the state' in the Swedish VAT act encompasses all organs of the state, with the exclusion of the commercial state organs (affärsdrivande verk). Thus, if Lund University is supplying a service to the tax authorities, this transaction takes place within the same entity for VAT purposes, the Swedish state.

As a consequence, all VAT on acquisitions by state entities is dealt with under the special scheme for state entities.

[B] History and Development of the Present Compensation Regulation

The VAT treatment of state entities in Sweden can suitably be divided into before and after 1991. Before 1991, state authorities were compensated for VAT incurred when acquiring goods and services for their activities via an increase in the appropriations. Thus, compensation for VAT paid on acquisitions was paid as part of the general appropriations. Costs were calculated as VAT inclusive.[3] In 1991, in a general tax reform, the VAT base was considerably broadened and also, services were generally included in the tax base. In connection herewith, the treatment of state organs and communes was also discussed. Above all, the issue was how they should be compensated for the increased cost that the VAT would entail when they bought services from external providers. The system was completely changed. After the tax reform of 1991, appropriations were calculated exclusive of VAT. VAT paid on acquisitions by state authorities was compensated for in direct relation to what was actually paid in VAT on acquisitions. The result was that state authorities could calculate prices from external providers exclusive of VAT. The amount of compensation paid to state authorities was deducted from the Swedish state's account for VAT income. Accordingly, a kind of net accounting was applied where VAT paid on acquisitions by state entities did not form part of the state's income from VAT.

The purpose behind the change was to make contracting out and self-supplying neutral, i.e., that it should be neutral for state entities to produce goods and services themselves (or purchase from other state entities) or to purchase them from external suppliers. This was achieved by linking the VAT compensation to VAT actually paid. In addition, the change was intended to be neutral to the state budget. The net accounting principle achieved this neutrality.

A particular feature of the compensation system enacted was the treatment of compensation to specifically defined state entities (mostly Universities) that also received external funds in the form of subsidies and contributions not liable to VAT because they were not consideration falling within the scope of the VAT system. As these entities now received full compensation for all VAT on acquisitions for their activities, and not only for the part corresponding to purchases linked to appropriations, they were over-compensated compared to the situation before the 1991 reform. To compensate the Treasury for the cost entailed in providing state entities with the right of compensation for VAT on acquisitions, Universities etc. were obliged to pay in 8% of any external funds received as *University VAT* (Högskolemoms), as it was conveniently named. The 8% was thus an estimation of the magnitude of VAT-to-be-claimed through the compensation scheme on purchases linked to activities financed

3. See with regard to the topic of this section ESV 2001:12.

through subsidies. The *University VAT* was increasingly questioned[4] and finally abolished in 2009, but then, it seems, not because of the criticism raised but as part of Government's policy to strengthen University research and increase resources for research.[5]

A Regulation governing the net accounting method was enacted in 1991 and replaced with a Compensation Regulation in 1993, which was in turn replaced by the Present Compensation Regulation in 2002.

According to the 1993 Regulation, the Ekonomistyrningsverket (the Swedish National Financial Management Authority, below referred to as the ESV) had the right to determine which authorities should have the right to compensation. What entities and which VAT (under what criteria) these entities should be compensated for were also left to the discretion of the ESV and not at all regulated in the Compensation Regulation of 1993. In an extensive report on the 1993 Regulation, the ESV discusses the shortcomings of the 1993 Regulation.[6] This report is of particular importance as the 2002 Regulation to a large extent reflects the position of the ESV in the report.

The ESV considers that it needs to be determined what entities a Compensation Regulation should cover. In connection herewith the ESV notes that the original purpose of the compensation scheme was to increase neutrality in competition between internally producing the goods and services necessary for the activities of state entities, and contracting out these to external providers. In addition, it is desirable that the system is neutral with regard to competition between the state sector, the commune sector and the private sector. Lastly, the administration of the system should be manageable.

Problems with regard to distortions of competition arise[7] in the situation where the state does not have to charge any output VAT but still, unlike private sector entities, can get compensation for input VAT incurred. This happens due to the combined effects of the presence of exemptions from VAT in the VAT Act and a Compensation Regulation for VAT incurred on acquisitions by state entities. However, according to the ESV, distortions of competition only arise in a market where there is actual competition between state and private entities.

In the report, the ESV goes through the exemptions from VAT in the Swedish VAT Act and evaluates where there probably could be a situation of actual competition between state and private entities.[8] How, and on what basis, the assessment has been made is not further discussed. It seems that it is not based on any empirical research but rather on the knowledge of the activities of the state and its organs, and those of private entities held by the author of the report. The level of competition, and thus also the level of distortions that the Compensation Regulation brings about, is not assessed based on empirical evidence but on assumptions. The assessment is thus highly subjective. According to the ESV, the assessment shows, however, that it is probably

4. ESV 2001:12 pp. 30 et seq. contains a description of the weaknesses and critique of the University VAT provision.
5. See prop. 2008/09:50 pp. 62 et seq.
6. See ESV 2001:12 pp. 28 et seq.
7. In my words. However, the same reasoning can be found in the report, *ibid.*
8. ESV 2001:12 pp. 38 et seq.

not especially common for real competition to arise in areas where the private sector does not have the right to input VAT deduction yet state entities have a right to compensation.

According to the ESV, state entities should be exempted from a Compensation Regulation if a real distortion of competition would arise (i.e., when a VAT exemption is present and the private sector entity cannot deduct input VAT) or when a state entity receives appropriations including compensation for VAT. This may be the case in a situation where the state entity in question receives a lot of external funds, and the Government does not want to compensate the entity for VAT costs linked to these external funds (compare the discussion on *University VAT* above). In addition, only VAT not deductible under the VAT Act should be compensated.

The ESV raises the issue of to what extent it should be possible for a commercial state organ (affärsverk) to receive compensation in relation to activities that are financed through charges that do not fall within the scope of VAT (due to the fact that the activities are public body activities; *myndighetsutövning*).[9] The ESV concludes that this should not be possible and that commercial state organs should be excluded entirely, for reasons of simplicity.[10]

[C] The Present Compensation Regulation

According to section 1 of the Compensation Regulation 2002, the Regulation is applicable for authorities under Government which are part of the state's accounting organisation, unless the ESV decides differently based on section 2. The Regulation is not applicable for commercial state organs (de statliga affärsverken). The scope of the Regulation is thus restricted and authorities under the Parliament, and those not part of the state's accounting organisation, are excluded.

In 2010, 391 authorities were subject to Government.[11] There were 12 organs subject to Parliament,[12] and 237 authorities were part of the state's accounting organisation.[13] Consequently, a significant number of authorities are not covered by the scope of the Compensation Regulation. Presumably these receive appropriations with VAT compensation included. As state authorities do not have the right to deduct any input VAT under the Swedish VAT act, one must assume that a disincentive to contracting out exists for state authorities not covered by the Compensation Regulation. The significant number of authorities not covered by the Compensation Regulation is therefore noticeable.

9. The ESV erroneously considers that some state authorities are probably not taxable person under European VAT since they do not aim to make a profit. The ESV thus ignores that under European VAT, it is sufficient that charges are made to cover costs of the activities in order for the activity to be an economic activity.
10. ESV 2001:12 pp. 54–55.
11. See Statskontoret (2010).
12. According to the homepage of the Parliament (www.riksdagen.se).
13. See http://www.esv.se/myndigheterstatligaredovisningsorganisationen.4.76b9ee0011a15907 24180003632.html, accessed on 21 October 2010.

According to section 2, of the Compensation Regulation, the ESV shall decide that an authority shall not be part of the compensation scheme if the ESV considers that it is more important that there is neutrality of competition in the market in question (where the authority performs activities in competition with private sector entities that are not allowed to deduct input VAT according to the rules in the VAT Act) than that the authority has the right to compensation for input VAT incurred under the Regulation. The ESV thus has complete discretion to determine which authorities shall be excluded.[14] According to the second paragraph of section 2, the ESV shall consult Konkurrensverket (the Competition Authority) before a decision in accordance with section 2 is taken.

Only eight of 237 authorities listed as being part of the state's accounting organisation in 2010 were not eligible for VAT compensation.[15] Of these, four are commercial state organs, excluded explicitly by section 1.[16] Consequently, the ESV considers that a situation of competition is present, rendering a decision according to section 2 necessary, only as regards four authorities. These are Bolagsverket, Exportkreditnämnden, Institutet för utvärdering av internationellt utvecklingsarbete och Myndigheten för internationella adoptionsfrågor.

Bolagsverket's (the Swedish Companies Registration Office) main functions are to register business enterprises and associations; to receive and store annual reports; to register corporate mortgages; to make decisions in liquidation; to make information from the registers available; and to register announcements in Post- och Inrikes Tidningar (The Official Gazette) and make them available to the public. The assignment from Government is to maintain good conditions for trade and industry. It should be noted that the Office makes available, on its homepage, standard documents such as articles of incorporation free for download.[17]

Exportkreditnämnden (the Export Credit Guarantee Board) is commissioned by the government to promote Swedish exports and the internationalisation of Swedish companies. It does so by insuring export companies and banks against the risk of non-payment in export transactions, thereby enabling them to conduct more secure export transactions. Government controls the Board.[18]

Institutet för utvärdering av internationellt utvecklingsarbete (the Swedish Agency for Development Evaluation) is a government-funded agency that evaluates Swedish international development cooperation and the reform cooperation in Eastern Europe. Evaluations address both results and effects of the development cooperation as well as efficiency of the use of development aid funds. The Agency distributes its

14. There are not even any criteria enacted in the law in relation to which the decision can be tried. Where a private sector entity considers that it is competing with a state authority but the ESV disagrees, the private sector entity will have a very weak case!
15. See http://www.esv.se/myndigheterstatligaredovisningsorganisationen.4.76b9ee0011a1590724180003632.html, accessed on 21 October 2010.
16. Statens Järnvägar, Luftfartsverket, Sjöfartsverket and Svenska Kraftnät.
17. See www.bolagsverket.se.
18. See the Export Credit Guarantee Ordinance, SFS 2007:656.

evaluations to decision-makers and other stakeholders in order to improve and strengthen the Swedish international development cooperation.

Myndigheten för internationella adoptionsfrågor (The Swedish Intercountry Adoptions Authority) is a government authority under the Ministry of Health and Social Affairs. The Authority is also the Central Authority under the 1993 Hague Convention on Protection of Children and Cooperation in respect of Intercountry Adoption. It is the task of the Authority to establish a high standard in intercountry adoption operation in Sweden. In particular it shall monitor that intercountry adoption intermediation in Sweden is conducted according to law and the principle of the best interest of the child as expressed in the UN Convention on the Rights of the Child and in the 1993 Hague Convention.

In the case of Bolagsverket and Exportkreditnämnden it is not hard to see that they are performing functions also performed by private entities - providing legal assistance and credit guarantees respectively. With regard to the other two authorities it is not as apparent in what way they are competing with the private sector.

According to section 4, the right to compensation encompasses an amount, which is equal to input VAT according to the VAT Act, and is attributable to the authority's activities (*verksamheten*).[19] Thus, only Swedish VAT charged can be compensated and only VAT actually charged, and properly defined as input VAT (and not, for example, VAT charged in other Member States) in the VAT Act. The wording here is similar, but not identical, to Chapter 8 section 3 of the VAT Act (the main material provision governing the right to deduct input VAT in the VAT Act), where it is stated that the right to deduct input VAT is present for VAT on acquisitions for the business (förvärv i *verksamheten*). I presume that the phrases have the same meaning - the VAT has to be attributable to the authority's activities/business (*verksamhet*), i.e., if pertaining to the private consumption of employees outside the scope of the authority's activities, the VAT is not refundable. That interpretation is furthermore confirmed by the second paragraph of section 4.

According to this paragraph, there exists no right to compensation when the input VAT is subject to a restriction in the right to deduct VAT according to Chapter 8 sections 9, 10, 15 or 16 of the VAT Act. These are the exclusions from the right to deduct VAT in Sweden (presumably based on Article 176 of the VAT Directive[20]) for acquisitions pertaining to permanent residences, representation costs and purchases and leasing (and similar costs) of certain cars and motorcycles. I submit, based on the fact that these exclusions exists also with regard to the compensation scheme applicable for communes etc. and based on the report of the ESV, that the exclusion exists for the same reason as it does with regard to the compensation scheme for communes (see further below). It would not increase neutrality in competition at all to compensate for input VAT that private sector entities cannot deduct.

Compensation is paid on a monthly basis and is based on the amount of input VAT booked in the accounts the preceding month. The tax authorities administer the repayment.

19. The concept of 'verksamhet' is further discussed in Chapter §6.03[B].
20. Thereby not said that they conform to the requirements of that provision.

One issue is how to deal with the fact that some public bodies are both engaged in public body activities (falling under Article 13 of the VAT Directive) and other economic activities falling within the scope of VAT. An illustrative example provided in the ESV report is that of the activities of the Swedish Maritime Administration (Sjöfartsverket). It is responsible for icebreaking, fairways, lighthouses etc. for which it charges dues and fees on merchant fishing, which are its main source of income.[21] These charges are considered to be made for public body activities and consequently excluded from the scope of VAT by the Swedish implementation (Chapter 4 section 7 of the Swedish VAT Act) of Article 13 of the VAT Directive. However, it is claimed to be very difficult to separate these charges, and activities connected therewith, from other activities liable to VAT, such as fees for pilots. As a consequence, it is also very difficult to attribute costs to either the public body activities or other VAT liable activities. These difficulties made the ESV draw the conclusion that public bodies engaged partly in VAT liable activities, such as the Swedish Maritime Administration, should be excluded from a Compensation Regulation, and that is now the case. As a consequence, a preference to self-supply is created and competition distorted.

The scope of the Compensation Regulation creates distortions of competition. To limit these distortions there are, in some cases, additional special compensation arrangements. For example, in Sweden, university education is in all but a few cases provided by state universities. As regards some private institutions which are running university education, special compensation arrangements have been put in place to compensate for VAT costs arising. The aim is again to create neutrality with regard to the impact of VAT on costs in the provision of University education.

According to the tax authorities, only VAT that is stated on an invoice or, when a simplified invoice is used, possible to calculate, is refundable under the Compensation Regulation.[22] This is not, however, stated anywhere in the Compensation Regulation which simply refers to input VAT according to the Swedish VAT Act. The requirement may be hard to maintain if an authority can, in a way other than by producing an invoice, prove that it has paid 'input VAT'.

The adjustments rules regarding input VAT on capital goods are not made applicable to state authorities. This is contrary to the case with regard to communes under their compensation scheme (see below). The absence of adjustment rules may lead to distortions of competition. Consider the situation with capital goods acquired for a taxed activity, which is changed to an exempt activity. Full compensation for input VAT might have been granted initially but no mechanism to adjust exists. The situation can be handled only by excluding certain authorities engaged in exempt activities from the Regulation.

21. See http://www.sjofartsverket.se/en/Infrastructure--Maritime-Traffic/Dues--Fees/, visited on 21 October 2010.
22. Skatteverket (2010), *Handledning för mervärdesskatt*, p. 1200.

§6.03 TREATMENT OF LOCAL AUTHORITIES (KOMMUNER)

[A] Introduction

The Swedish communes are autonomic and self-ruling, according to the Swedish constitution.[23] The communes are allowed to charge taxes to cover costs in fulfilment of their duties.[24] What falls within the scope of the communes' responsibilities (*den kommunala kompetensen*) must be laid down by law enacted by Parliament.[25] Parliament has regulated these issues in the Law of the Communes (*Kommunallagen*).[26]

In Sweden, a special system exists for handling input VAT incurred by local authorities, the Commune's Compensation Scheme, previously the Commune's VAT Account System.[27] In short, under the system, communes can apply for compensation for certain VAT paid on acquisitions which is not deductible under the Swedish VAT Act.

Communes finance almost all health care, education (except for higher education), and social care in Sweden. Even in the case that a hospital is private, for example, the commune[28] provides financing. The private hospital contracts with the commune providing its services. The patients (usually) also pay a fee to the hospital directly for health care services provided.[29] However, almost all health care, social care and education is mainly financed by communes.

[B] History and Development of the Present Compensation Scheme

Sweden introduced a VAT system as early as 1969.[30] However, most services were excluded from the scope of the system. Only services directly concerned with supplies of goods, such as transport services, were covered by it. Activities conducted by the state or a commune, were excluded from the scope of the system in so far as they related exclusively to the business[31] of the state or

23. Chapter 1 section 1 *Regeringsformen* (SFS 1974:152), RF.
24. Chapter 1 section 7 RF.
25. Chapter 8 section 5 RF.
26. SFS 1991:900.
27. *Ersättningslagen* and *kommunkontosystemet* respectively. It is applicable to *kommuner, landsting* and *kommunförbund*, i.e., the different forms of local authorities that exist under the Law on communes, *Kommunallagen*.
28. There are two kinds of communes in Sweden; 'kommuner' and 'landstingskommuner'. The latter are responsible above all for the health care within the area of the landstingskommun. No distinction is made between these two kinds here – both are treated the same in the relevant legislative acts.
29. A patient's fee is payable, unless the fees paid in a year exceeds a certain ceiling. When the ceiling is reached no fee may be charged to the patient.
30. SFS 1968:430, referred to as the Old VAT Act. The present VAT Act was enacted in connection with Sweden entered the EU.
31. The Swedish term used here is 'verksamhet'. It could be translated into 'activities' or 'business' or even 'activity type'. The word can be used as a reference to the type of activity conducted as well as to the generic business in itself. It does not have a clear and unambiguous meaning. In

the commune.[32] An exception from this exclusion was made for business conducted by a limited liability company or similar, owned by a state or commune. Such business did not fall under the exclusion. Since the exclusion only covered business *exclusively* related to the commune or state, when business was (also) provided for external entities (i.e., the activities were not exclusively conducted for the needs of the state or the communes[33]), the activities performed fell within the scope of the VAT system, but then only in so far as the activities entailed the provision of goods and services to external entities. All internal commune or state business fell outside the scope of the system. State organs and communes did not have the right to deduct input VAT, but had to carry the cost of the VAT to the extent that their activities fell outside the scope of the tax.[34]

As noted before, in 1991, in a general tax reform, the VAT base was considerably broadened. The Government found that communes should be compensated for the increased cost brought about by the inclusion of services in the VAT base. A system with a general right to deduct input VAT for state organs and communes was incorporated within the ordinary VAT system.[35] Even if there was a general right to deduct input VAT for communes and state organs, the prohibitions in the VAT Act against deduction of input VAT pertaining to permanent dwellings etc. were also applicable for state organs and communes. This was motivated by the fact that these types of costs were private living expenses that should not be excluded from the scope of taxation.[36]

The reason behind the introduction of a (general) right to compensation was the wish to equalise the VAT system's distorting effects on competition with regard to the choice of producing the services in-house or acquiring them from external suppliers.

In order to compensate the state for the reduced income that a general right to deduct input VAT for communes entailed, compensation for VAT costs was calculated and considered, in 1991 and 1992, when the, then applicable, *avräkningsskatten*[37] was charged by central government to the communes.[38] A motive for the adjustment through the *avräkningsskatten* was also not to intervene with neutrality in competition between self-supplying and contracting out that was achieved through the Communes'

---

the present context I read it, considering the context of the provision (the instructions to the second section of the law) as a reference to the activities conducted by the commune or state that they are performed as part of their public function rather than as a support for external parties. I have used the term 'business' as I perceive it to most closely resemble the meaning which I deduce from the Swedish term, viewed in the present context.

32. See prop. 1968:100 pp. 16–17.
33. This is a direct translation of the expression in Swedish 'icke uteslutande tillgodoser egna behov', see prop. 1968:100 p. 16. Exactly what is meant is thus not clearer in the Swedish text than in the English translation.
34. See prop. 1968:100 p. 114.
35. See prop. 1989/90:111 pp. 125 et seq. and the description of the changes in prop. 2001/02:112 pp. 16 et seq. The Swedish compensation model was said to built upon the Danish model, see prop. 1989/90:111 p. 126.
36. See prop. 1989/90:111 p. 127. Se also prop. 1997/98:153 concerning exemptions from the deduction prohibitions with regard to certain dwellings for disabled people etc. (särskilda boendeformer).
37. A direct translation would be 'the deduction tax'. It was a tax linked to the communes' own tax base which regulated the financial position between the states and the communes.
38. See prop. 2001/02:112 pp. 16 et seq.

Compensation System. Consequently, the *avräkningsskatten* was increased to cover for the state's costs under the Communes' Compensation System in 1991 and 1992. In 1993, the VAT compensation was considered when the new state equalisation regime for communes was established and through the health insurance scheme for the *landstingskommun*.

In connection with Sweden becoming a Member State of the EU in 1995, a new system, the commune's VAT accounts, was introduced.[39] The reason behind this was that the system with a general right to deduct input VAT for communes and payment of the state's cost for this general right of deduction through another part of the tax system, was not considered to be in accordance with the Sixth VAT Directive (77/388/EEC). Repayment of VAT to communes was however not abolished. Instead, the VAT repayments were allowed based on a separate law,[40] only valid in 1995 – awaiting a more sustainable solution.

A permanent system was introduced by the *Law on communes' VAT accounts* in 1995 (valid from 1 January 1996).[41] It is clear from the bill introducing the law that the system introduced was intended to correct distortions of competition arising between self-supplying and contracting out and was to be based on self-financing.[42] Self-financing was achieved by each commune being required to pay into a VAT account established for this purpose. Payments to the account were meant to equal payments from the account as compensation for VAT costs arising. The criterion for payment into the account was a certain amount per citizen in the commune, and the basis for payments from the account was the actual VAT costs incurred. According to the bill, the sole purpose of the system was, as far as possible and without any support from the state, to limit the distortions of competition within the VAT exempt areas that could otherwise occur, dependent upon whether the activities were carried out by a commune or privately.[43]

A not insignificant difference with the system, compared to its predecessors, was neutrality vis-à-vis the state as regards communes' payments into the system and compensation from the state. The exact amount paid by each commune to the VAT account was compensated for through an adjustment of the general contributions from the state to the commune. Over time, a change in the relationship between payments to, and repayments of input VAT compensation from the VAT account may change for each commune. In total, the level of payment was said to be set so that the payments to the accounts would not be greater than the withdrawals therefrom.

39. The developments have been described in prop. 2001/02:112 pp. 16 et seq.
40. Lagen (1994:1799 om kommuners och landstings hantering av mervärdesskatt för år 1995.
41. Lag (1995:1518) om mervärdesskattekonton för kommuner och landsting.
42. See, also in the following prop. 1995/96:64 pp. 51 et seq.
43. *Ibid*. The statement viewed in isolation is puzzling. The reference to neutrality could be read as a referring to neutrality in competition between private entities and communes in the sense that they are treated the same. However, that is obviously not the case – in VAT exempt businesses, private entrepreneurs cannot deduct input VAT whereas communes get compensation. The VAT Account System introduced in this regard distorts competition. The reference, viewed in the context of the bill (see the introductory text 'Propositionens huvudsakliga innehåll') is clearly to neutrality for communes in their choice between self-supplying or contracting out a particular activity.

The VAT account system was reformed substantially in 2003. According to the bill, the old system had a number of weaknesses.[44] First, the system brought about a redistribution of funds between communes. Some communes received more in compensation compared to what they paid into the accounts.[45] Second, the communes had a limited possibility to plan their budget. The charge to the communes was fixed at a not very desirable point in time, seen from the communes' point of view with regard to their need to plan their activities. Third, how the charge to the account was made - which was (now) by estimating the need for compensation for VAT costs based on last year's need - was increasingly unsatisfactory. Lastly, distortions in competition occurred.

The problems of planning etc., outlined above, were addressed in the reform by abolishing the system of payments into the accounts. Instead, the general contributions to communes from the state were lowered to provide for the costs in the system. The accounts were financed through the state budget. Just like the VAT, which appears on the state's budget net on the income side, the net position of the communes' VAT accounts was stated on the income side in the budget.[46]

The broad lines of development can be outlined as follows. As from 1991, a general right of deduction has been present for communes, first as part of the VAT Act and from 1996 as a special scheme. During the period 1991–1995, the system was financed through adjustments of state contributions to the communes. As from 1996, the adjustments were abolished and a separate account system, with payments made into and from the accounts by communes only, was introduced. In 2003, the direct payments into the accounts by communes were abolished and the system was financed (again) through adjustments of general contributions from the state to the communes. The VAT accounts lasted for 10 years - in 2006 the present compensation system was introduced.

[C] The Communes' Compensation Scheme

In 2006 the law on communes' VAT accounts was abolished and a new law, the Law on Communes' Compensation for VAT, the LCC, was introduced.[47] The main changes were to abolish the accounts from which refunds were claimed - instead the claims

44. Prop. 2001/02:112 pp. 18–19.
45. Shorter fluctuations were anticipated and acceptable. However, the system entailed long-term reallocation of resources between the communes, something which was clearly not acceptable nor foreseen.
46. Prop. 2001/02:112 pp. 20–21. A significant legal change was also made. Previously, *VAT that had not been deducted* was refundable. This was changed so that only *VAT not deductible* was refundable. As the wording was before the change, communes did not have to distinguish between input VAT that was deductible under the normal VAT rules and input VAT that was not deductible under the normal rules but for which a refund could be made. Consequently, there was a risk that communes only sought compensation from the VAT accounts system and not through the ordinary VAT system at all, or received double compensation.
47. Lag (2005:807) om ersättning för viss mervärdesskatt för kommuner och landsting (usually called Ersättningslagen).

were made directly on the state's budget. In addition, the whole procedure for claiming VAT compensation was digitalised.

A peculiarity of the compensation scheme[48] is that it is administered through the same system as the ordinary VAT system. As a consequence, payments from the system are administered through the tax account, an account every taxpayer has at the tax authorities where his net tax position is stated (and interest charged or paid, depending on whether there is a surplus or a debt). The refunds are thus in reality cleared against tax debts due by the commune to the state. In addition, the same procedures are applicable, except for where explicitly stated in the LCC (which is the case for the time frame for making adjustments, where a three year cap is applicable to a certain extent, the ordinary cap being six years).

According to section 2 of the LCC, communes have the right, after an application, to have compensation for input VAT that is neither deductible nor refundable according to the rules of the Swedish VAT Act. The LCC also refers to the rules in Chapter 8a of the VAT Act, which concerns adjustments in respect of capital goods, and deem those rules to be applicable.

The restrictions in the right to deduct in the VAT Act, in Chapter 8 sections 9, 10 (concerning permanent dwellings and business entertainment), and 15 and 16 (concerning leasing and purchases of cars used for personal transport), are made applicable also when the LCC is applied, section 4 of the LCC. The restriction with regard to deduct input VAT pertaining to a permanent dwelling is not applicable with regard to certain kinds of dwellings that are supplied for social reasons.[49]

The reasons behind the restrictions in the right to a refund have been discussed above in the historical section, see section §6.02[B]. The restrictions and adjustment provisions are identical in both the LCC and the VAT Act, except for the treatment of certain kinds of dwellings supplied for social reasons. However, there is no prerequisite in the LCC that requires that there is a link to the business as is the case in Chapter 8 section 3 of the VAT Act, where the right to deduct input VAT occurs in so far the input is related to the business ('hänför sig till förvärv eller import i verksamheten'). As a consequence, it has been found that a commune can get compensation for VAT paid on acquisitions not linked to its activities, such as acquisitions used solely by its employees.[50]

The treatment of certain kinds of dwellings supplied for social reasons was introduced by prop. 1997/98:153. It is clear from the bill that the general purpose of the restrictions in the right to deduct input VAT pertaining to permanent dwellings (also for communes) is that VAT should not be deductible on private living expenses. The reason why a right to a refund of input VAT incurred is in any event allowed with regard to certain kinds of dwellings is due to the fact that the interpretation of the phrase 'permanent dwellings' (stadigvarande bostad) has involved difficulties with

48. Both the Compensation Scheme discussed here and the one for 'hidden VAT' costs.
49. See Chapter 5 section 5 second paragraph and Chapter 5 section 7 third paragraph in Socialtjänstlagen (2001:453) and sections 8 and 9 in lagen (1993:387) om stöd och service till vissa funktionshindrade.
50. See the judgment in case No. 5629–5632-2000 from the Appeal Administrative Court in Gothenburg (Kammarrätten i Göteborg).

regard to the right to have a refund for certain types of dwellings where social care is supplied in connection with the rental of the dwelling. In the laws mentioned, such care is always provided in connection with the rental. In addition, to draw the line between permanent dwellings and premises for medical care or social care is often difficult and complicated, as the space used for medical and social care as compared to that used as a permanent dwelling needs to be estimated (especially with regard to spaces used for both activities, such as corridors). The change was motivated by a need to express more clearly when there was a right to compensation from the compensation system.

In the event that it is not possible to determine to what extent input VAT should be treated as deductible in accordance with the VAT Act or refundable in accordance with the LCC respectively, the attribution to each system shall be done based on what is fair and reasonable (skäligt), section 3 of the LCC. According to the VAT Act, when it cannot be determined to what extent an input relates to transactions that entail the right to deduct input VAT and transactions that do not entail such a right, the extent of deductibility shall also be determined based on what is fair and reasonable (skäligt), Chapter 8 section 13 of the Swedish VAT Act.[51] The question naturally arises of whether the same measure as to what is *fair and reasonable* should be used in both acts. If the concepts are not interpreted in conformity, the consequence would be double compensation or non-compensation. According to the bill, the rule in the LCC has been drafted with Chapter 8 section 13 of the VAT Act as a model.[52] It seems therefore likely that a court will make an interpretation of the Acts in conformity, were the provision to be tried.

It seems well established that, while the compensation system's purpose is to increase neutrality for communes in the choice between contracting out and self-supplying, problems of distortions of competition between supplies made by communes and private sector entities arise because of the system, especially in the health care and dental sectors.[53] The problem arises when compensation is paid for VAT costs incurred by communes on acquisitions when making VAT exempt supplies. Private sector entities do not have the possibility of having the VAT refunded. Private sector entities therefore have to carry an extra cost compared to communes.

[D] Compensation Schemes for 'Hidden' VAT Costs

In addition to the general right to receive compensation for input VAT, in 1991 a system was introduced whereby *communes* were compensated for certain hidden VAT costs arising when acquisitions were made from external parties for certain VAT exempt

51. Article 173 to 175 in the VAT Directive contains the equivalent rules in European VAT. Whether Chapter 8 section 13 of the Swedish VAT Act implements the VAT Directive satisfactorily could legitimately be questioned.
52. Prop. 2001/02:112 p. 24 and p. 37.
53. See Konkurrensverket, *Konkurrens i tandvården*, 1993 and Konkurrensen I Sverige: Åtgärder för bättre konkurrens, Konkurrensverkets rapportserie 2009:4. See also the report prepared by the Association for Private Dentists in Sweden, Privattandläkarna, *Hinder för konkurrens på lika villkor inom tandvården består – ett helhetsgrepp är nödvändigt*, April 2006.

activities (health care, dental care, social care and education) carried out by the communes.[54] When a commune acquires services from, for example, a self-employed dentist, the dentist has higher costs compared to a dentist employed by the commune, since the commune can get compensation for VAT on its costs through the compensation system, while such compensation is not available for the self-employed dentist. This creates a disincentive to contract out and distortions of competition. Based on (it is stated in the government's bill) a Danish model, a system of state contributions was enacted, which was totally self-contained and not related to the VAT system. Even though the need for such state contributions was considered to be limited in 1991, a system was enacted to avoid future distortions of competition arising.[55]

Communes accordingly have a right to compensation for hidden VAT under a Compensation Scheme for hidden VAT costs. Compensation is calculated based on fixed percentages that are intended to compensate for the lack of a right of deduction on behalf of the exempt supplier. The fixed percentages were set in relation to the cost of acquiring services concerning dental care, health care, social care and education.[56] Compensation was originally paid at 6% of the cost for acquiring services relating to one of these areas.

The system was reviewed in 2003 and problems with the fixed percentage points and remaining distortions of competition were noted, but no changes to the system were proposed.[57] It was noted that the VAT account system's purpose was to created neutrality in competition between contracting out and self-supplying. The system also solved most of the problems with distortions of competition that arose within the communes' sector as a consequence of the VAT rules. Nonetheless, there were some problems that the system did not solve. One was the problem with hidden VAT for main contractors, i.e., external entrepreneurs contracted by the communes, who were involved in VAT exempt activities. These main contractors could not deduct the VAT charged by subcontractors, so the VAT became a cost in the main contractor's business. In the choice of the main contractor to contracting out or self-supplying, there was a disincentive to subcontract. Another problem noted in the bill but not solved was also related to fact that the compensation was fixed in advance. This could bring about the position that contracting out was still not chosen, and distortions of competition remained.[58]

Yet another problem of distortions of competition appeared when communes were performing activities in competition with the private sector with regard to activities that were exempt from VAT and thus the private entrepreneur could not get

54. SFS 1990:578, prop. 1989/90:111 pp. 128 et seq.
55. See prop. 1989/90:111 p. 129.
56. SFS 1990:578 and SFS 1990:1374. It can be noted that the law stated that it was for the Government, or the agency that the government indicated, to fix the percentages to be used. I have not been able to find any reasoning concerning why 6% was chosen.
57. See prop. 2001/02:112 pp. 19 and 35 et seq.
58. Prop. 2001/02:112 p. 19.

any compensation for VAT costs arising but the communes did receive such compensation through the VAT accounts system. The bill does not contain any proposals on how to come to terms with any of the distortions.[59]

Today, the scheme is found in the LCC and a Regulation from Government.[60] According to section 5 of the LCC, communes have the right to compensation for the increase in costs that arises because of the rules on VAT when activities relating to health care, dental care, social care and education, and to premises for certain dwellings are contracted out. A right to compensation also arises when a commune pays subsidies to a private business involved in the activities mentioned. The magnitude of the compensation is left for Government to decide.

According to the Regulation on Communes' Compensation, enacted by Government, contributions are to be paid with:

- 6% of the cost to contract out, or of subsidies for the activities mentioned, or if it is apparent that a certain part is paid for the cost of premises, 18% for this part and 5% for the rest; and
- 18% in the case of costs for leasing premises used as certain dwellings used in social care.

Compensation with 18% is not paid when the premises leased are leased from the state or a commune.

The use of the word *subsidies* is interesting. In the bill introducing the system, it is clear that the word subsidies was to cover subsidies paid to external service providers that provided services relevant for the communes.[61] The word subsidies was inserted to cover not only the case where a particular activity was contracted out to an external supplier. It seems therefore clear that the word *subsidies* refers to payments where there is no direct link between the payment and the supplies made by the external service provider such that the payment falls within the scope of VAT. Consequently, compensation for hidden VAT costs of external service providers is also paid when funds are redistributed from a commune to an external service provider.

§6.04 CONCLUSIONS

Originally, the Swedish VAT system contained a complete right to compensation, or actually deduction, of all input VAT incurred by public bodies. As this was perceived as not being in conformity with the EU VAT system, the special compensation schemes were enacted. These schemes have been changed many times during a relatively short period of time. Some changes of the system relate to the functioning of the system, such as the introduction of adjustment rules etc. Most changes are however of technical character and concern foremost the issue of allocation of the cost of the scheme both in

59. Prop. 2001/02:112 pp. 35 et seq.
60. SFS 2005:807 and Förordning (2005:811) om ersättning för viss mervärdesskatt för kommuner och landsting respectively.
61. See prop. 1989/90:111 pp. 128–129.

terms of central and local government, whether the state or the communes or both should finance the system, and in terms of allocation between different communes.

The whole issue of allocation between the state and the communes has a certain unreal air around it. The communes in the VAT account systems paid into the account and the system was supposed to be self-contained, i.e., the state was not supposed to contribute. But where the system is administered through the state, the communes are actually, it may be argued, also carrying the burden of the cost of the system. The general contributions have been reduced to cover for the cost of compensating for VAT costs arising. So, in reality, VAT *is* a cost factor for the communes, yet, the communes are tricked into thinking it is not. Agreeably, in each decision to self-supply or contract out, the funding of the system is not an issue. The fiction is only on a macro level, not on a micro level.

Overall, whether distortions between self-supplying and contracting out are neutralised is uncertain. I am not aware of any economic appraisal of the efficiency of the system. However, it seems to be working provided that each decision to contract out is taken without considerations being had as to the overall position of the commune vis-à-vis the state.

Distortions are created under the system in Sweden between communes making exempt supplies and private sector entities making the same supplies. In the state system, the ESV has been given total discretion to deal with this situation whereas under the commune compensation scheme, the situation is not handled at all.

The effects of the compensation scheme for indirect VAT costs are hard to measure. Clearly, it reduces the self-supply bias inherent in the exclusion for public bodies. How the levels of compensation were set is not clear and whether they do at all reflect indirect VAT costs is doubtful. They may even be working as an incentive to contract out.

CHAPTER 7

Other VAT Compensation Schemes

§7.01 INTRODUCTION

In the following sections, the VAT compensation systems in Canada, and in the EU countries of the United Kingdom, Austria, Finland, France, the Netherlands and Portugal are discussed.[1] In addition, sector specific systems for compensating for VAT costs arising are present in various other Member States. As these have been dealt with in the study by Copenhagen Economics and KPMG, they are not dealt with further here.[2] Instead, Norway's system is dealt with briefly in a section, as this system has also been the subject of discussions with relation to state aid issues (dealt with in Chapter 8).

§7.02 CANADA

As pointed out in section §4.03, the Canadian VAT system is very complex.[3] Canada operates a GST on a federal level alongside provincial VATs operating in most, but not all, provinces with some provinces also operating retail sales taxes RST.[4] In principle, all supplies of public bodies fall within the scope of Canadian VAT (both the federal and provincial systems). Thereby Canada can be said to apply a full tax model where public bodies are not generally excluded from the scope of the VAT system.

1. The study of these systems is not a comparative legal study but rests heavily on secondary sources.
2. Copenhagen Economics and KPMG (2011), pp. 58 to 80.
3. Bird & Gendron (2009) state that 'Canadians developed and implemented a sales tax system that no one in their right mind would have designed from scratch'.
4. See Gendron, *Bulletin* (2005) and Bird & Gendron (2009) for a general description of the Canadian VAT system. See also van Dijk & Lubber *IVM* 2000.

However, Canada operates exemptions for a variety of supplies made by public bodies, such as health, education, social welfare and public administrations.[5] In principle, VAT is not deductible on acquisitions for exempt supplies. However, the VAT costs arising due to this are mitigated by a rebate system. VAT paid on acquisitions is partly refunded/rebated. This rebate may be up to 100%, i.e., in practice some sectors are zero-rated. The rebate system prescribes a specific rebate for specific public bodies (such as municipalities, universities etc.). The system is complex, and careful accounting is required to ensure that inputs used to provide a list of acquisitions are excluded.[6]

§7.03 UNITED KINGDOM

A VAT refund scheme has been in place in the United Kingdom since the introduction of the VAT in 1973.[7] It is applicable to VAT payable under the UK VAT Act 1994 and thus not applicable to foreign VAT.[8] VAT is refundable when pertaining to non-taxable activities. VAT pertaining to exempt activities is also refundable when 'insignificant'. According to the VAT Act, the Commissioners have the power to determine when an insignificant proportion of acquisitions pertains to exempt activities. In a notice, HM Revenue & Customs has declared that limit to be 5% of acquisitions. This special de minimis rule is only applicable to certain listed authorities, including local authorities.[9] Consequently, when VAT paid on acquisitions for exempt activities is less than 5%, it is deductible based on the de minimis rule.[10]

The scheme is applicable to those authorities listed in the law, such as local authorities, certain river purification boards, police authorities, the British Broadcasting Corporation and nominated news providers.[11] The scheme, according to section 33.3(k) of the UK VAT Act, extends to 'any body specified for the purposes of this section by an order made by the Treasury'. HM Revenue & Customs has announced two conditions which it considers when taking a decision under this provision. The body must undertake a function ordinarily carried on by local government and it must have the power to draw its funding directly from local taxation.[12] It has been claimed that this list covers only a limited number of designated public sector bodies.[13]

All VAT paid on importation or acquisitions pertaining to the activities of the authority is refundable, as long as it is not deductible under the normal rules. The capital goods scheme is applicable, i.e., adjustments must be made when the usage of

5. Gendron, *Bulletin* (2005).
6. Bird & Gendron (2009), p. 13. See also Millar (2012).
7. Wassenaar & Gradus (2004), p. 385.
8. See section 33.1 of the UK VAT Act and HM Revenue & Customs Notice 749 (April 2002).
9. See also Copenhagen Economics and KPMG (2011), pp. 90–91.
10. Section 33(2) of the UK VAT Act. HM Revenue & Customs Notice 749 (April 2002), Chapter 4.2 and 8.2 and Wassenaar & Gradus (2004), pp. 385 and 392 and Copenhagen Economics and KPMG (2011), p. 91.
11. See section 33.3 of the UK VAT Act 1994 for details.
12. HM Revenue & Customs Notice 749 (April 2002), Chapter 2.4.
13. van Dijk & Lubber *IVM* 2000.

capital goods acquired changes so that the right to a refund increases or decreases.[14] Wassenaar and Gradus claim that VAT is not refundable for certain acquisitions such as VAT paid on acquisitions of motorcars.[15]

The scheme is funded by central government and local authorities do not contribute.[16]

§7.04 FINLAND

The Finnish VAT refund scheme seems to be very similar to the Swedish VAT Account Scheme if assessed based on secondary sources.[17] As in Sweden, the state cannot deduct input VAT, Art 116 of the Finnish VAT Act.[18] So all claims for VAT compensation are handled through the refund schemes.

Articles 130 and 130a of the Finnish VAT Act regulate refunds to communes.[19] They were introduced in 1994 when Finland introduced its VAT prior to entering the EU in 1995. The Scheme was introduced to compensate local authorities for extra costs due to the broadening of the VAT base.[20]

VAT paid on acquisitions for both non-taxable transactions and exempt activities is refundable. The right to a refund does not however extend to VAT that is excluded under the normal VAT scheme, such as acquisitions for private dwellings, business dinners etc.[21] Acquisitions for private consumption are also explicitly excluded, section 130 of the Finnish VAT Act.

Compensation is also paid for 'hidden' VAT on acquisitions relating to certain specified activities, section 130a of the Finnish VAT Act. These are health care, social care and dental care. When an external supplier supplies a commune with health care services etc., the commune can get a compensation of 5% of the costs of acquisition. This is said to be an approximation of the hidden VAT element in the external supplier's business.[22]

The communes themselves fund the scheme, according to some sources, yet others claim that the scheme is partly state financed.[23] Due to the fact that the scheme seems to be part of the general budget allocation between the communes and the state,

14. HM Revenue & Customs Notice 749 (April 2002), Chapter 10.6.
15. Wassenaar & Gradus (2004), p. 385. See also Dijk & Lubber *IVM* 2000.
16. Wassenaar & Gradus (2004), p. 385.
17. Wassenaar & Gradus (2004), p. 386 and Copenhagen Economics and KPMG (2011), p. 87.
18. See also Yang, *IVM* (2005).
19. Mervärdesskattelag 30.12.1993/1501.
20. Wassenaar & Gradus (2004), p. 386.
21. See section 130 referring to section 114 and 114a of the Finnish VAT Act which contains the restrictions on the right to deduct VAT.
22. See Skatteförvaltningens Anvisning DNr 41/40/2002 10.01.2002 *Avstående från att återkräva mervärdesskatt och kalkylerad återbäring av kommunernas skattefria anskaffningar i anslutning till hälso- och sjukvård.*
23. See Wassenaar & Gradus (2004), p. 386 and van Dij, & Lubbers *IVM* (2000), pp. 6–9 on the one hand and Copenhagen Economics and KPMG (2011), p. 87 on the other.

the decrease in subsidies paid to the communes as compensation for VAT compensation paid to the communes may not be readily apparent. That can explain the difference in opinion. It seems that the system is meant to be self financed.

§7.05 FRANCE

In France, a compensation system is operating whereby local government authorities receive a fixed percentage (15.482%) as compensation for VAT payable on investment expenses.[24] Central government entities are excluded from the scheme. Input VAT linked to exempt activities is not refundable.

The refund system is funded by central government, yet an adjustment has been made in the contributions from central to local government to partially finance the system. Importantly, compensation is not paid continuously (every month or trimonthly as in the other compensation systems) but two years after the investment costs. Copenhagen Economics and KPMG note that since the reduced VAT rate of 5.5%, that is often applicable to supplies made by local governments, is significantly lower than the compensation paid, local governments can be in a positive, overall VAT position.[25] In principle, the French system does not exclude the possibility that compensation is paid for foreign VAT costs arising.

§7.06 NORWAY

Norway operates a VAT which shares the key characteristics of the European VAT (as discussed in Chapter 1). It is a general, indirect tax on consumption expenditure levied at all stages of production and distribution. As such it is thus comparable to the European VAT system.

According to § 2-1 of the Norwegian VAT Act, public bodies are liable to register for VAT under the same conditions as other businesses.[26] However, § 3-9 exempts the supply of services in connection with the exercise of official authority, the supply of services between participants in a public service office concerning the operation of such offices and certain services performed in connection with forced sales of property. Furthermore, § 3-10 exempts services supplied between state entities, in so far as the supplier is not involved in an economic activity. Lastly, § 3-28 exempts the application of goods and services from a public body when the main objective is to take care of its own requirements. However, the exemption only applies when the application does not exceed 20% of the total production of the public body.

The right to deduct input VAT exists only in so far as acquisitions are used in the business, § 8 of the Norwegian VAT Act. Consequently, § 8-2 also states that public bodies performing exempt activities under § 3-28, have the right to deduct input VAT only in so far as it relates to external supplies.

24. Copenhagen Economics and KPMG (2011), pp. 87–88.
25. Copenhagen Economics and KPMG (2011), p. 88.
26. 2009-06-19 Lov om merverdiavgift (merverdiavgiftsloven) last changed through Lov 2011-06-24–27.

Norway operates a compensation scheme for communes, private or non-profit organisations that are supplying education, health and/or social services that the commune is obliged to provide under law, Kindergartens and churches.[27] The explicit purpose of the compensation scheme is to prevent distortions of competition resulting from the VAT system through the provision of compensation for VAT costs arising.[28]

Compensation is paid for all VAT pertaining to the activities that give rise to a right to compensation. No compensation is allowed for deductible VAT under the VAT Act and input VAT pertaining to: (1) certain restrictions in the VAT Act (such as entertainment costs and personal transport), (2) certain acquisitions of real property, and (3) when the activities of a commune are of an economic character and this activity may be in competition with businesses that are not eligible for compensation.[29] The system should, according to an explicit provision in the Kompensasjonslov, 'generally' (*som hovedregel*) be financed through a reduction of the transfers from central government to the communes.[30] Only Norwegian VAT is refunded.[31]

The Norwegian scheme shows a number of interesting features. First, the explicit provisions in the actual law on the purpose of the scheme and its financing are notable. It seems to me that this may be a reaction to the state aid issue that has arisen with the Norwegian system (see Chapter 8).

Second, the system extends to non-profit making entities that are involved in exempt activities. Thus, a private law entity supplying hospital services, which seems to be a service which a commune is obliged to supply under law, is entitled to compensation for VAT costs arising. This effectively deals with the problems with distortions of competition between public bodies and private bodies supplying exempt services (that arise in Sweden for example). These services are in fact zero-rated.[32]

Third, a guarantee is also inserted in this regard with the provision that in so far as an activity may be performed by a commune in competition with entities that are not allowed compensation for VAT, compensation shall not be paid. In the choice of distorting competition between public bodies and private bodies, and distorting the choice between contracting out and self-supplying, the legislator has taken a clear stance that the previous is the most important.

Lastly, the provisions discussed do not cover state entities.

---

27. See § 2 of the Lov 2003-12-12 nr 108: Lov om kompensasjon av merverdiavgift for kommuner, fylkeskommuner mv. As per 2011-01-01 (Kompensasjonsloven). The refunds to NPOs have been commented on by Gjems-Onstad *International VAT Monitor* (2004).
28. §1 of Kompensasjonsloven.
29. See § 4 of Kompensasjonsloven. In addition, a point 5 provides that no compensation is allowed unless payment is made through the bank's payment system when the payment exceeds 10 000 NOK. This corresponds though to a general rule in the Norwegian VAT Act, § 8-8, and is thus not specific for the repayment scheme.
30. §5 of Kompensasjonsloven.
31. Compare § 3 of Kompensasjonsloven.
32. The approach is similar to the Austrian one.

§7.07 THE NETHERLANDS

A compensation fund was introduced in 2003 in the Netherlands. It was motivated primarily by the view that a level playing field between self-supply and contracting out should be created.[33] The Scheme applies to municipalities, provincial authorities and designated regional governments.[34]

Compensation is paid only for non-deductible VAT connected with activities that fall outside the scope of VAT.[35] Compensation is also paid for foreign VAT paid, as long as it originates within the EU or an EES country (Norway, Liechtenstein and Iceland).[36]

The VAT compensation fund was intended to have a budgetary neutral effect on all parties involved.[37] The VAT compensation fund is to be established yearly and the capital is to equal the amount of VAT repaid to local authorities. The fund is maintained by a reduction in the contributions from the Dutch state, a reduction in general payments from state funds (the Municipal Fund and the Provincial Fund) and by an increase in VAT receipts.[38] However, it has been claimed that the system is not completely neutral to state resources as 'over compensation' (above designated resources budgeted through reductions in the general payments) is financed through the state budget.[39]

§7.08 PORTUGAL

Portugal is reported to have a compensation system for certain entities in certain sectors, such as churches, political parties and the army.[40] Compensation is paid both for VAT pertaining to exempt activities and non-taxable activities. The system is exclusively financed by the state.

33. Wassenaar & Gradus (2004), p. 388.
34. Copenhagen Economics and KPMG (2011), pp. 88–89.
35. Copenhagen Economics and KPMG (2011), pp. 88–89.
36. Wassenaar & Gradus (2004), p. 388.
37. van Dijk & Lubbers *IVM* (2000).
38. Van Dijk & Lubbers *IVM* (2000).
39. Copenhagen Economics and KPMG (2011), pp. 88–89.
40. Copenhagen Economics and KPMG (2011), p. 89.

CHAPTER 8

State Aid and Compensation Schemes

§8.01 INTRODUCTION

According to Article 107(1) TFEU, any aid granted by a Member State or through state resources in any form whatsoever which distorts or threatens to distort competition by favouring certain undertakings or the production of certain goods shall, in so far as it affects trade between Member States, be incompatible with the internal market. In one decision from the EFTA Surveillance Authority, the Communes' Compensation Scheme for VAT costs in Norway has been declared to be illegal state aid within the meaning of Article 61(1) of the EEA Agreement (the equivalent of (now) Article 107(1) TFEU).[1] This indicates that there may be difficulties in aligning compensation schemes for VAT costs of public bodies with EU competition law.

In this chapter the prohibition against state aid is dealt with in relation to compensation schemes for VAT costs of public bodies. The study does not aim at a detailed appraisal of each compensation scheme and the compatibility with Article 107 TFEU, but seeks to identify the core problems arising with the compensation schemes' compatibility with Article 107(1) TFEU.

§8.02 STRUCTURE AND CONTEXT OF THE STATE AID PROVISIONS

Title VII of the TFEU is 'Common rules on competition, taxation and approximation of laws'. The Title comprises three chapters; Chapter 1 'Rules on competition', Chapter 2 'Tax provisions' and Chapter 3 'Approximation of laws'. Chapter 1 comprises two sections; section 1 'Rules applying to undertakings' (Articles 101–106) and section 2 'Aids granted by states' (Articles 107–109). Despite the fact that Chapter 1 has two

1. The EFTA Surveillance Authority Decision, No. 155/07/COL of 3 May 2007 on state aid granted in connection with Article 3 of the Norwegian Act on compensation for value added tax (VAT) (Norway), OJ 18.9.2008, L 249/35.

sections, both the rules applying to undertakings and the rules on state aid refer to practices etc. and aid received by 'undertakings'. It is clear from case law that the concept has the same meaning throughout Chapter 1.[2] As public bodies are principally not 'undertakings', EU competition law is in principle not applicable to public bodies. However, this is true only in so far as the public body is acting as a public authority as defined in competition law case law from the Court of Justice.[3] When a public body is involved in an economic activity, EU competition law is applicable.

In so far as the rules applying to undertakings are concerned, regard is had to the fact that some public bodies are providing public goods. Article 106(1) states that in the case of public undertakings and undertakings to which Member States grant special or exclusive rights, Member States shall neither enact nor maintain in force any measure contrary to the rules contained in the Treaties. However, undertakings entrusted with the operation of *services of general economic interest* (often abbreviated SGEI) or having the character of a revenue-producing monopoly shall, according to Article 106(2), be subject to the rules contained in the Treaties, in particular to the rules on competition, only in so far as the application of such rules does not obstruct the performance, in law or in fact, of the particular tasks assigned to them.

The Commission has issued *inter alia* a decision and framework concerning the SGEI.[4] A number of legal instruments are applicable to SGEI, divided by sector (land transport, air transport, maritime transport, broadcasting, telecommunications, post and energy).[5] The treatment is currently under review.[6] Apart from the special provisions dealing with SGEI, no special regard is had, in section 1 on the rules applying to undertakings, to the fact that a public body is dealt with or that public goods are provided.

In contrast thereto, the section on state aid is full of considerations taken with regard to the special functions of a state. First, even if state aid is found to exist based on Article 107(1) TFEU, a number of aids shall be considered to be consistent with the common market. According to Article 107(2) TFEU the following shall be compatible with the internal market:

(a) aid having a social character, granted to individual consumers;
(b) aid to make good the damage caused by natural disasters or exceptional occurrences; and
(c) aid granted to the economy of certain areas of the Federal Republic of Germany affected by the division of Germany.

---

2. See generally on state aid and taxes, Schön (1999), Aldestam (2005) and Mamut (2010). Interesting points are also raised in Luja (2007).
3. This crucial distinction is discussed further below.
4. See Commission Decision of 28 November 2005 on the application of Article 86(2) of the EC Treaty to state aid in the form of public service compensation granted to certain undertakings entrusted with the operation of services of general economic interest (2005/842/EC) and a Community framework for state aid in the form of public service compensation.
5. A compilation can be found in the Annex to COM(2011) 146 final.
6. *Ibid.*

Second, according to Article 107(3) TFEU, the following aid may be compatible with the common market:

(a) aid to promote the economic development of areas where the standard of living is abnormally low or where there is serious underemployment, and of the regions referred to in Article 349, in view of their structural, economic and social situation;
(b) aid to promote the execution of an important project of common European interest or to remedy a serious disturbance in the economy of a Member State;
(c) aid to facilitate the development of certain economic activities or of certain economic areas;
(d) aid to promote culture and heritage conservation where such aid does not affect trading conditions and competition in the Union to an extent that is contrary to the common interest;
(e) such other categories of aid as may be specified by decision of the Council on a proposal from the Commission.

It is clear from the wording of Article 107(1) and the case law of the Court of Justice that state aid shall be declared as incompatible with the internal market when four conditions are met:

(1) The aid is an intervention by the state or through state resources.
(2) the intervention is liable to affect trade between the Member States.
(3) the intervention confers an advantage on the recipient.
(4) the aid distorts, or threatens to distort, competition.[7]

These requirements will be dealt with in turn and their application to the compensation schemes for states and communes reflected upon. First it must be determined under what conditions refunds of VAT costs constitute 'aid' within the meaning of Article 107 and when a public body may be classified as an 'undertaking' for the purposes of competition law.

§8.03 THE CONCEPT OF 'AID'

In order for Article 107(1) TFEU to be applicable, 'aid' has to be granted. The Court of Justice has held that the concept of 'aid' is a legal concept which must be interpreted on the basis of objective factors.[8] That concept is very wide. It is more general than that of a subsidy. It embraces not only positive benefits, but also measures which, in various forms, mitigate the charges which are normally included in the budget of an undertaking and which, without therefore being subsidies in the strict meaning of the

7. See, for example, Case C-172/03 *Heiser*, p. 27.
8. Case C-83/98 P *Ladbroke racing*, p. 25.

word, are similar in character and have the same effect.[9] What is decisive is whether the aid confers an economic advantage on the recipient.[10]

Some payments are not aid but compensation paid for services provided. These payments do not fall under Article 107(1). According to the Court of Justice, where a state measure is compensation for services provided by the recipient undertakings in order to discharge public service obligations, so that those undertakings do not enjoy a real financial advantage and the measure thus does not have the effect of putting them in a more favourable competitive position than the undertakings competing with them, such a measure is not caught by (now) Article 107(1) TFEU.[11] The Court has laid down four conditions that must be satisfied in order for a payment to be classified as compensation and not aid (the so-called Altmark test). First, the recipient undertaking must actually have public service obligations to discharge, and the obligations must be clearly defined. Second, the parameters on the basis of which the compensation is calculated must be established in advance in an objective and transparent manner. Third, the compensation cannot exceed what is necessary to cover all or part of the costs incurred, taking into account the relevant receipts and a reasonable profit for discharging those obligations. Fourth, where the undertaking, which is to discharge public service obligations, is not chosen pursuant to a public procurement procedure, the level of compensation needed must be determined on the basis of an analysis of the costs which a typical undertaking would have incurred in discharging those obligations, taking into account the relevant receipts and a reasonable profit for discharging the obligations. A state measure, which does not comply with one or more of those conditions, must be regarded as state aid. Compensation paid under the Compensation Schemes researched falls short of the Altmark test and constitutes aid within the meaning of Article 107(1).

As is clear from case law, as soon as the economic effect is that of mitigating charges normally included in the budget of an undertaking, an aid has been granted. Tax concessions, reduced rates, deduction or a refund of VAT, delayed payment of VAT etc. all potentially constitute state aid. In European VAT there exists in principle no right to deduct input VAT incurred that pertains to an activity falling outside the scope of VAT or falling within the scope of VAT but exempt. Compensation paid to public bodies under the compensation schemes researched concerns precisely the VAT not deductible under the normal VAT rules. It can therefore be concluded that a repayment of VAT on acquisitions by public bodies constitutes 'aid' within the meaning of Article 107(1) TFEU.[12]

§8.04 THE CONCEPT OF 'UNDERTAKINGS'

According to Article 107 TFEU, the prohibition against state aid is only applicable when an aid favours certain 'undertakings'. The compensation schemes researched for

9. Case C-172/03 *Heiser*, p. 36.
10. Case T-67/94 *Ladbroke Racing*, p. 52.
11. See, also in the following, Case C-280/00 *Altmark*, pp. 87–94.
12. See also Chapter §8.07.

central and local government authorities for VAT costs arising favour certain entities, namely public bodies. It must therefore be ascertained when public bodies can be regarded as 'undertakings' within the meaning of Article 107 TFEU.

The Court has held that as regards the possible application of the competition rules, a distinction must be drawn between a situation where the state acts in the exercise of official authority and that where it carries on economic activities of an industrial or commercial nature by offering goods or services on the market.[13] In that connection, it is of no importance that the state is acting directly through a body forming part of the state administration or by way of a body on which it has conferred special or exclusive rights. In order to make the distinction between the two situations of acting as official authority and engaged in economic activities, it is necessary to consider the nature of the activities carried on by the public undertaking or body on which the state has conferred special or exclusive rights. Consequently, the definition of 'undertaking' for the purposes of competition law is any entity engaged in an economic activity, regardless of the legal status of the entity and the way in which it is financed.[14]

Public bodies are as such thus not excluded from the scope of EU competition law, just because they are public bodies. Instead, an assessment needs to be made of the nature of the activities carried out.

In *Cali*, the Court found that anti-pollution surveillance activities were tasks in the public interest which form part of the essential functions of the state as regards protection of the environment in maritime areas.[15] Such surveillance was connected by its nature, its aim and the rules to which it is subject with the exercise of powers relating to the protection of the environment which are typically those of a public authority. The Court therefore considered that the entity performing them was not conducting activity of an economic nature justifying the application of the Treaty rules on competition.

In *Poucet, Pistre*, the Court found that an organisation entrusted with the management of the public social security system was not an 'undertaking' for competition law purposes.[16] The Court noted that the systems pursued a social objective and embodied the principle of solidarity. They were intended to provide cover for all the persons to whom they applied, against the risks of sickness, old-age, death and invalidity, regardless of their financial status and their state of health at the time of affiliation. The principle of solidarity was embodied in the fact that the scheme was financed by contributions proportional to the income from the occupation and to the retirement pensions of the persons making them; only recipients of an invalidity pension and retired insured members with very modest resources were exempted from the payment of contributions, whereas the benefits were identical for all those who received them. Furthermore, persons no longer covered by the scheme retained their entitlement to benefits for a year, free of charge. Solidarity entailed the redistribution of

13. Case C-343/95 *Cali*, pp. 16–18.
14. Joined Cases C-180/98 to 184/98 *Pavlov and others*, p. 74.
15. Case C-343/95 *Cali*.
16. Joined Cases C-159/91, C-160/91 *Poucet, Pistre*.

income between those who were better off and those who, in view of their resources and state of health, would be deprived of the necessary social cover. In the old-age insurance scheme, solidarity was embodied in the fact that the contributions paid by active workers served to finance the pensions of retired workers. There was also solidarity between the various social security schemes, in that those in surplus contributed to the financing of those with structural financial difficulties. Furthermore, the schemes were entrusted by statute to social security funds whose activities were subject to control by the state. In the discharge of their duties, the funds applied the law and thus could not influence the amount of the contributions, the use of assets and the fixing of the level of benefits. Based on the above, the Court found that the organisation was not an 'undertaking' for the purposes of competition law.

In *Sat Fluggesellschaft* the Court found that Eurocontrol's activities, by their nature, their aim and the rules to which they are subject, are connected with the exercise of powers relating to the control and supervision of air space which are typically those of a public authority.[17] They were therefore not of an economic nature justifying the application of the Treaty rules of competition.[18]

In *Wouters*, the question was whether the members of the Bar in the Netherlands, as well as the Bar itself, were undertakings for the purposes of competition law. The Court found that the members carried on an economic activity and that the complexity and technical nature of the services provided, and the fact that the practice of the profession was regulated, did not alter that conclusion.[19] The Court thereafter dealt with the question of whether the Bar, when adopting the disputed Regulation in question, was acting as an association of undertakings or, on the contrary, as a public authority.[20] The Court recalled that according to its case law, the rules on competition were not applicable to those not belonging to the sphere of economic activity.[21] The Bar was however not fulfilling a social function based on the principle of solidarity, unlike certain social security bodies (dealt with in *Poucet, Pistre*), nor exercising powers which are typically those of a public authority. It acts as the regulatory body of a profession, a practice which constitutes an economic activity.[22]

Consequently, whether a public body is an 'undertaking' for the purposes of competition law must be assessed based on a careful appraisal of the activity in question. When a public body is involved in the essential functions of the state, perhaps exercising powers which are typically those of a public authority, or fulfilling

17. Case C-364/92 *Sat Fluggesellschaft*. See also Case T-189/03, pp. 72–79 for an interesting assessment by the General Court of an aid in the form of an income tax exemption and its relationship with the public services sector.
18. See also Case C-113/07 P, *SELEX*, pp. 69–77, where the Court found that the assistance which Eurocontrol provides to the national administrations, when so requested by them, in connection with tendering procedures carried out by those administrations for the acquisition, in particular, of equipment and systems in the field of air traffic management, could not be considered as an economic activity for the purposes of competition law.
19. Case C-309/99 *Wouters*, p. 49.
20. Case C-309/99 *Wouters* p. 56.
21. Case C-309/99 *Wouters* p. 57. The Court referred to Joined Cases C-159/91, 160/91 *Poucet, Pistre* and Case C-364/92 *Sat Fluggesellschaft*.
22. Case C-309/99 *Wouters* p. 58.

a social function based on the principle of solidarity, and the aim and rules governing its activities are those of a public authority, this indicates that it is not an undertaking. In short, activities that are an exercise of sovereign power or are social activities based on solidarity are exempted from competition law. Undertakings engaged in economic activities are subject to competition law, unless the 'services of general interest' exemption applies.[23]

With regard to the compensation schemes researched, it needs to be assessed whether compensation paid is linked to an economic activity performed by the public body within the meaning of the case law described. In that context, it must be noted that the concept of 'undertakings' shows clear similarities with the VAT concept of economic activities in Article 9(1) of the VAT Directive. 'Undertakings' for competition law purposes are those engaged in economic activities entailing providing goods or services on a market (and then, by necessity, for payment). This similarity raises the issue of to what extent case law in the field of VAT is relevant in competition law when determining whether an activity performed falls under the concept of 'undertaking'.

There are clear indications that case law in the field of VAT is relevant in competition law. The Commission has explicitly inferred VAT case law on the concept of economic activities in a Decision on an Italian state aid.[24] The Decision concerned whether SICAV funds were undertakings for the purposes of competition law. The Commission found that they were and motivated its decision as follows:[25]

> The Commission considers that specialised investment vehicles perform an economic activity and constitute undertakings within the meaning of Article 87(1). This is confirmed by the case law of the Court in the VAT field. In particular, the Court recently held (17) that transactions carried out by SICAVs and consisting in the collective investment in transferable securities constitute an economic activity carried out by taxable persons within the meaning of Article 4(2) of the Sixth VAT Directive [now Article 9(1) of the VAT Directive, OH]. According to the case law, it is evident from the preamble to the First Directive that VAT harmonisation aims to eliminate factors which may distort conditions of competition and therefore to secure neutrality in competition. Given that the State aid rules and the VAT harmonisation directives share the same purpose, the Commission considers it appropriate to refer to the case law concerning the latter, which confirms that the investment vehicles in question, whether or not they have corporate form, perform an economic activity and therefore constitute undertakings within the meaning of Article 87(1).

The Commission explicitly referred to *BBL*, where the Court of Justice had found that a SICAV did perform economic activities for VAT purposes.[26] In the field of competition

23. Lear, Mossialos and Karl (2010), p. 340.
24. See European Commission Decision of 6 September 2005 on the aid scheme implemented by Italy for certain undertakings for collective investment in transferable securities specialised in shares of small- and medium-capitalisation companies listed on regulated markets, OJ L268/1, 27 September 2006. See also Luja (2006).
25. European Commission Decision of 6 September 2005 on the aid scheme implemented by Italy for certain undertakings for collective investment in transferable securities specialised in shares of small- and medium-capitalisation companies listed on regulated markets, OJ L268/1, 27 September 2006, paragraph 38. Footnotes omitted.
26. Case C-8/03 *BBL*.

law, case law on the VAT concept of economic activity is thus relevant in the eyes of the Commission.

The position must in my view be criticised. Defining the concept of economic activities in the field of VAT has less to do with ensuring neutrality in competition and elimination of distortions of competition than with defining the scope of the VAT system.[27] VAT is a tax on consumption. Savings is not consumption. There is therefore a need to distinguish production and consumption activities from savings activities. This fundamental problem underlies the difficulties in defining what economic activities are for VAT purposes, rather than a need to ensure neutrality in competition.

Anyway, public bodies perform economic activities for both VAT and competition law purposes, such as activities exempt from VAT in Article 132 of the VAT Directive. The question which arises is whether it should matter whether an activity is excluded from the scope based on Article 13 of the VAT Directive or due to its non-economic character (i.e., based on Article 9). Activities excluded from the scope by Article 13 of the VAT Directive may still be of such a nature that it is possible to supply them on a market. Furthermore, the Court has held that prior to determining whether a public body is covered by Article 13 of the VAT Directive, it needs to be determined whether the public body performs an economic activity within the meaning of Article 9(1) and thus if it at all falls within the scope of the VAT system. I therefore submit that case law on VAT is solely relevant in competition law for determining the concept of 'undertakings' when it concerns (now) Article 9(1) of the VAT Directive.

§8.05 INTERVENTION BY THE STATE OR THROUGH STATE RESOURCES

According to Article 107(1) TFEU, aid has to be 'granted by a Member State or through State resources' to be caught by the provision. The phrase as such raises the question of whether it is enough that aid is granted by an organ of a Member State or if it is also required that the aid emanates from state resources. The Court has commented on this stating that the distinction made in the provision between 'aid granted by a Member State' and aid granted 'through State resources' does not signify that all advantages granted by a state, whether financed through state resources or not, constitute aid. It is intended merely to bring within that definition both advantages which are granted directly by the state and those granted by a public or private body designated or established by the state. Only aid granted directly or indirect through state resources falls within the scope of the provision.[28]

Consequently, it is now clear that the essential requirement is that the aid emanates from state resources. Whether it is actually paid by an organ of a Member State or another entity is irrelevant.

27. See, for a discussion on the concept of economic activities and the fundamental characteristics of the VAT system, Henkow (2008), Chapters 3 and 5.
28. Case C-379/98 *PreussenElektra*, p. 58.

It is also necessary to define which entities fall under the concept of the 'state' within the meaning of Article 107(1) TFEU. It is clear from case law that the provision should be interpreted by reference to its purpose of ensuring that competition is not distorted. It follows from such an interpretation that it is not necessary for subsidies to be granted by the government or by a central administrative authority of a Member State.[29] The Court has held that the concept of the state also includes regional and local bodies of a Member State, whatever their status or description.[30] All aid financed with public resources is thus granted through state resources.[31] Consequently, state resources may be central or local – as long as they are public resources they fall under the provision. This interpretation finds support in the purpose of the provision: to ensure that competition is not distorted.

With regard to the communes' compensation schemes discussed in Chapters 5–7, these are financed by central government, by the municipalities through contributions to a common account or jointly by both central and local government (or it is unclear how they are financed). It seems clear from case law that either way, the compensations are granted from public resources. When the municipalities or communes are themselves financing a contribution to an activity that falls under the state aid provisions in the Treaty[32], there is, under one condition, an intervention through state resources. The condition is that financing is not ear-marked so that only resources emanating from activities classified as an 'undertaking' for competition law purposes is used to compensate VAT costs arising in such activities and that resources emanating from the communes' public body functions, within the meaning of competition law, are not ear-marked for such activities.

The funding of the refund schemes applicable in the Member States is not easily grasped. In the in-depth study of the Swedish system, it was found that the intention of the legislator was that the communes should carry the costs of the system themselves. As seen from the description above, some countries, like Denmark, have clearly stated in their law or *travaux preparatoire* that their communes' compensation scheme should not be financed through the state budget but by the communes themselves. In EU competition law this is of no importance – resources emanating from the communes' public funds are also resources of the state. Furthermore, none of the compensation schemes researched involved ear-marking the resources used in the way discussed above.

Interestingly, the Norwegian authorities argued, in the EFTA Surveillance Authority decision mentioned above, that the fact that the VAT compensation scheme was self-funded, since general transfers from the state budget were reduced, meant that it did not constitute state aid. The Authority replied that it was not relevant whether the funds from the state were reduced. What was important was whether 'undertakings' for the purpose of competition law received financial support through state resources.

29. Case T-358/94 *Air France*, p. 56.
30. Case 248/84 *Germany v. Commission*, p. 17.
31. Case 248/84 *Germany v. Commission*, p. 17.
32. An activity that is economic and thus the commune or municipality is acting as an 'undertaking'.

Whether the state's cost of compensation at the central level is counterbalanced by reduced transfers to local and regional authorities as such does not alter this conclusion. The refund for input VAT paid was financed from the state budget and therefore constituted state resources. The Authority added that '[m]oreover, in the Authority's understanding, each municipality does not get a reduction in the State transfer exactly corresponding to the exact VAT compensation it receives'.

As noted above, the new Norwegian rules state in the law that the system should be self-financed. It seems likely that this is at least partly a response to the decision of the Surveillance Authority. However, the Authority just added this to a list of reasons supporting the position that the aid emanated from state resources. Case law is clear. All public funds are state resources. Whether the aid is financed locally, centrally or jointly is of no importance.

§8.06 LIABLE TO AFFECT TRADE BETWEEN MEMBER STATES

The measure must affect competition and trade between the Member States. It seems that this condition is met, according to the case law of the Court of Justice, as soon as the activity in question is also carried out in another Member State and cross-border trade exists. The Commission has summarised the situation as follows:[33]

> the criterion of trade being affected is met if the recipient firm carries on an economic activity [for the purposes of competition law/OH] involving trade between Member States. The mere fact that the aid strengthens the firm's position compared with that of other firms which are competitors in intra-Community trade is enough to allow the conclusion to be drawn that intra-Community trade is affected. Neither the fact that aid is relatively small in amount, nor the fact that the recipient is moderate in size or its share of the Community market very small, nor indeed the fact that the recipient does not carry out exports, or exports virtually all its production outside the Community, do anything to alter this conclusion.

It needs thus to be determined whether the aid is granted to any activity that is carried out elsewhere and also whether the activity involves cross-border trade to any extent. It cannot be ruled out that an activity that constitutes an 'undertaking' for competition law purposes does not involve any cross-border trade. However, it seems most likely that such activities are also performed elsewhere and that some cross-border trade exists somewhere in the EU. The Norwegian compensation scheme was found to be capable of affecting trade by the EFTA Surveillance Authority.

§8.07 FAVOURING CERTAIN UNDERTAKINGS: SELECTIVITY

According to Article 107(1), state aid has to distort competition 'by favouring certain undertakings or the production of certain goods' in order to be declared incompatible with the internal market. General aid is thus allowed – only selectively granted aid, i.e.,

33. Commission notice on the application of the state aid rules to measures relating to business taxation, OJ C 384/3, 10.12.98, p. 11. Footnotes and references have been omitted.

aid favouring certain undertakings, is not permitted. As a consequence, measures whose scope extends to the entire territory of the state have been considered to be non-selective. Regional and local aid may however favour certain undertakings, as could aid granted for a specific sector.[34]

Tax measures open to all economic agents operating within a Member State are in principle general measures.[35] Tax measures not open to all economic agents are in principle selective. Such measures may however be justified by the nature or general scheme of the tax system and therefore not favouring certain undertakings within the meaning of Article 107(1).[36] It ought to be mentioned that selectivity relates to de facto effects of tax provisions and not their form.[37] Furthermore, selectivity can easily be established if a tax provision leaves it to the discretion of the tax administration to grant the incentive as it sees fit.[38]

As the Commission has noted, following from the above, the main criterion with regard to the application of Article 107(1) on tax measures is that the measure provides, in favouring certain undertakings, an exception to the application of the tax system.[39] A 'normal' tax system needs to be established and the tax measure in question needs to be 'benchmarked' against the 'normal' tax system to see whether it is in line with the nature of the system or design thereof, or if it in contrast is selective and derogates from the 'normal' system.[40] The proper benchmark is thus the situation of other taxable persons' vis-à-vis the benchmark tax system.[41]

To establish a benchmark system that is the normal situation without encroaching upon the right of Member States to manage and structure their tax systems as they see fit is a delicate matter. But it seems to be necessary to draw a line between the difficulties encountered in direct taxes and indirect taxes, and the VAT in particular. The vast harmonisation of VAT in the EU has created a special situation with regard to the presence of a benchmark tax system.[42]

The Commission has noted[43] that to:

34. See Commission notice on the application of the state aid rules to measures relating to direct business taxation, OJ C 384/3, 10 December 1998 paragraphs 18 and 19, Schön *CMLR* (1999) and Aldestam (2005), pp. 186–191 for different views of the test to be made.
35. See on the selectivity criterion Schön *CMLR* (1999) and Aldestam (2005).
36. See Case 173/73 *Italy v. Commission*, p. 15, where this derogation was established and Schön *CMLR* (1999).
37. Case 173/73 *Italy v. Commission*, p. 13 and Commission notice on the application of the state aid rules to measures relating to direct business taxation, OJ C 384/3, 10 December 1998 paragraph 15.
38. See Schön *CMLR* (1999) and Commission notice on the application of the state aid rules to measures relating to direct business taxation, OJ C 384/3, 10 December 1998 paragraph 21.
39. Commission notice on the application of the state aid rules to measures relating to direct business taxation, OJ C 384/3, 10 December 1998 paragraph 16.
40. See Schön *CMLR* (1999) for a discussion of the problems inherent in this approach.
41. Schön *CMLR* (1999), pp. 923–924 and Case C-6/97 *Netherlands v. Commission*, p. 16, discussed also in Aldestam (2005), p. 187.
42. On state aid and VAT, see generally Terra (2011), who provides an overview of the few cases dealt with by the Court of Justice and the General Court dealing with VAT and state aid as well as an explanation to the limited number of cases that have been decided.
43. Report on the implementation of the Commission notice on the application of the state aid rules to measures relating to direct business taxation, C(2004)434, 09.02.2004.

> be caught by the concept of State aid, measures must favour certain undertakings by reducing the charges normally borne by them. In this connection, VAT reductions are subject to strict Community rules and conform to the principle of equality of taxation for similar products. Such reductions are therefore not usually caught by Article 87(1).

Terra has submitted that the strict harmonisation also provides an autonomous general description of a 'normal' VAT system which functions as a benchmark.[44] I will proceed based on the position that the EU VAT Directive constitutes the proper benchmark towards which national measures should be compared.

The character of European VAT was discussed in Chapter 1. It is clear from the nature of the tax system that it entails a right for taxable persons to be fully relieved of the burden of the VAT in so far as their transactions are themselves subject to VAT. Except for in specific circumstances, as provided for in Article 169(c) of the VAT Directive, when a right to a refund of input VAT incurred for transactions which are exempt from VAT arises, and in cases where an exemption applies for technical reasons when taxing rights (the place of supply) have been allocated to another country, as provided for in Article 169(b), there exists no right to deduct or receive a refund of VAT incurred for transactions that bear no output tax. In addition, the Court has held that VAT incurred in relation to non-economic activities that do not fall within the scope of VAT is, in principle, not deductible either.

Accordingly, refunds of VAT pertaining to non-taxed output must be considered to deviate, in principle, from the general scheme of the EU VAT system. Two issues arise, whether it is of any importance that the compensation scheme is there to increase neutrality in competition between contracting out and self-supplying, and whether Article 13 of the VAT Directive on public bodies should entail a different conclusion with regard to non-deductibility of VAT pertaining to non-economic activities, as Article 13 deems certain activities to be non-economic rather than that these are inherently non-economic. With regard to the latter issue, it seems to me that case law indicates that Article 13 should not in this regard lead to special treatment. In *Waterschap Zeeuws Vlaanderen*, the *Lennartz*-principles, applicable to acquisitions by a person not acting as a taxable person when acquiring goods, was considered applicable *mutatis mutandis* to public bodies covered by Article 13.[45] The Court thus did not choose, in a case concerning deduction of input VAT incurred, to infer any special meaning to activities covered by Article 13 with regard to deduction of VAT compared to 'normal' persons covered solely by Article 9.

With regard to the first issue, this was discussed in the EFTA Surveillance Authority decision on the Norwegian compensation scheme. The Norwegian authorities argued that VAT compensation is justified by the nature or general scheme of the tax system in question. It is a fundamental principle that the VAT system should be neutral and non-discriminatory. Neutrality may therefore be seen as inherent in the VAT system itself. Neutrality, which is inherent to the VAT system, was also the objective assigned to the VAT compensation scheme. Therefore, the Norwegian

44. Terra (2011).
45. Case C-378/02 *Waterschap Zeeuws Vlaanderen*.

authorities believed that it was fair to consider the VAT compensation scheme to be in line with the nature and logic of the VAT system itself. The authorities also pointed to the fact that the scheme rather increased neutrality in competition, since it remedied the distorting effects against outsourcing that would arise were compensation not to be granted.

The Authority considered that the scheme implied a relief from the obligation that follows from the general VAT system applicable to all buyers of goods and services. It was thus selective and may only be justified based on the nature and general scheme of the VAT system. The Authority assessed the Norwegian VAT system and the existence of exemptions from VAT in that system. It concluded that the consequence of the logic of the system was that exempted supplies of goods and services and final consumers bear input tax without having the possibility to deduct it.

The Authority continued[46]:

> This logical consequence of system had created, however, a distortion at another level, which the Norwegian authorities have tried to offset with the introduction of the VAT Compensation Act. Thus, it follows that the logic of the VAT Compensation Act is to counterbalance the natural logical consequence of the VAT system when exempting certain supplies. Hence, the logic of the VAT Compensation Act is not to tax end users, as it is in the general VAT system, but to alleviate a certain group of final consumers to avoid distortion of competition between 'in-house' and outsourcing for transactions subject to VAT.
>
> The Authority considers that to compensate for paid input tax for other reasons than the ones set in the VAT system, is not justified by the objective of taxation of a given activity, which primarily inspires the VAT system. The objective pursued by the Norwegian authorities in creating a level playing field between self supply and outsourcing by public entities of goods and services subject to VAT should be seen as commendable as such but can hardly be said to be in the nature and logic of the VAT system itself. In this sense, the Authority refers in particular to the Heiser jurisprudence according to which the mere fact that a measure has a laudable purpose does not suffice to exclude it from classification as aid within the meaning of Article 61(1) of the EEA Agreement. Article 61(1) of the EEA Agreement does not distinguish between measures of state intervention by reference to their causes or aims, but defines them in relation to their effects.
>
> The Authority does not ignore that the aim pursued by the Norwegian authorities with the introduction of the VAT Compensation Act was to create neutrality in the procurement of goods and services subject to VAT for the public administration. This neutrality cannot be confused with the neutrality inherent in the VAT system.

Based on the above, the Authority concluded that the system was selective and could not be justified. I find the reasoning convincing and equally relevant for the Member States of the EU and the EU VAT System. The distortions appearing are inherent in the system as it is presently laid down.[47] Despite the fact that a refund of VAT on acquisitions for producers of goods and services (such as public bodies) is in line with

46. Footnotes omitted, p. 42.
47. NB. In Chapter 9 it is advocated that the system should be changed.

a view of the VAT as a tax on consumption (proper), the VAT system actually also treats acquisitions by exempt taxable persons and public bodies as non-deductible.

§8.08 THREATENS TO DISTORT COMPETITION

Aid granted must 'distort or threaten to distort competition by favouring certain undertakings or the production of certain goods' in order to fall within the scope of Article 107(1) TFEU. It has been claimed that unlike the competition tests in EU competition law in general, the test here does not focus on measuring the extent of distortion of competition.[48] Instead, the Court has consistently held that the Commission is required, not to establish that the aid has a real effect on trade between Member States and that competition is actually being distorted, but only to examine whether that aid is liable to affect such trade and distort competition.[49] Consequently, when financial aid granted by a Member State strengthens the position of an undertaking compared with other undertakings competing in intraCommunity trade, the latter must be regarded as affected by that aid.[50]

Moreover, there is no threshold or percentage below which trade between Member States can be said not to be affected. The relatively small amount of aid or the relatively small size of the undertaking which receives it does not as such exclude the possibility that trade between Member States might be affected.[51]

It seems evident that a right to a refund of VAT incurred on acquisitions for an economic activity where such a right does not exists under the normal VAT scheme strengthens the position of the undertaking receiving the aid. In so far as compensation is paid for VAT incurred that is not deductible for those not covered by the refund scheme, competition must be considered to be threatened to be distorted in accordance with the relevant case law.[52] Thus, when a public body makes exempt supplies and input VAT is refunded the compensation scheme (threatens to) distorts competition.

§8.09 CONCLUDING REMARKS

The legal situation in competition law is not especially clear with regard to public services. Put into the context of a specific public service (health care) in competition law, Prosser has made the following reflections:[53]

---

48. See Karlsson (2011), Chapter 2.7.
49. See, for example, Case C-148/04 *Unicredito*, p. 54.
50. Case C-372/97 *Italy v. Commission*, p. 52.
51. See Case T-189/03 *ASM Brescia*, p. 69. It should be noted that aid of a small value is excluded from the application of the state aid regime, see the Commission Regulation (EC) No. 1998/2006 of 15 December 2006 on the application of Articles 87 and 88 of the Treaty to de minimis aid, OJ, L 379, 28.12.2006.
52. As noted by Karlsson (2011), Chapter 2.7, the issue of whether an aid distorts competition seems to be linked to whether the aid is selectively granted. When the aid has been granted to only some undertakings, it is strengthening those undertakings positions vis-à-vis its competitors. That is enough to pass the test in Article 107(1). The requirement that competition must be distorted seems thus to be fulfilled when an aid is selectively granted.
53. Prosser (2010), p. 315.

> The treatment of health care by European competition law encapsulates more clearly than almost any other public service a key dilemma: to what extent are public services subject to the norms of competition law and the internal market, or are they characterized by quite different principles of solidarity and citizenship, which make the application of market and competition principles inappropriate? As we shall see, neither the European courts nor the Commission has so far provided a completely clear set of answers to these questions [...].

Activities of public bodies are not always 'undertakings' falling within the scope of Article 107 TFEU. Activities such as anti-pollution surveillance activities, the management of public social security systems, the supervision of air space and other essential functions of the state where the public body is exercising public powers or fulfilling a social function based on the principle of solidarity are not 'undertakings'. As regards these activities, a repayment of VAT costs does not constitute illegal state aid.

Furthermore, it cannot be ruled out that Article 107(3)(d) or (e) may be applicable, to a certain extent, to repayments of VAT costs and thus compensation schemes may not, on this ground, in all respects be incompatible with the common market.

Despite this, compensation schemes are problematic in relation to Article 107. To a large extent they may be incompatible with the provision. The best way of ensuring that they are not is to make them an integral part of the EU VAT system.[54]

54. The Commission has stated that 'closed' compensation schemes do not constitute illegal state aid, se Question to the EP, PWQ 2000, P-2861/99, OJ C225 E/211, 7 January 2000. The present analysis shows that this statement should not be considered as a *carte blanche* for compensations schemes – they are problematic from a state aid perspective.

CHAPTER 9

Concluding Discussion

Public bodies engaging in transactions as public authorities fall outside the scope of EU VAT not only as a result of the explicit exclusion in Article 13 of the VAT Directive but also since their activities or the consideration received for them fall outside the scope of VAT. Specific to public bodies, some public activities, such as issuing licences to exploit a specific part of the electromagnetic spectrum, are not considered to be economic activities for VAT purposes. Also excluded are supplies which do not result in any consumption, i.e., activities performed for the benefit of society as a whole.

As regards the supplies made and income received by public bodies, it should first be noted that pursuant to an explicit provision in the VAT Directive, it does not matter whether the supply arises from a legal obligation or a contract – in both cases it could be a supply falling within the scope of VAT. However, income in the form of taxes or pure transfers from other parts of government, as well as fees and charges not linked to supplies made (i.e., payments that are more fees than consideration in the strict sense), fall outside the scope of VAT.

The grant of a subsidy by a public body may constitute consideration for supplies if the subsidy is (almost) directly linked to the price paid for supplies. The scope of VAT is thus broadened to include also income being almost directly linked to supplies, and not only income directly linked to supplies. In principle, however, there is no reason to interpret this broadening of the scope especially widely with a view to mitigating distortions of competition. Distortions in competition resulting from not taxing subsidies is not a flaw of the VAT system but inherent in the granting of a subsidy.

It may occur that VAT is collected by central government, or a federal government, while the subsidy in question is paid by a local government entity, or a state in the federation. In such a situation, when the subsidy is paid by a part of government that is not the tax collector, the granting of a subsidy not subject to VAT will potentially result in a more advantageous position for the entity receiving the subsidy vis-à-vis a competing private business that must charge VAT on the full price (and cost) of providing the same services. In that case, the grossing up of the subsidy with VAT would result in extra cost for the local authority or state granting the subsidy and equality of competition would be restored.

As concerns the explicit exclusion from the scope of the VAT system for public bodies in Article 13 of the VAT Directive, the overall question is of course how this exclusion must be considered to function.

Jimenez has made a predominantly secondary sources review of the implementation of Article 13 in the Member States of 2008.[1] He divides the Member States in the following categories:

- States that clearly respect Article 13 and merely reproduce the text of the provision in their national law (Portugal, Greece, the Czech Republic, Cyprus and Bulgaria).
- States whose legal texts originate from the structure of the Directive, but do not copy it and add references and definitions of some concepts (Belgium, France, Luxembourg, Lithuania, Sweden, Poland, Hungary, Malta and Romania).
- States that, although using the terms of the Directive, drift away from it considerably in some aspects (Estonia, Slovakia and Latvia).
- States using general criteria for determining taxable persons, although they include necessary modifications (Italy, United Kingdom, the Netherlands, Denmark, Finland and Slovenia).
- The German and Austrian system.
- Ireland.

Even if some of the classifications can be disputed, and above all its implicit statement on whether the various forms of implementation are in conformity with the Directive, the list provides an interesting display of the diversity in how Article 13 has been implemented. That implementation and application of the exclusion for public bodies acting as such varies is confirmed in Copenhagen Economics' study. Considering the fact that Article 13 refers to the national legal regime, this is far from surprising. Public bodies are subject to very different environments in states, depending on public administration practices and history. It is foreseeable that implementation of the provision in question may look very different depending on the Member State that one looks at. It is an inherent complication in a common treatment that EU legislation needs to be workable in different legal settings. Public administration is closely linked to the culture of a state and having a very uniform way of implementing common EU wide provisions may therefore very well be more problematic than is the case in other areas of law.

If the goal of Article 13 is to create a common treatment in the EU, the provision has failed. Public bodies are treated differently in the Member States and that difference in treatment result in distortions.[2] These distortions are not dealt with through limitations for situations when competition is distorted, as distortions do not only arise

1. Jimenez *Intertax* (2008).
2. For example, taxable persons are faced with different VAT costs depending on whether public bodies charge VAT or not. And so on.

when a public body is making supplies in competition with a private sector entity in the relevant market, but also through the very existence of the exclusion itself. In order to increase harmonisation the reference to national law needs to be abolished.[3]

A number of activities typically engaged in by public bodies are exempt from VAT under the EU VAT system. Deduction of input VAT under the VAT system is linked to outputs provided. As a consequence, and as a result of the mixed nature of public body activities (exempt, taxed, inside the scope and outside the scope of VAT) determining when VAT is deductible is a very complex matter.

Some provisions in the VAT Directive seem only to have been included in order to deal with some of the consequences of the fact that public bodies are excluded from the scope of the system or exempt from VAT.

VAT compensation schemes have been enacted for local authorities in a number of countries. In Chapter 5 and 6, the Swedish and Danish VAT compensation schemes were discussed in detail and other European systems where briefly outlined in Chapter 7. The aim of those schemes is to eliminate the self-supply bias, which is created because of the fact that local authorities are excluded from the scope of VAT and cannot deduct VAT charged on acquisitions. In the choice of contracting out or self-supplying a certain function, a preference is created to self-supply since if the function is contracted out, non-deductible VAT will be charged. This is sometimes referred to as a distortion of competition. Under the VAT compensation schemes, VAT charged to the local authority is compensated for, outside the VAT system.

Two types of compensation are paid under the communes' compensation systems. Both direct VAT costs arising are reimbursed as well as indirect VAT costs, i.e., VAT costs arising at an exempt supplier to which a function has been contracted out by the local authority. As regards indirect VAT costs, the compensation levels used are said to reflect the VAT cost arising at the exempt supplier. However, I have not found any calculations or closer assessment on which these levels are based. Generally speaking the Danish model, the 'positivliste', is more detailed and differentiates between different categories of activities, whereas the Swedish model only differentiates between VAT costs linked to immovable property and other VAT costs.

The VAT compensation schemes in some cases create distortion of competition. When VAT compensation is paid for VAT costs linked to exempt supplies (on which input VAT is not deductible) made by a local authority, the local authority gets compensation for VAT on acquisitions while private entrepreneurs will not get compensation. This distortion created by the VAT compensation scheme could be

3. De la Feria *Intertax*, considers that the terms are unclear and that the provision is out-dated. Many provisions of the VAT Directive contain concepts that are not defined. In Article 13, the reference to public law is quite clear – if this is the level of harmonisation aimed at, the terms are in my view clear enough. I cannot see in what sense the provision is out-dated. The problem of having a definition referring to public law has always been a problem considering the various forms of public administration both in the original Member States and in the acceding states. The increased deregulation and privatisation that are the most fundamental changes since the original enactment of the provision are actually dealt with, from a system design point of view, satisfactorily in the flexibility of the distortion of competition provision. Agreeably, Annex 1 ought however be updated, if possible, to reflect other sectors where it can be presumed that there is competition between the public and private sectors.

handled in different ways. Compensation could not be paid when exempt supplies are made or compensation could not be payable when a local authority is involved in an activity in competition with entities that are not allowed compensation for VAT, or compensation could also be paid to those involved in activities exempt in competition with public bodies (zero-rating). Norway extends its compensation schemes to private law entities involved in certain exempt activities. Norway does not pay compensation if a local authority is acting in competition with entities not entitled to compensation. I find the Norwegian system particularly interesting. In the choice of distorting competition between public bodies and private bodies, and distorting the choice between contracting out and self-supplying, the legislator has taken a clear stance that the former is the most important.

A distinction must be made between the treatment of state and local authorities. State authorities are part of central government, which is the recipient of the revenue from the VAT. Local authorities are not recipients of the revenue from the VAT.

As regards state authorities, under the Swedish system VAT is typically, but not always, accounted for on a net basis, i.e., VAT on acquisitions is accounted for not as a cost, but as directly reducing the income from VAT on the state's income statement. However, in many cases VAT is not eliminated as a cost factor and appropriations must be increased to cover for non-deductible VAT. In those cases, the preference to self-supply is of course present and a disincentive to contract out is created.

As regards local authorities' compensation schemes, there are a number of differences between the various systems. First, there is a difference in how the compensation systems are funded. Wassenaar and Gradus distinguish between 'open' and 'closed' models.[4] In an open model, extra costs for refunding VAT when more activities are contracted out are funded by the extra VAT receipts of government. In the closed models the local governments themselves are funding the schemes and extra costs.

The difference between the models lies in the budgetary flows between central and local government. In an open model, any contracting out is reflected in a decrease of receipts by central government. What is decisive for local government in the choice to outsource or in-source is then exclusively (with regard to the economics of the decision) whether the activities can be bought for a cheaper price, exclusive of VAT, than what the authority itself can produce the activities for.

In a closed model, the economic decision of the local authority must in addition take into consideration any increases in payments to the funding of the scheme that result from outsourcing.

It seems to me that provided adjustments are made in the general contributions from central government to local government, based on the level of refunds paid for non-deductible VAT, the system cannot properly be denoted as 'open'. Even if central government initially finances the refunds, it will eventually take back the funding through a reduction in its general contributions. The overall position of the local authority will then, in the final analysis, be no different from under a closed model.

4. Wassenaar & Gradus (2004), p. 391.

However, both systems can be considered to be carried out within the context of the budget mechanism.[5] When VAT paid by local authorities is refunded, money collected is merely transferred back to the authority. There is a, from a budget perspective, equivalence between setting appropriations/contributions to local authorities paid from central government as inclusive of VAT and exclusive of VAT, but in the latter case allowing for separate repayment of VAT costs actually incurred. In both cases a local authority's VAT costs are covered![6]

Second, there seems to be a difference in what VAT is refundable. In some systems, the UK and the Netherlands, only VAT pertaining to an activity that does not fall within the scope of VAT is refundable. In other countries, Sweden, Denmark and Finland, VAT pertaining to acquisitions linked to activities falling within the scope of VAT but exempt therefrom is also refundable.[7]

Third, only the Netherlands scheme allows for compensation of non-national VAT. When foreign VAT is not refunded, a disincentive is created to contract out to companies that have to charge foreign VAT. In so far as these companies are also foreign companies (in the normal course of events), the Treaty freedoms or prohibition against discrimination on grounds of nationality are infringed (or perhaps Article 110 TFEU). With regard to compensation schemes for indirect VAT costs, this discrimination seems obvious; typically only domestic suppliers incur domestic VAT on most of their acquisitions.

Consider the situation where a public authority in Sweden purchases goods in Denmark below the acquisition threshold.[8] Danish VAT is charged when the recipient public body is not identified for VAT. This VAT is not refundable under the Danish compensation scheme. However, a Danish public body would receive a refund of VAT on purchases of goods in Denmark. There is a preference created for the public authority in Sweden to purchase goods in Sweden rather than in Denmark due to this treatment. The Danish public body has a competitive advantage compared to the Swedish public authority as it receives compensation for VAT costs. That competitive advantage is created for the Danish public body since it will not have any (Danish) VAT costs. A distortion of competition however only arises in cases where the suppliers are actually in competition with each other. In that regard, it must be noted that if distortion is 'significant' the public body is not 'acting as such' within the meaning of Article 13 of the VAT Directive and excluded from the scope thereof, but should be treated as a taxable person. The public body could then receive a refund of the VAT as any foreign taxable person. In that case, the distortions created by the compensation scheme are no different than those arising in relation to private entrepreneurs.

5. Compare Yang *IVM* 2005.
6. Yang IVM 2005 notes with regard to the Finnish compensation system, which is found in the VAT Act itself, that it would increase transparency of the financial relationship between the state and the local authorities if the refunds of VAT formed part of the budget legislation and procedure. I can definitely see his point.
7. Wassenaar & Gradus (2004), p. 392 also make this distinction.
8. According to Article 3 of the VAT Directive, a non-taxable legal person must register if acquisitions are made above the threshold specified therein.

The purpose of the compensation schemes is to create neutrality between contracting out and self-supplying. The current main rule for trade in services is that VAT is due in the Member State of the recipient of the supply (Article 44 of the VAT Directive). Thus, also with regard to foreign suppliers of services falling under the main rule, VAT will be charged in the country where the recipient public body, provided it is identified for VAT, is established. If that country operates a compensation scheme, the domestic VAT should be refundable (provided that other conditions are met). No discrimination can then be said to be present.

In other situations, the place of supply is abroad and foreign VAT may be chargeable. In that case, however, both suppliers established in the country where the supply takes place, and those outside the country, would have the same obligation to charge VAT in the country of the supply. In those cases there is no discrimination either as neither the foreign nor the domestic suppliers' VAT is compensated for.

However, there are situations where domestic suppliers charge domestic VAT (which may be compensated for) but foreign suppliers charge foreign VAT (which is then not compensated for). This is the case, for example, when a public body is not registered for VAT purposes and Article 44 does not apply. In these situations there is discrimination against foreign suppliers. In addition, such discrimination also arises when indirect VAT costs (in domestic VAT) are compensated for. Typically, domestic suppliers incur more domestic VAT than foreign suppliers. In that situation there is therefore clear discrimination against foreign suppliers.

Compensation schemes may constitute illegal state aid. It is clear from the assessment in Chapter 8 that it seems likely that most national compensation schemes to some extent do constitute illegal state aid. This calls for an initiative to introduce compensation schemes on an EU wide basis and make them an inherent feature of the VAT system and therefore allowed.

The compensation schemes for communes in Denmark and Sweden are not easily grasped. They have also been changed substantially over a relatively short period of time. The systems are linked to public administration in the countries and how the system of public administration is set up.

Lastly, it can be concluded that the present treatment of public bodies in the EU VAT legislation is rather complex. It contains a number of safeguards against creating distortions of competition, because of the exclusion from the scope and the existence of exemptions. The presence of VAT compensation schemes alleviates some of the problems of distortions of competition but also creates new ones. Only in a system where all supplies are taxed and all entities involved in economic activities are included within the scope of the tax can a real level playing field be achieved.

PART III
Full Taxation Models

In this part, the full taxation model adopted by the modern GST systems is discussed. In contrast to the EU VAT system, the scope of these GST systems extends to public bodies. These systems are also characterised by the fact that they contain fewer exemptions than the EU system.

The New Zealand system is discussed in detail in this part. Other systems employing full taxation models are only briefly referred to.

CHAPTER 10

New Zealand's GST System and Public Management

§10.01 INTRODUCTION

New Zealand's Goods and Services Tax Act 1985 (the GST Act) is commonly recognised to be a model VAT system.[1] It is the most broadly based VAT in the world, containing very few exemptions.

The modern and legislative history of New Zealand has been very influenced by Britain. New Zealand was a British colony in its own right in 1841 and remains part of the British Empire. When New Zealand considered introducing a broad-based consumption tax in the 1980s, to finance its running deficit, it looked at the UK and its VAT (i.e., the European VAT system). Due to various reasons, the end product was much different, and contained a true novelty in the world of VAT – the full inclusion of all government and local authorities within the scope of the tax.

New Zealand is a democracy and a constitutional monarchy. The Governor-General normally exercises the powers of the sovereign (the Crown).[2] The political executive is established by convention rather than by statute and comprises the Prime Minister and cabinet. The Constitution Act constitutes a House of Representatives as the legislature and those persons elected as Members of Parliament.[3] Parliament enacts laws and scrutinises the actions of the executive, and authorises Government to spend public money and to incur costs. Parliament is thus formally the supreme lawmaker.

A variety of public bodies exist, such as Government departments, Crown entities and Local authorities.[4] These are not regulated in the Constitutions Act.[5]

1. Cnossen, in White (2007), footnote 3, and Due *CTJ* (1988). Even though it is called a GST it has the same basic characteristics as a VAT. In the following the terms GST and VAT are both used.
2. See, also in the following, Boston et al. (1996), pp. 43–53.
3. Constitution Act 1986 (Public Act 1986 No. 114, Date of assent 13 December 1986).
4. See Gill (2002).
5. Local Authorities are regulated in the Local Government Act 2002 (Public Act 2002 No. 84, Date of assent 24 December 2002).

Each bill that becomes law receives three readings in Parliament as well as examination in two different kinds of committee stages. Statute law, such as the GST Act 1985, is primary law in New Zealand.[6] Court decisions are recognised as another source of primary law. Secondary sources of law are doctrine, discussion documents etc. These are subordinate to primary sources.

The Judiciary is the fourth component of the constitutional structure.[7] The courts have a clear hierarchy, which is as follows (in relation to tax issues)[8]:

(i) District courts (about 100 in number).
(ii) The High Court.
(iii) The Court of Appeal.
(iv) The Supreme Court (until 1 January 2004 appeal was made to the Judicial Committee of the Privy Council in London).

In addition, a Taxation Review Authority (TRA) exists to hear and determine objections and challenges to assessments of tax or other decisions, or determinations regarding tax by the Inland Revenue. The TRA is a tribunal, not a court, and anonymity of the taxpayer is preserved. Decisions can be appealed to the High Court.[9]

The doctrine of *stare decisis* is applicable in New Zealand. The lower courts are thus obliged to follow the ruling of a higher court, provided the material facts are not different, in which case the higher court's judgment may be 'distinguished'. A court may depart from its own decisions, but is likely to follow them unless it was divided the last time the issue was heard.[10]

In this chapter, the treatment of public bodies under New Zealand GST is discussed in some detail. In section §10.02, public management in New Zealand, which is vital to the treatment of public bodies for GST purposes, is discussed. Sections §10.03 and §10.04 provide an overview of the New Zealand GST system and its introduction.

§10.02 PUBLIC MANAGEMENT IN NEW ZEALAND

[A] The Evolution of Present Public Management

When New Zealand introduced its unique treatment of public bodies in the 1980s, no other country included public bodies within a VAT system. The treatment of public bodies in the GST system is however not the only unique feature of the treatment of public bodies in New Zealand. The structure and organisation of government, and the

6. Alley et al. (2010), p. 42.
7. Boston et al. (1996) and White (2005).
8. Specialist courts exists, but not for tax matters.
9. White (2005) and Alley et al. (2010), pp. 52–53.
10. Alley et al. (2010), pp. 53–54.

public management in general, were also uniquely reformed at the same time.[11] The public management system in New Zealand has also been considered to be a model worldwide. In New Zealand, public bodies are in principle treated as any service provider in society. It has been noted[12] that New Zealand has 'gone the farthest along the entrepreneurial path'. New Zealand has done away with its old civil service system, freeing department managers to negotiate their own contracts with their employees. It has eliminated regulations that inhibited competition in both the private and public sectors. And it has adopted a budget system focused on performance and an accrual accounting system modelled on business accounting.

To understand the reforms to the Government introduced in 1986, it is necessary to go back to the economic and political situation before their introduction.[13] A new Government was elected in 1984 and the fiscal crisis brought about a quick reform of both the public management system and the indirect tax systems. The whole process of introducing the GST, which was the first broad-based indirect tax in New Zealand, from its first announcement to introduction was almost precisely two years.[14]

Scott, Ball & Dale describe the situation before the reform of government management as follows:[15]

> Government management in New Zealand prior to the reforms was based on a fairly standard program budgeting system in common with most Organization for Economic Cooperation and Development (OECD) countries, but an unusually large proportion of the economy was in the hands of traditional government bureaucratic organizations. The prevailing macro- and microeconomic policies at the time were heavily interventionist, perhaps the most interventionist in the OECD.
>
> A fiscal policy crisis occurred in the early 1980s as a result of years of steady growth in the proportion of government expenditure to gross domestic product, erosion of the revenue base due to concessions and subsidies, and a fragmented indirect tax system. By 1984 the ratio of government expenditure to GNP was near 40 percent. A weak world economy eroded revenue collections and an aggressive incomes policy, which relied on large personal tax cuts in order to restrain wage increases, resulted in a fiscal deficit of 9 percent of gross domestic product.
>
> Government-owned businesses run from government departments generated 12 percent of gross domestic product and 20 percent of national investment. Because they were part of the budget sector and entirely under the control of the executive, these state enterprises were used to promote public employment and deliver a wide array of non-commercial services and patronage benefits to various segments of the community. They were largely captured by provider interests, which substantially controlled advice about funding and service configurations. Not only were these organizations in general poorly managed, but they were also

11. See, Boston et al. (1996).
12. By David Osborne and Ted Gaebler, in *Reinventing Government* (1993), p. 330, quote from Boston (1996), p. 2.
13. See, concerning the economic and political situation, Graham, Ball & Dale (1997), Muir (1993) and Dickson (2007).
14. The historical background and introduction of the GST have been described by Due *CTJ* (1998), Douglas (2007), Green (2007), Todd (2007), Dickson (2007) and Stephens (2007).
15. Scott, Ball & Dale (1997), pp. 357–358.

> often constrained by government directives not to install modern business planning and financial management practices. Lack of transparency was used to conceal cross subsidies that might not have been sustainable politically if their true costs were open to public gaze. Examples included cross subsidies between local and intercity telephone calls and between mainline railway freight and services to rural areas.

It is important to note that the Government intervention had gone very far. All but one or two departments of the New Zealand Government were engaged in some kind of commercial and quasi-commercial activities alongside the more traditional governmental functions.[16] The new liberal government's response to this was to liberalise and reform government budgeting etc. with a view to treating government agencies similar to private entities when they were dealing with commercial activities. When the initial experience in 1984 of reform of these state-owned enterprises was successful, the issue was raised of why could the underlying thinking not be applied to activities where objectives were not commercial and why could output not be measured in monetary terms.[17]

The underlying idea of the reforms of public administration in the 1980s was thus to equalise government agencies with businesses. With this new perspective, a shift came regarding how performance of government departments and the like was looked at. First, instead of focusing on the outcomes of government activities when measuring performance, the focus shifted to the outputs – the services provided – by government agencies.[18] Second, in order for government officials to be held accountable for the performance of their departments, the officials had a higher degree of control over the aspects of the performance for which accountability was sought. Third, an analogy with businesses was taken as regards the investor and customer perspective of a firm. Ministers were considered as being both customers of government agencies and investors in them. These perspectives were applied to all government activities.[19]

This way of looking at performance was reflected in how departmental budgets were set, how appropriations were paid and reporting through annual statements of service performance. In order to measure performance, it was necessary to move away from cash basis accounting and adopt accrual accounting and financial reporting. In New Zealand, no public money can be spent by a government department except by way of an appropriation by an Act of Parliament. Separate appropriations are required for each group of goods and services (class of outputs) to be produced by a department, any capital contribution being made by the Government to a department and any payments of benefits or grants by a department on behalf of the Crown.[20] Financial statements of both sub-entities of the government (departments and statutory authorities) and the government as a whole must report on an accrual basis by including in

16. Dickson (2007), p. 54. See also Barrand (1990), p. 36 on local authority services provided in New Zealand charged for by rates and direct charges.
17. Scott, Ball & Dale (1997), p. 359.
18. Scott, Ball & Dale (1997).
19. Scott, Ball & Dale (1997). See also, for a more moderate assessment and discussion of the limits of the approach, Boston et al. (1996), pp. 7–15.
20. Barrand (1990), p. 31 and below on the New Zealand Public Finance Act.

their financial statements balance sheets (statements of financial position), the equivalent of profit and loss statements (operating statements, or statements of financial performance) and cash flow statements. Also, to provide input to the customer dimension, a Statement of Service Performance is required.[21]

It is noticeable that at the time of the reform, accrual accounting had not been implemented for public bodies. On introduction, government departments used single entry cash accounting systems and accordingly reported GST on a payment basis.[22] Still, the GST Act provides for the possibility for accounting on a payments basis for some local authorities.[23]

[B] The Public Finance Act 1989

As noted in the previous section, New Zealand has a quite unique public administration. In this section, crucial rules governing the fiscal administration in New Zealand, which can be found in the Public Finance Act 1989 (PFA), are discussed. The PFA is referred to in the GST Act in a provision governing the treatment of public bodies (see further below).

The PFA contains rules on how tax money may be spent. According to the act, section 4(1), the Crown or an Office of Parliament must not incur expenses or capital expenditure, except as expressly authorised by an appropriation, or other authority, by, or under, an Act. Furthermore, according to section 5, the Crown or an Office of Parliament must not spend public money, except as expressly authorised by or under an Act (including the PFA). In so far as expenditure is not regulated in another act, the general provisions on appropriations in the PFA are applicable.

According to section 7(1), separate appropriations are required for the following types of expenses and capital expenditure:

(a) each category of output expenses (definition just below);
(b) each category of benefits (to specific persons) or other unrequited expenses;
(c) each category of borrowing expenses (defined as any interest or other financing expenses in respect of any loan or under any public security);
(d) each category of other expenses (defined as expenses measured in accordance with generally accepted accounting practices including costs);
(e) each category of capital expenditure (defined as the costs of assets acquired or developed, including tangible, intangible, or financial assets and any ownership interest in entities, but excluding inventories);
(f) expenses and capital expenditure to be incurred by each intelligence and security department.

An *output* is defined in section 2 of the PFA as goods or services that are supplied by a department, Crown entity, Office of Parliament, or other person or body, including

21. Scott, Ball & Dale (1997), p. 367.
22. Barrand (1990), p. 32.
23. See section 19AB of the GST Act.

goods or services that such an entity has agreed or contracted to supply on a continuing basis, but that have not been supplied. The term *output expenses* includes the full cost of producing and supplying outputs (including full allocation of overhead costs).

Appropriations may not be used for other purposes than those for which they were distributed, section 9(1) of the PFA. It should be added to this that according to the Guide to the PFA, capital contributions to departments do not require appropriations under the PFA. However, acquisitions of shares in subsidiaries do, as capital expenditure, and likewise are appropriations needed to cover for depreciations of departmental assets (which are considered as output expenses).[24]

§10.03 THE INTRODUCTION OF THE GST

New Zealand had, at the time of the introduction of the GST by the Goods and Services Tax Act 1985, a Wholesale Sales Tax (WST) that was not considered to work properly.[25] The announcement to introduce a GST was in November 1984 in the budget of 1984.[26] It is clear from those documents that the intention was to introduce a broad-based, low rate tax that was as neutral as possible. In fact, there was a very strong commitment to these characteristics, and the traditional New Zealand approach to look at the UK did this time not mean that the UK/EU approach was followed. Rather to the contrary the tax was called a GST (and not a VAT) in order to distinguish it from the UK/EU VAT with all its exemptions etc.[27]

The question of whether to introduce a GST and its coverage etc. was the subject of a public discussion in September 1984.[28] It emerges from the documents leading up to the introduction, that public utilities and government departments were not originally intended to be fully included within the scope of the GST.[29] It is noted in the budget report of 1984 that a major feature of the VAT[30] is that the seller does not need to now the status of the customer; VAT is always chargeable. Under the WST, exemptions were granted on certain sales to non-trading departments. This would be undesirable in the case of a VAT. The most straightforward, and theoretically correct, way was considered to be to tax the inputs of non-trading departments. The report continues:[31]

> In effect, non-trading departments are treated as final consumers. The value added by these departments produces no marketable output and is thus not subject to tax. This treatment would raise the operating costs of departments by an amount

24. See *A Guide to the Public Finance Act* 2005 p. 22.
25. See *Goods & Services Tax; A booklet explaining measures announced in the 1984 budget, 8 November 1984*. See also Todd (2007), p. 29, Due (1988), pp. 129–131 and Muir (1993).
26. Muir (1993) and Due *CTJ* (1988).
27. Dickson (2007).
28. White (2005), p. 213.
29. See Budget Report No. 68 of the New Zealand Treasury of 24 September 1984 to the Minister of Finance, entitled 'Value Added Tax: Public Utilities and Government Departments'.
30. A reference is made to 'VAT' and not 'GST'. It is thus obvious that the name GST was chosen for political reasons and not to mark any legal difference between the systems.
31. See the Budget Report No. 68. *Votes* are a type of appropriations; see section 2 of the Public Finance Act.

> equal to the tax revenue collected. Some general adjustments to Votes may be required to compensate.

Furthermore, according to the Report, government organisations that engage in trading activities would be registered and liable to charge VAT on the same basis as any other trader. That would include the postal services, electricity as well as departments supplying services exclusively to the public sector. The report concludes by noting that the ownership of an undertaking in itself should have no bearing on its treatment for VAT purposes. The key test is whether or not the organisation trades in taxable goods and services.

In the White Paper on Goods and Services Tax from March 1985, the attitude has changed.[32] In addition to the inclusion of trading governmental departments and agencies, it is also proposed that goods and services produced by government departments and agencies, which are consumed in the governmental process, shall be treated as having been supplied commercially to the Crown.[33] The proposal, it is stated:

> avoids the need for decisions as to which departmental activities are considered to be trading, which are considered to be non-trading – a significant administrative problem in other countries with GST type taxes – and the need to design a basis for apportioning GST invoiced, overheads and joint costs among the classified functions.... In line with the principles applying to the treatment of government departments and other public bodies, it is proposed that registered persons who receive subsidies from the Crown be regarded as receiving those subsidies in payment for the provision of services to the Crown.

With regard to local authorities the paper notes that these provide goods and services paid for by consumers by way of rates, fees and other charges:

> Treatment of local authorities in a manner consistent with other suppliers of goods and services will mean that the tax will alter the level of rates and other charges levied by the authorities in line with changes in the price level of other supplies that will be subject to tax.

Local authority revenue subject to the GST therefore includes rates, inspection and licence fees and service fees.[34]

Thus, between November 1984 and March 1985, the idea arose within the Treasury to include government and local authorities within the GST system. Barrand notes that the treatment was designed to ensure that the tax applied in a neutral manner to both the public and private sector.[35] He claims that the treatment enables this to be achieved with compliance costs significantly lower than would be the case if the more conventional treatment was adopted. He states that four arguments supported the inclusion of public bodies within the scope of VAT:[36]

32. Governmental Paper B 27, Proposals for the Administration of the Goods and Services Tax (the White Paper).
33. White Paper, p. 34.
34. *Ibid.*
35. Barrand (1990), p. 3 and Barrand (1991).
36. Barrand (1990), pp. 29–30.

(1) *Administrative simplicity.* The difficulties in allocating costs and revenues between commercial and non-commercial activities are avoided.
(2) *Accountability and Transparency of Government Operations.*
(3) *Comprehensiveness of GST Coverage.* If the Government had exempted services which it consumes, a strong case could be made for applying concessions to other forms of supplies and therefore weakening the commitment to the broad-based approach.
(4) *Economic Management.* Barrand states that there seemed no reason in principle why, when tax changes alter the balance between savings and consumption in the economy, the public sector should be immune to the change. Nor is there a reason to suggest that if the tax rate increases, public sector consumption should automatically become a larger share of total final consumption expenditure – as would happen if only private consumption expenditure is taxed.

It cannot be a coincidence that the new thoughts on public management, the idea to apply an entrepreneurial approach also for core government functions, arose at exactly the same time as the idea to include public bodies fully within the GST system. Actually, the novelty of the GST approach is just that – extending the idea of government as a producing entity not just to pure production of goods and services, but also to traditional functions of authorities, the output of which cannot easily be measured. The new way of looking at public bodies and an even more neutral treatment vis-à-vis private sector entities – the new economic management perspective – is the same in the reforms of the GST and the public administration. The treatment in GST actually only seems to be a natural consequence of the changes proposed with regard to public administration. It is hard to imagine the public sector reform without the GST reform (and possibly vice-versa). The idea was to put the public sector on equal footing with the private sector – with regard to all aspects of their activities. Consequently, public bodies were therefore obliged to account for GST as any other trader, filing VAT returns and so on.[37]

A most controversial aspect of the reform with regard to the inclusion of local authorities in the GST system was the imposition of GST on rates. Rates are a sort of local property taxes charged by local authorities.[38] Rates take different forms.[39] Basically, they are charged on land in some relation to the funding impact. The different forms are:

- General rates, which are set either as uniform rates or different rates based on categories.[40]

37. See Barrand (1990), p. 30.
38. See on this Dickson (2007), p. 54; Green (2007), p. 20 and Barrand (1990), pp. 36–37.
39. See Local Government Rating Act 2002, Part 1 section 5 and Barrand (1990), pp. 36–37.
40. Local Government Rating Act 2002, Part 1, section 13.

- Targeted rates, which are set for a specific activity or group of activities, and can be levied on a uniform basis or differentially for different categories of rateable land.[41]
- Uniform Annual General Charges, a fixed amount per rating unit or part of a rating unit.[42]

One argument against levying GST on rates was that it would be strange to impose a tax on another tax. Another argument was that if rates are taxed, then the income tax should also be taxed and include GST. The last argument does have merits. General rates and Uniform Annual Rates are not charged for specific supplies but for funding the local authorities' activities in general. The income tax is no different – it is 'charged' to fund the activities of government (without it being more specific than general or uniform annual rates).

§10.04 AN OVERVIEW OF THE GST ACT 1985

In blunt contrast to the simplicity of the underlying policy of the New Zealand GST Act, the actual text of the Act is not easily accessible. This is not (only) attributable to the fact that the Statute has never been recast – the Act is simply not user-friendly.[43]

The GST Act is structured in 12 numbered 'parts':

(1) *Interpretation*, containing definitions of various terms, such as financial services, supply, taxable activity etc. but notably not all definitions. Some are 'hidden away' elsewhere.
(2) *Imposition of tax*, containing provisions concerning when GST is due, on what value, zero-rating of goods and services, exempt supplies etc.
(3) *Returns and payment of tax*, containing provisions on taxable periods, GST returns, accounting basis, calculation of tax liability, attribution of input tax, payment of tax, tax invoices etc.
(4) *Assessment of tax*, (repealed).
(5) *Objections*, (repealed).
(6) *Recovery of tax*, containing provisions on that topic and deduction of tax from payment due to defaulters.
(7) *Refunds and relief from tax*, concerning refund of excess tax, Commissioner's right to withhold payments etc.
(8) *Registration*, on who needs to be registered, when a registration is cancelled etc.
(9) *Special cases*, on Group of companies, unincorporated bodies, agents and auctioneers etc.
(10) *Penalties*, (repealed).

41. Local Government Rating Act 2002, Part 1, section 16.
42. Local Government Rating Act 2002, Part 1, section 15.
43. Blanchard (2007).

(11) *General provisions*, on record keeping, avoidance etc.
(12) *Transitional provisions*, concerning the introduction of the GST.

Section 8(1), in Part 2, is the main charging provision in the GST Act and defines the scope of the GST:

> Subject to this Act, a tax, to be known as goods and services tax, shall be charged in accordance with the provisions of this Act at the rate of 15 percent on the supply (but not including an exempt supply) in New Zealand of goods and services, on or after the 1st day of October 1986, by a registered person in the course or furtherance of a taxable activity carried on by that person, by reference to the value of that supply.

Section 2(1) states that a *registered person* is a person who is registered or is liable to be registered under the Act. It follows from section 51(1) that any person, who carries on any taxable activity, and is not (yet) registered, is liable to register. Section 6(1)(a) defines the term *taxable activity* as:

> any activity which is carried on continuously or regularly by any person, whether or not for a pecuniary profit, and involves or is intended to involve, in whole or in part, the supply of goods and services to any other person for a consideration; and includes any such activity carried on in the form of a business, trade, manufacture, profession, vocation, association, or club.[44]

Goods and *services* are defined in section 2(1),[45] where the definition of the term *supply* as 'any forms of supply', is also found.

According to section 10(2), *the value of a supply* shall be such amount as, with the addition of the tax charged, is equal to the aggregate of (a) to the extent that the consideration for the supply is consideration in money, the amount of the money; (b) to the extent that the consideration for the supply is not consideration in money, the open market value of that consideration:

> The *consideration* is defined in Section 2(1) as
>
> any payment made or any act or forbearance, whether or not voluntary, in respect of, in response to, or for the inducement of, the supply of any goods and services, whether by that person or by any other person; but does not include any payment made by any person as an unconditional gift to any non-profit body.

As pointed out by Blanchard, even though it is not immediately discernable, in order for there to be a taxable supply, the supply has to be in the course of or in furtherance of a taxable activity.[46] This in turn requires that the supply is made for consideration.

44. Section 6(2) states that anything done in connection with the beginning or ending, including a premature ending, of a taxable activity is treated as being carried out in the course or furtherance of the taxable activity. Section 6(3) contains limitations with regard to hobbies (in (a) and (aa)), employment contracts (in (b)) and similar contracts and, notably, any activity to the extent to which the activity involves the making of exempt supplies (in (d)). Thus, an exempt activity is treated as a non-taxable activity.
45. It is not necessary to describe those here for the purposes of this research.
46. Blanchard (2007), p. 94.

It is however immediately apparent that the definition of what constitutes consideration is very broad, which, together with the fact that the term supply is also very broadly defined, implies that the coverage of the GST Act is very broad.

Sections 20 and 20A(4) provide that input GST incurred is *deductible*, if incurred for the principal purpose of making taxable supplies by the registered person. That is, as long as an acquisition is made for the principal purpose of making a taxable supply, all input GST is deductible, and vice-versa. There is no partly deductible GST.[47] If an output is split into several supplies, the input GST is determined for each supply.[48] However, a single supply is in some situations split into several supplies.[49]

As noted in the historical section, public and local authorities are deemed to supply services to the Crown remunerated by transfers from central government. Rates charged by local authorities are similarly considered as remuneration for services. Even though the idea and basic rule are simple as such, the New Zealand GST Act contains numerous provisions on the treatment of public bodies. Many of these concern specific fees and bodies, a fact discussed further below.

The meaning of the term *taxable activity* is extended by section 6(1)(b) to include 'the activities of any public authority or any local authority'. In addition, section 5(6) deems every public authority to *supply goods and services:*

> where, within the meaning of the Public Finance Act 1989, any amount is brought to charge by the public authority as revenue from the Crown for the supply of outputs.

Public authority is defined in section 2(1) as:

> all instruments of the Crown in respect of the Government of New Zealand, whether departments, Crown entities, state enterprises, or other instruments; and includes offices of Parliament, the Parliamentary service, and the Office of the Clerk of the House of Representatives; but does not include the Governor-General, members of the Executive Council, Ministers of the Crown, or members of Parliament.

---

47. McKenzie (2008), p. 210. However, adjustments for non-taxed use may have to be made. The rules seem quite complex, see McKenzie (2008), pp. 339–358.
48. McKenzie (2008), p. 212 points at *Wairakei Court Limited v. Commissioner of Inland Revenue* (1999) 19 NZTC 15,202 as being the leading judgment. The following description of the principle purpose test is taken from Chisholm J's judgment in that case at p. 15, 206:
The word purpose is a reference to the object that the taxpayer had in mind or in view. This is not synonymous with intention or motive. Moreover, care must be taken to avoid confusing the means by which the taxpayer achieves its purpose with the purpose itself.
The principal purpose is the main, primary or fundamental purpose. This does not equate with a more than 50% test.
Where the taxpayer is a company, its purpose is to be determined by examining the collective purpose of those in control.
The principal purpose is to be ascertained as at the time the goods and services were acquired. The focus should be on individual supplies.
49. See sections 5(14), 5(15) and 10(18) in the GST Act and McKenzie (2008), p. 340.

A public authority could also encompass a state-owned entity, such as Telecom Corporation of New Zealand Limited (which is thus an 'instrument' of the Crown), an organisation subject to the provisions of the State Owned Enterprises Act 1986.[50]

Revenue from the Crown is defined in section 2(1), as:

> any amount brought to charge from the Crown (not being revenue received from any other public authority) by any public authority for the supply of outputs (within the meaning of the Public Finance Act 1989) by that public authority

The GST itself and revenue collected by the public authority as agent on behalf of the Crown are explicitly excluded from the definition.

Some charges made by public authorities are specifically regulated. According to section 5(6A):

> any registration fee paid pursuant to section 7(3) of the Transport (Vehicle and Driver Registration and Licensing) Act 1986 (and prescribed in Part 1 of Schedule 2 to that Act, and any annual licence fee paid pursuant to section 10(2) of that Act (and prescribed in Part 2 of Schedule 2 to that Act), shall be deemed to be consideration for a supply of services in the course or furtherance of a taxable activity carried on by the New Zealand Transport Agency.

In a similar manner, section 5(6AB) deems a levy paid to the Fire Service Commission under the Fire Service Act, that is not a penalty surcharge or interest[51], to be consideration for a supply of services; section 5(6AC) states that a levy paid under the Waste Minimisation Act shall be treated as consideration for a supply of services, defining those levies in detail; section 5(6B) states that any amount of road user charges paid shall be deemed consideration for services performed by the Transport Agency; section 5(6C) deems the amount of any deposit specified in certain sections of the Electoral Act to be consideration for the supply of services.

Local authorities are defined in section 2(1) with reference to the Local Government Act 2002. Every local authority is deemed to *supply goods and services* 'to any person where any amount of rates is payable by that person to that local authority' (section 5(7)(a)). In addition, the local authority is deemed to supply goods and services 'if the local authority requires a contribution from the person as a financial contribution or a development contribution' (further defined by reference to certain acts, see section 5(7B)). A territorial authority is treated as supplying goods and services under certain conditions, see section 5(7D). A territorial authority is defined in section 11B(2). In addition, the Chatham Islands Council is treated as supplying goods and services to a person if an amount of council dues is payable, see section 5(7)(b).

Local authority land transactions receive special treatment in section 5(7C) and anyone providing housing under an authority's affordable housing policy is treated as supplying goods and services to the authority, section 5(7E).

50. Case *M40* (1990) 12 NZTC 2,247.
51. *N.B.* financial services are exempt from GST and as such fall outside the scope of GST. The exclusion seems necessary in order for interest charged in this particular situation not to be taxed based on the principle of *lex specialis*.

Payments in the nature of *a grant or subsidy* are deemed to constitute consideration in certain situations. According to section 5(6D):

> For the purposes of this Act, where any payment in the nature of a grant or subsidy is made on behalf of the Crown or by any public authority to –
>
> (a) Any person (not being a public authority) in relation to or in respect of that person's taxable activity; or
>
> (b) Any person for the benefit and on behalf of another person in relation to or in respect of that other person's taxable activity, –
>
> that payment shall be deemed to be consideration for a supply of goods and services by the person to whom or for whose benefit the payment is made in the course or furtherance of that person's taxable activity.[52]

Benefit paid under the Social Security Act is excluded, as are payments for the personal use and benefit of specific persons, section 5(6E)(b). In addition, any payment of a kind that is declared by the Governor-General by Order in Council to be considered as a payment of a grant or subsidy for the purposes of section 5(6D), or not considered as such, shall be treated accordingly, section 5(6E). Lastly, section 5(6CA) deems amounts of any deposit referred to in section 55 of the Local Electoral Act to be consideration for services supplied by the relevant local authority in the course or furtherance of a taxable activity.

Lastly, with regard to the time of the supply, section 9(1) deems a supply of goods and services to take place at the earlier of the time an invoice is issued by the supplier or the recipient, or the time any payment is received by the supplier, in respect of that supply.[53]

52. Input GST is deductible, I presume, by the person deemed to have received the supply.
53. See, as regards jurisdictional issues, sections 11 et seq. See also Millar (2009) for a useful comparison with European VAT (and further references).

CHAPTER 11

The Inclusion of Public Bodies in New Zealand

If we look at the core provisions defining the scope of the GST, they are clearly the provisions of a general, indirect consumption tax. Taxable persons, or registered persons as they are called in the GST Act, are those engaged in supplies for consideration and the only exclusions are for persons' hobbies and employed persons.

The core provisions are supplemented by provisions 'deeming' certain bodies, activities and transfers to be registered taxpayers, taxable activities and consideration respectively. The scope of the GST system is herewith substantially extended. Many (or even almost all) of these provisions concern public bodies, which are deemed to be performing taxable activities and supply goods and services for consideration.

In the New Zealand GST Act, a most remarkable feature is the inclusion, by way of deeming, of public bodies within the scope of VAT. Public bodies are clearly intended to be totally equalised with entrepreneurs engaged in taxable activities. This is done both for reasons of simplicity and theory – it relieves the system of the burden of having to decide when a public body shall charge VAT (as in the European system) and it conforms to the theory of a consumption tax with a coverage as broad as possible.

It is not apparent from the Act itself, but I have been informed that even the Crown is registered for GST in New Zealand! The Crown does not deduct any input GST, however, for the reason that it would make no sense to deduct a tax that it is ultimately collecting itself anyway. However, other Crown entities than the Crown itself do charge and deduct GST on their (deemed) supplies.

It seems evident from the history of the New Zealand GST Act that it is intended to cover all public bodies and subject them to the deeming provisions of the GST Act. The technical way of achieving this is by defining public authorities as all instruments of the Crown etc. (see definition above). Local authorities are defined with reference to the Local Government Act 2002.

However, these general references are not the only ones present. There are also, as noted above, a number of specific provisions that deem certain fees/levies etc. from certain bodies (such as the New Zealand Transport Agency, the Fire Service Commission and the Transport Agency) to be consideration for services preformed by the Agency etc. in question. The question therefore arises whether all public bodies are really covered by the general rule and/or the specific rules.

Actually, the wording of the general provision of inclusion, the history and context, all suggest that the specific provisions ought not to be necessary. This is confirmed in my contacts with people of the policy division at the Inland Revenue. The specific deeming provisions have been enacted to deal with interpretation issues – i.e., when doubts have arisen whether a particular body is really covered by the main provisions, the response has been to enact a particular provision deeming the body in question to be a public body. Though effective in the short run, the structure of the act, with a general provision and specific provisions regulating situations or bodies that one thought ought to be covered by the general provision, makes the interpreter question the field of application of the general provision. Based on a contextual analysis, it should not be so broad as to cover the bodies covered by specific provisions, as those latter provisions would be redundant if the general provision was applicable anyway. Considering this, and the general rule in interpretation that a text should be interpreted in a manner where all provisions are considered to have a meaning and a thought through relation to other provisions of the same act (at least), one may question the reach of the general provision.[1] However, based on the historical context, there can be no doubt as to the intentions of covering all public bodies with the general definitions entailed in the act. Based on this, it must be concluded that the specific provisions should not be interpreted in such a way as to limit the reach of the general provisions.

The question arises of whether the specific provisions are strictly necessary, if the general provision is broadly construed based on a historical, purposive interpretation. It seems to me that the entities the specific provisions regulate are public bodies, i.e., they are instruments of the Crown. If so, the reason why they are specifically mentioned presumably has to do with the kinds of services and charges made, and whether they are covered by the general provision on revenue from the Crown (in section 2(1)).

1. I submit that it would be more suitable to issue a statement on the interpretation of the general provision, and what it should cover, or make a legal instrument where the main provision is explained. The difficulties in interpreting the act pointed out would then not arise.

CHAPTER 12

The Treatment of the Income of Public Bodies

§12.01 CONTEXT AND HISTORY

The consideration is, when expressed in money, the payment. According to the main rule, there is a requirement that the consideration is a payment made 'in respect of, in response to, or for the inducement of', the supply - i.e., that some kind of link is established between the supply and a payment.[1] In addition, a number of specific levies charged by specific public bodies are deemed to constitute consideration (see sections 5(6A), (6AB), (6B), (6AC) and (6C) of the GST Act). Furthermore, deeming provisions extend the scope of the tax to cover, first, amounts received (appropriations) by a public body from the Crown for the supply of 'outputs' (section 5(6)), and second, grants and subsidies paid by public bodies to a registered taxpayer in relation to or in respect of that person's taxable activity (section 5(6D)). In relation to local authorities, rates charged are liable to GST (section 5(7)(a)), the Chatham Island Council's dues are likewise liable to GST (section 5(7)(b)), but also contributions (in some situations monetary contributions and in other situations contributions in land) acquired and required to be paid by local authorities in some specific situations (section 5(7B) and (7C)). Finally, deposits under the Local Electoral Act 2001 are liable to GST (section 5(6CA)).[2]

The same considerations can be made here as in the preceding chapter as regards the general and specific rules defining public bodies. The general rule on what constitutes a consideration for a supply is potentially very broad, covering all kinds of transfers, even if they are only for the inducement of a supply and not really consideration for services received. Based on the wording of the provision, it would not

1. The wording implies a broader scope than under European VAT, see Chapter 2.
2. See also Millar (2012).

be totally impossible to argue that subsidies are to a large extent covered, as are a number of specific payments now specifically regulated in the GST act. However, in a contextual analysis considering the specific provisions present, the general rule should, it may be argued, have a more limited scope. Again, this is not in line with the history of the Act. For example, section 5(6D) was introduced as a response to *Case M129* and in order to restore the original intent that subsidy payments should be included within the wording of the General rule.[3] In addition, the case law does not support such a restrictive view of the general provision. Instead, there are statements that imply that the specific provisions and the general provision overlap.[4]

In the next section, the quite extensive case law on these provisions is discussed.

§12.02 CASE LAW ON THE NEXUS BETWEEN A PAYMENT AND A SUPPLY

There are a number of cases decided by the TRA and courts in New Zealand on the issue of when a payment is made for a supply and therefore liable for GST.

In Case *M129*, the issue was whether the payments received by the taxpayer from the Department of Labour pursuant to a Job Opportunities Scheme (JOS) constituted consideration for a taxable supply, the taxable supply being the provision by the taxpayer of employment under the scheme.[5] The judge of the TRA, Barber DJ, held that it was necessary to ascertain the true nature of the transaction. He found that the taxpayers were motivated to employ the person by a combination of altruistic feelings and the knowledge that the employment could be effected under the Scheme in question, which would entitle them to a subsidy. The judge found that the taxpayer did not supply anything to the Department of Labour. The realistic and commercial approach to this situation shows a supply of services by the employee to the employer and, perhaps, the supply of a job from employer to employee. Section 6(3)(b) excludes that type of engagement or employment from the meaning of 'taxable activity'.[6]

In *Turakina Maori Girls College Board of Trustees*, the question before the Court of Appeal was whether attendance dues paid to integrated schools' 'proprietors' were paid as consideration for a 'service'.[7] The proprietors' contributions to the schools were to supply the school building, contribute to assuring the maintenance of the special character of the school and to enter into contracts with parents, which entitle

3. See the New Zealand Inland Revenue, *Tax Information Bulletin*, vol. 3, no. 1 at p. 30. See further – on the case – the next section.
4. See *The Director-General of Social Welfare v. De Morgan and Anor* (1996) 17 NZTC 12,636, dealt with in the next section, where payments made are found to 'fall within the meaning of "consideration" in section 2 *and* [my emphasis] come squarely within section 5(6D)'.
5. Case *M129* (1990) 12 NZTC 2,839.
6. The payments would now be covered by section 5(6D) and liable to VAT, see further section § 12.04.
7. *Turakina Maori Girls College Board of Trustees & Ors v. C of IR* (1993) 15 NZTC 10,032.

the pupil to attend the school in question. The Court ruled that the GST Act does not require that the supply be to the person who pays the consideration. It is clear from the definition of the consideration in section 2 that the supply of any service for consideration is part of a 'taxable activity' under section 6, even though it is to a person other than the person who provides the consideration. Parents paid the attendance dues to proprietors responsible for the above-mentioned areas. This was 'clearly' made 'in respect of, in response to, or for the inducement of' the things mentioned. Attendance dues were paid to secure enrolment in the school in question, which was itself a supply of a service.

It is clear from this case, and other cases[8], that at one and the same time a supplier may be making a supply to two different recipients. The supply can be to any person, not just the one paying the consideration.

Case *S77* concerns out-of-court settlements following a dispute over negligence.[9] Barber DJ found, in short, that the payment was not made for a supply. All that passed between the parties was the payment and, in the abstract, the surrendering of the right to proceed with the claims against the other party. That surrender is not a supply. No legal right or anything else has been forgone. It is however different if a settlement payment relates to a supply.[10]

An interesting case that also deals with the relationship between the concept of consideration and grants and subsidies is *De Morgan and Anor*.[11] The case concerns payments made by the Department of Social Welfare under a Rest Home Subsidy Scheme. Essentially, owners of a rest-home signed a written contract with the Department in question under which the owners were retained to provide rest-home services to residents in return for an agreed fee. The case primarily concerned the effects of the rate increase from 10% to 12.5%, yet, in order to determine those effects, it was necessary to ascertain whether the consideration for the supply was in the nature of a grant or subsidy. The Court of Appeal found, in a judgment delivered by Richardson P., that it is the character or quality of what is to be paid, and of the consideration that is given, which is crucial. The transaction reflected in the contract in question was much more than an ordinary commercial contract specifying a commercial fee for a commercial service. The payments were made for the purpose of 'granting' special assistance under the programme. The contractor rest-home owners participated in the scheme and were 'retained' to provide the services. The Director-General, in turn, performed a standard function on behalf of the state of providing financial support. The payments made to the owners pursuant to the agreements entered into

8. *Suzuki New Zealand Limited v. Commissioner of Inland Revenue* (2001) 20 NZTC 17,096. See Blanchard (2007), p. 96.
9. Case *S77* (1996) 17 NZTC 7,483.
10. See also Case *T22* (1997) 18 NZTC 8,124 on a settlement between the crown and a crayfish farming business, and instructive discussions on what may constitute a supply and what is not.
11. *The Director-General of Social Welfare v. De Morgan and Anor* (1996) 17 NZTC 12,636.

under the scheme were considered to fall within the meaning of 'consideration' in section 2 and come squarely within section 5(6D).[12]

For me, this seems clearly to be a payment for the inducement of a supply. It would have been strange if it would have been decided any other way. However, in the light of earlier case law, the fact that the issue lead to a court decision is not that strange, see *Case M129* above. The Government's payments under the JOS dealt with in that case may very well be considered to be made for the inducement of a supply. One may ask what the difference is between the subsidy to rest-home operators (as was the case in *De Morgan and Anor*) and the employment of a person under the JOS. One possible explanation to the different outcomes can be the fact that in the latter case, there existed an employment situation, which is explicitly excluded from the scope of the GST Act. Apart from that, the payment seems clearly to constitute a payment for a supply within the meaning of the GST Act. I submit that *M129* should not be conferred any higher value.

Taupo Ika Nui Body Corporate was a body corporate comprising the registered proprietors of a timeshare resort.[13] Taupo Ika Nui took over the management of the resort's affairs in 1988. The proprietors each paid the body an assessed sum per week, based on an annual budget, which paid for the resort's upkeep and maintenance. The Commissioner contended that the taxpayer was obliged to charge GST on the administration and maintenance levies it made on the proprietors. The Court considered two issues on appeal: (i) whether the taxpayer was a separate entity from the proprietors; and (ii) whether the taxpayer's activities were carried out for a consideration.

The Court, Gallen J., came to the conclusion that all the pointers (in the legal treatment of the body) indicated that the appellant had an identity separate from the proprietors who constituted it. It had powers and liabilities which the proprietors did not individually possess. It was furthermore subject to at least one restriction to which they were not individually subject, that is the prohibition on trading.

With regard to the question of whether the activities were carried out for a consideration, Gallen J. stated that there is a distinction between the cost of the services and collecting the cost of those services. The corporate body did not receive or obtain anything for its own benefit in respect of the organisation which it performed. The whole of the sums supplied by the proprietors were used for the payment of the independent contractors either in respect of the immediate obligations, or accumulated for the provision of future obligations. The services of collection, management and payment carried out by the appellant were gratuitous. The appellant received nothing for what it did.

Furthermore, the concept of consideration must be considered to contain an element of reciprocity. There is no such element in a situation where a corporate body merely collects the contributions from its members and passes them on, i.e., a mere handling of the funds. Further, while the term 'in respect of', in the definition of the

12. In *Kena Kena Properties Limited v. Attorney-General* (2002) 20 NZTC 17, 433, the Privy Council's majority essentially agreed with (the conclusions and reasoning of) the Court of Appeal in *De Morgan*.
13. *Taupo Ika Nui Body Corporate v. Commissioner of Inland Revenue* (1997) 18 NZTC 13,147.

consideration in the GST Act, is unrestricted and wide enough to encompass a meaning which would include what took place in this case, it must be construed in relation not only to the use of the term 'consideration', but also to the allied concepts of 'response to' or 'inducement of', both of which involve an element of reciprocity.[14]

I find this judgment rather confusing. Payments were made in respect of supplies. Considering that the GST Act defines the consideration as payments made 'in respect of, in response to, *or* [emphasis added] for the inducement of' a supply, there was certainly room for the interpretation that the payments were 'consideration'. That interpretation would also better conform to the broad-based character of the GST. The fact that all compensation was merely forwarded to suppliers seems to have led the judge to conclude that no real supplies were made by Tauop Ika Nui. The body seems not to have acted as a financial payment intermediary however, but to have acquired services performed by contractors in its own name. I recognise that I may not have fully understood the legal situation prevailing, it is not particularly clear in the case.

In *New Zealand Refining*, the issue was whether certain payments made by the government to New Zealand Refining were consideration for services performed.[15] In the 1970s, New Zealand Refining received Governmental support, loans and encouragement to expand its business of processing oil products in return for fees. In the 1980s, Government changed policy to one of deregulation and passed legislation effectively taking back their support. An agreement was reached between the Crown and the taxpayer in which the Crown agreed to repay the taxpayer's loans and pay NZD 85 million over three years with the condition attached that the refinery remained operational on each payment date. The question was whether GST was due on the payment of the 85 million.

Judge Blanchard delivered the judgment of the Court of Appeal.[16] He viewed the payments as contributions to the operating expenses of New Zealand Refining. They were not part of the value of the supply of services to the oil company. Moreover, the Crown did not require the taxpayer to keep the refinery open, or prohibit closure. There was, significantly, no stipulation for the supply of services to any buyer or buyers. To qualify for the money, New Zealand Refinery simply had to keep the refinery operational. The payments were to compensate the taxpayer for the removal of the protections given and its exposure to the hot winds of competition. The payments were received in the course of the taxable activity, but they were not in consideration for any supply made by it, accordingly they were not subject to GST.

---

14. Blanchard (2007), pp. 100–101 comments on the case and compares it to a UK case, *Eastbourne Town Radio Cars v. Customs and Excise Commissioners* [2001] 1 WLR 794 (House of Lords), where the subscriptions of members of the association were fixed by dividing on a pro rata basis the association's expenses, including the costs of staffing and facilities. The decision was that the association was making taxable supplies to its members, even though its constitution provided that staff were employed by the members and not by the association. Blanchard submits that the distinction between the two types of situations may be a rather fine one, but he suggests that it makes practical sense in a society in which so much residential occupation is under unit title legislation (as was Taupo Ika Nui).
15. *C of IR v. New Zealand Refining Co Ltd* (1997) 18 NZTC 13,187.
16. He has also commented on the case, Blanchard (2007), pp. 97–98.

The judgment in *New Zealand Refining* concerned a period before section 5(6D) was introduced. It seems to me that the payments made to the refinery would have fallen under that provision, had it been applicable.

In the *Chatham Island* case, the question was whether an endowment of NZD 8 million, paid in two instalments, to the Chatham Islands Enterprise Trust was consideration in respect of, in response to, or for the inducement of a supply.[17] The trust was set up to acquire certain Crown assets and undertakings integral to the Chatham Islands' infrastructure and commercial activities. Trading companies owned by the trust were charged with running the port, the airport, the meat works and generating electricity for the island. However, most of the objects of the trust concerned promoting the economic development and well-being of the Chatham Islands' community. On appeal to the Court of Appeal, the Commissioners argued that the Trust was carrying out its functions pursuant to the trust deeds, and in doing so was making a supply of services to the Crown. This was done for a consideration because the payment of the NZD 8 million induced the Trust to carry out its functions. In the alternative, the supply induced by the payments was to the people of the Chatham Islands.

Judges Keith and Blanchard[18] found that the argument by the Commissioner was ingenious but had an unreal air about it. Although the linkage or nexus between a payment and the activity to which it gives rise may be very broad, it is still necessary to have regard to the legal form which is being employed. In taxation disputes, the Court is concerned with the legal arrangements actually entered into, not the economic or other consequences of the arrangements. The tax being one on transactions, it is necessary to pay close attention to the legal nature of what has been done.

The judges found that the trust did not assume a contractual or even a voluntary obligation to the Crown. The payments were not made pursuant to any covenant by the Crown involving reciprocal obligations by the Trust. What actually occurred was that, in a process governed by principles of equity, the Crown vested two sums of money in trust for the people of the Islands and the trustees, to hold the fund and apply it in a specified way. The trust was not making a supply of anything to the settler in exchange for, or induced by, the payments; it was the recipient of an endowment.[19] Neither could section 5(6D)(a) (concerning grants and subsidies) be applicable, as there was no taxable activity performed. The trust did not make any supplies for a consideration.

In *Pacific Trawling Ltd and Anor*, the High Court dealt with *deemed value payments* made pursuant to two versions of the Fisheries Act (1983 and 1996) and whether those payments constituted consideration for supplies for GST purposes.[20] Under the quota management system, a commercial fisher may take and sell quota species only if it holds a valid fishing permit and a share of the total allowable commercial catch for the relevant species. When fishing for species for which it holds

17. *Chatham Islands Enterprise Trust v. Commissioner of Inland Revenue* (1999) 19 NZTC 15,075.
18. In a judgment delivered by Blanchard, Judge Tipping agreed with the outcome but with a different legal reasoning.
19. *Chatham* at p. 15,079.
20. *Pacific Trawling Limited & Anor v. Chief Executive of the Ministry of Fisheries & Anor (2005) 22 NZTC 19,204.*

quota, a fisher frequently catches other quota species for which it does not hold quota. These fish are called by-catch. A fisher that caught by-catch, which was not covered by his quota, could surrender the by-catch, buy quota, or pay deemed values. The mechanism under the relevant Fisheries Acts provided that there was a general prohibition on taking fish except under the authority of a current fishing permit. The issue before the Court was whether the Ministry made a taxable supply for GST purposes in return for deemed value payments.

The Court, Miller J., found that the fisher must be considered to own the fish (including the by-catch) which he caught. The payment of deemed values was a necessary but not sufficient condition for authorising what would otherwise be the unauthorised possession and sale of by-catch where the fisher did not elect to surrender the fish to the Crown. It followed that something was supplied in consideration for the payment in the form of authority to keep and sell the by-catch covered by the payment where the fisher could also prove that it was genuine by-catch. Under the 1996 version of the Fisheries Act, a fisher who had taken by-catch secured, in return for deemed value payments, the continued right to use its fishing permit. Deemed value payments were not analogous to a levy or a penalty. Although nothing in the Goods and Services Tax Act expressly excluded fines, levies or penalties, they were excluded because they were not taxable supplies in which a good or service was provided in consideration for payment. In addition, the deemed value payments were not compulsory. Consequently the deemed payments constituted consideration falling within the scope of the GST act.

Blanchard has commented on the case and stated that the case illustrates the breadth of the concept of a supply under the GST Act.[21] Provided a nexus can be seen between the consideration and the supply, a taxable supply is likely to be found.

§12.03 DISCUSSION AND CONCLUSIONS

The definition of the consideration in section 2 of the GST Act ends with stating that the consideration 'does not include any payment made by any person as an unconditional gift to any non-profit body'. *Unconditional gift* is defined in section 2(1) as:

> a payment voluntarily made to any non-profit body for the carrying on or carrying out of the purposes of that non-profit body and in respect of which *no identifiable direct valuable benefit arises* or may arise in the form of a supply of goods and services *to the person making that payment, or any other person* where that person and that other person are associated persons; but does not include any payment made by the Crown or a public authority (emphasis here)

As can be seen, payments made by the Crown or a public authority are not included, which is probably due to the fact that these payments are deemed to constitute supplies. I note here that the definition of unconditional gifts conforms to a concept of consumption, of yielding direct utility (or benefit) to identifiable consumers/tax payers. At first sight, one may wonder why the provision is needed. Clearly, its

21. See Blanchard (2007), pp. 93–95.

existence implies that the definition of consideration is so wide as to also include payments that are not for the direct benefit of anyone. That impression is enforced by the fact that only payments made to non-profit bodies are included, and consequently unconditional gifts paid to any one else seem therefore to be taxed.

According to section 2(1), the consideration includes payments 'whether or not voluntary'. From the wording of that definition, and considering the fact that payments for the inducements of supplies are also covered by the scope, it seems clear that mandatory charges are also covered by the provisions as long as a service is indeed supplied to someone. In *Pacific Trawling*, the Court noted that nothing in the GST Act excludes fines, levies or penalties from GST. They are excluded because they are typically not consideration for a taxable supply.

The case on JOS (the jobs opportunity scheme) shows that borders still need to be defined even if one applies a very broad nexus in other cases. However, in my view one may question why the service to society was not characterised differently, perhaps as the relief of having to pay unemployment contributions to the previously unemployed or a similar service. Certainly from a European VAT perspective, such reasoning would probably not be too far fetched.[22] In addition, *De Morgan and Anor*, on a Rest Home Subsidy Scheme, shows, as pointed out above, that the JOS-case should not be extensively applied.[23]

Taupo Ika Nui Body Corporate shows that the question of whether a person is separate or part of an entity, i.e., the scope of the taxable person, needs to be determined – there are no supplies made between different establishments of the same legal entity/taxable person. Furthermore, the case also contains the important statement that even though the wording of the provision is very broad, the wording entails a requirement that there is some kind of reciprocity between a supply and the payment for the payment to constitute consideration. Pure transfers of wealth (e.g., pure subsidies) do not fall within the scope of the GST act. A supply has to be for something.

That impression is enforced when reading *New Zealand Refining*. In that case the service of keeping the refinery operational was not considered as a supply for consideration (not even the inducement of a supply!). In my view, to keep the refinery operational is definitely a service provided to the community, if not to a specific person. The judgment implies that for there to be a supply, a specific benefit, or utility, has to be awarded to some specific person(s) and not to society as a whole. But the judgment can also be explained by the circumstances. In the situation at hand, the payments were simply not linked to the performance of any service whatsoever, not even keeping the refinery operational. The government simply wanted to settle and get out of a relationship that it did not want to continue. The latter explanation seems the most plausible in my view. The facts of the case are very peculiar.

---

22. Compare the Court of Justice's discussion in Case C-55/09 in Joined Cases C-53/09 and C-55/09 *Loyalty Management UK*.
23. In addition, the case pre-dates the introduction of section 5 (6D) on subsidies. As McKenzie (2008) notes on p. 86, that provision reverses the effect of the judgment, i.e., the payments would be liable to GST today. See also *Tax Information Bulletin*, vol. 3, no. 1, pp. 30–31.

In *Chatham Islands,* the transfers in that case could very well be considered to be made for supplies made by the Council to the Crown (relieving it of the obligation to care for the infrastructure and companies which the Council undertook to invest in). Yet, the courts have not endorsed such a broad notion of services (and consumption).[24] Rather, the courts seem to have recognised that pure redistributions of wealth do not constitute consideration - however broad a scope of consumption one applies. Importantly, in their interpretation of the circumstances in the actual case, the courts seem, quite strictly, to follow the legal form employed.

§12.04 GRANTS AND SUBSIDIES

Section 5(6D) of the GST Act specifically deals with grants and subsidies. It was introduced as a response to the ruling in *CaseM129* on the JOS. As is evident from the historical documents, the Inland Revenue's presumption was that the subsidies etc. covered by the provision were originally intended to be covered by the main rule.[25] In any event, the provision as it currently reads deems payments made *in the nature of a grant or subsidy* by or on behalf of the Crown or any public body to any person not being a public body in relation to or in respect of that person's taxable activity to constitute consideration for goods and services.

Whatever the name given to it, a grant or subsidy for the purposes of section 5(6D) is a gift or assignment deemed to be beneficial to the public interest from the point of view of the provider of the grant or subsidy.[26]

The requirement of the payment being made 'in relation to or in respect of that person's taxable activity' was discussed in sections §12.02 and §12.03. It is especially noticeable that a payment is only consideration when received in the course or furtherance of 'that person's taxable activity', i.e., it must be related to a taxable activity. If received by a person neither required to be registered or registered, the provision is not applicable. This is as would be expected, considering the history of the provision and considering that the provision is not intended to extend the scope of who should be a registered taxpayer. Actually, it seems to me that the only effect section 5(6D) has is that it releases the tension from the fact that sometimes consideration is stipulated as subsidies in contracts and not as consideration. Since it has to be in respect of or in relation to a person's taxable activity, there still needs to be a link to taxable activities - which means to supplies for consideration in New Zealand GST. The provision does not extend to cover subsidies paid that are not connected with an already existing taxable activity. There is thereby also a similarity with the European provision, extending the taxable amount to include 'subsidies directly linked to the

24. Notably, no specific services were provided by the Council directly to third persons - the Council merely invested in companies and was not engaged in taxable activities, compare McKenzie (2008), p. 86.
25. See *Tax Information Bulletin*, vol. 3, no. 1, p. 30.
26. See McKenzie (2008), p. 85 and *Kena Kena Properties Limited v. Attorney-General* (2002) 20 NZTC 17, 433 at p. 14 and 15.

price'. In my view, section 5(6D) only restores what presumably was the intended scope of the general rule/definition of the consideration.

The scope of the provision apparently does not include grants or subsidies paid by one public body to another public body. In addition, section 5(6D) is not applicable to local authorities and grants and subsidies paid by them. The potential scope of the main provision is therefore still of interest with regard to grants and subsidies paid in circumstances where section 5(6D) is not applicable. And that scope is far from clear.

§12.05 APPROPRIATIONS BY THE CROWN

According to sections 2(1) and 5(6) of the GST Act, any amount brought to charge from the Crown (appropriations) by any public authority for the supply of outputs (within the meaning of the Public Finance Act 1989) by that public authority is consideration for supplies made within the meaning of the GST Act. It seems evident from the historical context of the GST Act that the intention of the provision is to cover all transfers from the Crown to any instrument of the Crown and thereby fully include public bodies within the GST system - alleviating them of the need to distinguish between outputs to the Crown or to other entities; all income is liable to GST. However, the provision entails certain phrases that potentially limit the reach thereof.

First, only outputs 'within the meaning of the Public Finance Act' are covered. Consequently, if there are payments made that do not fall under the Public Finance Act, then they are not covered by the provision.

Second, only appropriations transferred 'for the supply of outputs' are covered, i.e., if there is no 'output' for which the transfer is made, the provision does not cover the transfer.

It was noted above that an output in the Public Finance Act is a good or services supplied by a public body. Appropriations are needed for various categories of expenses, but also for capital expenditure (costs of assets acquired or developed or financial assets and ownership in entities). Furthermore, according to the guide to the Public Finance Act, capital contributions to departments do not require appropriations under the Public Finance Act.

It seems therefore clear that not all transfers of the Crown to public bodies are liable to GST. 'Outputs' seems not to include capital contributions in the form of investments. The scope of the GST is thus not extended to include pure transfers of wealth in the form of capital investments. In accounting terms, when an investment is made which shows on the balance sheet, it seems not to be for an output. The latter concept relates to incomes and costs and not assets and liabilities.

However, the distinction when funds are transferred to a public body may not be that clear. Take the example of the building of a road or a school. Is the money used to build the road or school an output, or is it not rather an investment for the later provision of outputs in the form of access to the road and provision of educational services? It is these latter services that yield utility to consumers and not the investments as such. It should also be remembered that a transfer to invest seems not to be seen as consideration for an output under the normal GST rules. If total equalisation with private sector is sought – pure financial investments should, also for public bodies, be treated as falling outside the scope of GST as these are not supplies for GST purposes. In the alternative, the investments could be taxed as pre-payments for future road-services/education services.

§12.06 LOCAL AUTHORITIES

Section 5(6D) is not applicable to subsidies paid by local authorities. If the Crown is to transfer money directly to local authorities, no rule deems this to be consideration for supplies; sections 2(1) and 5(6) on appropriations are not applicable to local authorities. Specific rules on contributions to local authorities exist (section 5(7C) and (7B)). These were introduced as a response to the judgments in *New Zealand Refining* and *Chatham Islands*.[27] Thus, in the view of the Government and the Inland Revenue, it is clearly so that the courts' approach is not in line with the original intent of the legislator and that the specific deeming provisions are merely restoring things as they originally were intended to be.

§12.07 MANDATORY CHARGES

According to section 2(1), the consideration includes payments 'whether or not voluntary'. From the wording of that definition, and considering the fact that payments for the inducements of supplies are also covered by the scope, it seems clear that also mandatory charges are covered by the provisions as long as a service is indeed supplied to someone (compare the conclusions of the case law). In *Pacific Trawling*, the Court noted that nothing in the GST Act excludes fines, levies or penalties from GST. They are excluded because they are not taxable supplies.[28] It is inherent in the character of penalties and levies that they are not paid as consideration for any services.

And this also raises the issue of whether the payment includes charges such as taxes and the like that are imposed by Act of Government or Local authorities, in so far as they can be considered to be paid 'for the inducement of' a particular supply. Indeed it does. General rates are clearly taxes and are deemed to be consideration.

27. See *Inland Revenue Department Tax Information Bulletin*, vol. 16, no. 1 (February 2004), pp. 88–89.
28. *Pacific Trawling* at p. 49.

CHAPTER 13

Other Issues and Conclusions

§13.01 DEDUCTION OF INPUT GST

The consequences of receiving income that does not constitute consideration is quite different under New Zealand's GST compared to European VAT. The right to deduct input GST is not affected as long as the acquisition is for the primary purpose of an activity that generates a GST-liable output. I have found no discussion concerning a restricted right to deduct input GST in cases where income not giving rise to output GST-liability has been received, except for in the sphere of supplies of exempt financial services. It is noticeable that deduction is an all or nothing question, either the GST is deductible or it is not, there exists no partial deduction.[1] Consider the case of a company issuing shares to fund its taxable activities. In European VAT, the activity of issuing shares correctly falls outside the scope of VAT, as it is neither production nor consumption but a pure transfer of wealth. Yet, the right to deduct input VAT on shares connected with the issue exists, also correctly, as the acquisitions are an input to the taxable business activities and acquiring funds for that activity. In a New Zealand approach of all or nothing, there is a risk that input GST pertaining to share issues is considered to be non-deductible.

§13.02 ON PURE TRANSFERS OF WEALTH AND CONSUMPTION

I have in previous research noted that pure transfers of wealth correctly, from a system design point of view, fall outside the scope of European VAT. Considering the similarities of VAT-type consumption taxes, the same ought to be true of the New Zealand GST. Also under this tax, pure transfers of wealth ought not to be taxed.

1. McKenzie (2008), p. 210.

Despite the broad scope intended, and despite the amendments enacted to include transfers not directly linked to a supply discussed in the preceding sections, not all transfers of funds are covered by the act. There is, first, a requirement that payments are made for a taxable activity, or for specific outputs. When a payment is not made for outputs, the payment does not constitute consideration. Second, fines and penalties are not subject to GST. Third, capital contributions are not paid for any output activity and thus not taxed.

The correct treatment of transfers of wealth not evidently linked to outputs is a difficult issue in New Zealand, as shown by the above discussions. The courts have been struggling with these transfers and the Government has enacted legislation concerning such transfers and deeming them to be included within the scope of the tax. Government simply considers that it is restoring the original intended scope of the GST Act.

The Courts in New Zealand have thus taken a narrow approach to the concept of consumption applicable under the main rule – utility to the society as a whole is not considered as a service falling within the scope of the GST Act. Despite the broad coverage implied by the wording and context, the actual scope and consequential required link between a payment and a supply is surprisingly similar to the one established in European VAT.

§13.03 CONCLUSIONS

New Zealand has strived towards equalising the public sector with the private sector in terms of management, and the treatment for VAT purposes reflects this. Transfers to public bodies are deemed payments for deemed supplies. A fiction is created and the sector is fully incorporated within the VAT system. The most relevant question in this study is how the fiction is working.

Problems have surfaced. The deeming provisions and broadly construed concepts under GST in general have not been enough to cover transfers that were obviously intended to be covered from the beginning. Additional 'deeming provisions' have been inserted to deal with specific activities. Based on the research here, it can also be presumed that these difficulties will continue. The Public Finance Act does not define all income of public sector bodies as paid for outputs provided. An assessment needs to be made in each specific situation on the appropriation and whether it is payment for an output. There is here clearly a risk that some income may be considered to fall outside the scope of the provision – necessitating additional deeming provisions to be enacted.

As regards the general definition of the consideration and required nexus between a supply and the consideration, it is, for a European lawyer, remarkable that the Courts have not interpreted the provision based on the purpose of the GST as a general tax on consumption. The deeming provisions on grants and subsidies, unconditional gifts paid to non-profit making bodies and appropriations from the Crown reduce the pressure on the fundamental distinctions. Yet, complicated issues arise when the provisions are not general enough to cover a certain transfer. That is the case when transfers are made by local authorities that are not subjected to the same rules as Government authorities. That is also the case in the private sector when transfers are made that are on the verge of being consideration. These problems are not unique to New Zealand, they are also present in EU VAT. But one would expect that the broad definition would relieve the pressure on the distinction to a larger extent.

Overall, the impression is of a system that works reasonably well. Whether that is because of the, in the European perspective, minor pressure on the system due to the size of the country and the number of advisors in indirect taxation, and its location, or due to the sustainability of the system is not evident. It seems to me that the system is working well and that the fundamental structure works very well in the context of New Zealand.

CHAPTER 14

Other Full Tax Systems and Evaluation

§14.01 INTRODUCTION

In this chapter, full tax systems other than the New Zealand one are discussed. These have not been separately researched and descriptions rest heavily on secondary material.

§14.02 AUSTRALIA

Australia has a general indirect tax on consumption, sharing the characteristics outlined in Chapter 1.[1]

Section 9-20 1-20 (g) of the Australian GST Act provides that an ***enterprise*** is an activity, or series of activities, done by, *inter alia*, the Commonwealth, a State or a Territory, or by a body corporate, or corporation sole, established for a public purpose by or under a law of the Commonwealth, a State or a Territory. Thus, public bodies are in principle fully included in the GST system as taxable persons in EU VAT terminology. The inclusion is extended to cover also government units that are not legally separate entities which should be registered separately. These units are also enterprises when they are not carrying on an enterprise for the purposes of the general definition, Division 149-5 of the Australian GST Act.[2]

In so far as input VAT relates to the enterprise making taxed supplies for consideration, it is deductible. The input VAT relates to the enterprise if it pertains to acquisitions you make carrying on your enterprise.[3] According to Division 149-15 of the Australian GST Act, a Government entity that is registered for GST purposes is

1. Millar (2012).
2. See Millar (2012).
3. Sections 11–15 of the Australian GST Act and Millar (2012).

treated as if it was an entity carrying on an enterprise. As a consequence, all input GST incurred is deductible.[4]

Transfers between government entities are excluded from the scope of GST as non-taxable transactions. Division 9-15(3)(c) provides that a payment made by a government related entity to another government related entity is not the provision of consideration if the payment is specifically covered by an appropriation under an Australian law. In addition, grants and subsidies not sufficiently linked to a specific supply are not taxed.[5]

Most notably, consideration under Australian GST explicitly does not include taxes (however described),[6] neither are certain fees or charges such as fees for authorisations, licences, permissions etc. and fees or charges relating to certain provisions of information paid to an Australian government agency.[7] Millar reports that the intention has never been to tax collective consumption with all taxes, fees and charges being grossed up for GST. Australia intends to tax only commercial activities of government and to effectively zero-rate non-commercial activities.[8] As is clear from the GST Act, the Government may, by regulation, provide for exceptions to the explicit exclusion of taxes, fees and charges in certain situations.[9] Regulations also exist through which certain fees, such as parking fees, road tolls and fees to use waste disposal are taxable.[10]

In effect, all transfers between government entities are zero-rated unless they entail consideration for exempt supplies in the case where input VAT is not deductible to the extent that exempt supplies are made.

Importantly, Australia does not have many exemptions (in comparison to the EU system). In addition, key areas where the Government supplies services in competition with private entities which are of social importance, notably health care, they are zero-rated; i.e., no output is charged but a full credit is allowed - also for private entities.

§14.03 CANADA

The Canadian VAT system is very complex.[11] Canada operates a GST on a federal level alongside provincial VATs operating in most, but not all, provinces with some provinces also operating retail sales taxes RST.[12] In principle, all supplies of public bodies fall within the scope of Canadian VAT (both the federal and provincial systems).

4. See also Millar (2012). Input VAT is deductible in so far it does not relate to input taxed supplies.
5. See GSTR 2000/11 and Millar (2012).
6. See section 81-5 of the Australian GST Act.
7. See section 81.10 of the Australian GST Act. See also Millar (2012).
8. Millar (2012).
9. Section 81.5 and 81.15 of the Australian GST Act.
10. Millar (2012).
11. Bird & Gendron (2009) state that 'Canadians developed and implemented a sales tax system that no one in their right mind would have designed from scratch'.
12. See Gendron, *Bulletin of International Taxation* (2005) and Bird & Gendron (2009) for a general description of the Canadian VAT system. See also van Dijk & Lubber *IVM* (2000).

Thereby Canada can be said to apply a full tax model where public bodies are not generally excluded from the scope of the VAT system.[13]

§14.04 EVALUATION

All states assessed which have a full tax model fully include public bodies within the scope of their GSTs/VATs. In that respect the treatment is quite straightforward - there is simply no exclusion for public bodies from the scope of the definition of taxable persons (taxpayers). In Australian GST, the concept of enterprise explicitly includes public sector bodies, mentioned in one of the indents of the definition. Similarly, in New Zealand GST, the main provision defining what is a taxable activity contains two parts, one dealing with activities in the form of a business, trade manufacture, profession, vocation, association or club and the other with activities of any public authority or any local authority. Both are taxable activities for the purposes of New Zealand GST. In both acts, public sector bodies are also defined with reference to national law.

Here, however, the similarities end. In New Zealand, a number of deeming provisions supplement the definitions of consideration and supplies. With reference to national law, activities performed by public authorities are deemed to be supplies of goods and services, and revenue received for the deemed supplies is deemed to constitute consideration. In Australia, the activities are not 'deemed' to be supplies of goods and services. Activities are only 'taxable transactions' in EU terminology when falling under the general definitions of the Act. A Government entity is treated as if it was carrying on an enterprise (taxable transactions in EU terminology) and input GST is therefore deductible. Consequently, where New Zealand completes the fiction of a public body making supplies for consideration and therefore eligible for deduction of GST on its input, Australia is reported to operate a model where input GST is simply deductible by definition for Government entities, unless linked to supplies for which the GST is not deductible.[14]

At first sight, the New Zealand model seems superior from a system design point of view due to its adherence to the structure of a VAT system, with tax charged on all outputs and tax deductible on all related inputs. Deeming activities to be supplies for consideration is part of its basic structure. However, the model's weakness lies precisely in the extension of its field of application to transactions not (potentially) resulting in expenditure for consumption (as will be discussed in Chapter 15).

As can be seen from the legal appraisal in Chapter 12 that the general deeming provisions have had to be complemented with specific deeming provisions to cover income that the legislator obviously considered ought to have been covered by the general deeming provisions. It has proved difficult to have as broad a scope as originally intended. Agreeably, the interpretation of the GST provisions has also been remarkable in the sense that the fundamental principle underlying a VAT, the

13. See further Chapter 7 section §7.02.
14. Millar (2012).

neutrality of the tax, has not been considered in the interpretation to the extent that one would assume, considering the strong political devotion to the general characteristic of the tax. Importantly, overall the New Zealand system, which is the one researched here, seems to be working well in the context of New Zealand.

The Australian system may seem simpler - public sector bodies are simply allowed to deduct input VAT but the (unnecessary) charging of output VAT on appropriations is done away with. An additional benefit of the Australian system can be found in the reasons for its adoption in Australia, rather than the New Zealand approach. Millar notes the following:[15]

> A key reason why Australia chose to adopt the GST-free approach rather than to follow the New Zealand approach is its federal structure. If revenue from the Crown, and grants by one part of government to another, were deemed to be consideration for a taxable supply, the result would be a redistribution of revenue from one government to another.

In a country with a federal structure, these reasons are of course important.

15. Millar (2012), p. 14.

PART IV

Evaluation

In this part the results of the findings regarding the exemption and full taxation models researched in part II and part III are evaluated against two benchmarks; the coherence between the fundamental character of a VAT/GST system, as established in part I, and political philosophy.

Overall recommendations are made as to what should be considered as best practice whenever a change in the treatment of public bodies in a VAT/GST system is contemplated.

CHAPTER 15

Towards a 'Best Practice'

§15.01 INTRODUCTION

Commentators seem to be in total agreement as regards the question of whether public bodies should be included within the field of application of a consumption-type VAT. While Tait seems to have been the first in the international arena to point at the New Zealand approach as the best one, Aujean, Jenkins and Poddar were the first to develop and convincingly describe the conceptual thinking behind a move to a full tax system with a VAT in their leading article from 1999.[1,2] Since then, the approach to include public bodies within the scope of a VAT has been supported by, *inter alia*, Terra and Kajus[3], Gendron[4], Millar[5] and de la Feria.[6] To move to a full tax option is also the approach advocated in the study by Copenhagen Economics commissioned by the Commission.[7] Gendron summarises the position in his conclusions:

> A few main conclusions emerge. First, the case for the status quo is extremely weak, while the case for taxing such services at any positive rate is quite strong. Second, the options to replace the exemption regime dominate the options to modify it. Third, considering the tax policy constraints facing DTEs, the Australian-New Zealand system appears to be the best option to replace the current treatment. Under that system, all the goods and services supplied by public sector bodies, non-profit organisations and charitable organisations are within the scope of GST (or VAT) and treated like any supplies from the private sector. Those models feature very few instances of zero-rating or exemptions.[8]

1. Tait (1988), p. 78.
2. Aujean, Jenkins & Poddar *IVM* 1999.
3. Terra & Kajus (2012), Chapter 9.5.
4. Gendron, *Bulletin* (2005) and *Tax Law Review* (2010).
5. Millar (2012).
6. De la Feria, *Intertax* (2008).
7. Copenhagen Economics and KPMG (2011).
8. Gendron *Bulletin* (2005).

As was noted in the first chapter of this book, the case for keeping the status quo is weak due to the fact that the exclusion system results in distortions. In the appraisal of the EU VAT system, a number of further legal problems where discussed. As will be seen below, the appraisal confirms that the case for keeping the status quo is indeed weak. However, the appraisal of the New Zealand system also showed that it would be difficult to transpose that system into the EU context. Furthermore, abolishing exemptions and introducing zero-rates may not be politically possible, despite the clear advantages it might offer both in reducing economic distortions and decreasing administrative burden. The question thus remains, as to how the exclusion system could be reformed.

The following sections, commence with a discussion of the considerations relating to political philosophy followed by an appraisal of the issue of the treatment of public bodies in the light of the character of the VAT. The last two sections deal with designs; one of a preferred treatment if an exclusion system is to be retained and one of a preferred treatment in an inclusion system.

§15.02 CONSIDERATIONS RELATING TO POLITICAL PHILOSOPHY

The issue of how to treat state and local authority entities suitably under an indirect tax on consumption is clearly related to one's views on the role of the state vis-à-vis its citizens and its role in relation to the economic system. The view on the role of the state in a totalitarian state or planned economy, that is the limits and role of the state and its organs, is presumably very different from that of the state in a liberal, parliamentary democracy. This difference in views may also potentially influence the opinion on how to treat public bodies in a VAT system. In a very liberal regime, like that of New Zealand in the mid-1980s, the equalising of state and local entities with service providers and private law entities (and full inclusion in the consumption tax system) is consonant with the New Zealand view of the role of the state in society. However, in a totalitarian state, or a state operating a planned economy, the idea to view the state as an external service provider sounds alien to the view of the appropriate role of the state. One of the main arguments for inclusion of public bodies within the VAT system - distortions of competition arising - is presumably much less aligned with the philosophy of a totalitarian state or planned economy compared to that of a liberal, parliamentary democracy.

If one traces the origin of liberal values and the idea of equality of state agencies and private entrepreneurs, one finds that the notion of equality is closely linked to the Rule of Law and the principle of equal treatment, which in turn are very much a product of the Enlightenment. Political philosophers of the Enlightenment, like John Locke, Rousseau and Montesquieu, attributed great importance to the principle of equality.[9] Montesquieu writes in *The Spirit of Laws*:

9. See Tridimas (2006), p. 59. See also his division of types of general principles of law where one category is principles which derive from the rule of law, pp. 4–5.

> For the better understanding of the first four books of this work, it is to be observed that what I distinguish by the name of virtue, in a republic, is the love of one's country, that is, the love of equality.[10]
>
> ...
>
> ... constant experience shows us that every man invested with power is apt to abuse it, and to carry his authority as far as it will go. Is it not strange, though true, to say that virtue itself has need of limits? To prevent this abuse, it is necessary from the very nature of things that power should be a check to power. A government may be so constituted, as no man shall be compelled to do things to which the law does not oblige him, nor forced to abstain from things which the law permits.[11]

He thereafter establishes his division of powers in government, all under the rule of law as expressed in the quote. Needless to point out, the Rule of Law has also since, in parliamentary democracies, been a fundamental building block. In Europe, and European Law, the Rule of Law and the liberal values connected thereto are enshrined in the constitutional traditions of the Member States and in the EU itself.[12]

Thus, from a philosophical perspective, the view on how to treat public bodies for VAT purposes, is linked to the particular view one has on the role of the state. However, as long as the Rule of Law is embraced as the basic building block, it does not matter to what extent, or exactly how, one actually views the degree of involvement and the more exact role the state should have in society. In this respect it should be noted that, it is not even clear in countries or regions where a free market (and the Rule of Law) is considered a leading principle, what a free market actually is; as pointed out in an article on the Role of the State by Chang:[13]

> Don't we know that a 'free' market is a market without state intervention? Of course, the argument may go, we may have disagreements on which is a 'good' state intervention and which is a 'bad' one, but don't we all know what state intervention means? I am not actually sure that we do. The trouble is that the same state action can be, and has been, considered an 'intervention' in one society but not in another (which could be the same society in a different point of time).... depending on which rights and obligations are regarded as 'legitimate' by the members of the society, the same action could be considered an 'intervention' in one society and not in another. And once something is not even considered to be an 'intervention' in a particular society at a given time (e.g., ban on child labour or slavery in the OECD countries), debating their 'efficiency' becomes politically unacceptable – although there is no God-given reason why this should be the case. The corollary is that, depending on the rights-obligations structure, the same market with the same state 'intervention' in the same area – for example, regarding child labour – can be seen as 'free' (from state intervention) in one society and not in another.

Also, the rhetoric in a country or region may be of a liberal, *laissez faire*, economy but the reality may be different:

10. Montesquieu (1748), p. 17.
11. Montesquieu (1748), p. 172.
12. See, as regards the EU Articles 2-6, 19 and 21 TEU and Tridimas (2006), Chapter 1.
13. See Chang (2000).

> For example, some commentators point out that the US federal state, despite its laissez faire rhetoric, has strongly influenced the country's industrial evolution through defence procurement programmes and defence-related R&D contracts – especially in industries like computer, telecommunication, and aviation. [...] So, again, the prevailing vision of the role of the state, where 'defence' is accepted as one of the 'minimum' functions of the state (almost shading into 'non-intervention'), makes people underestimate the importance of the US federal government in the country's industrial development.[14]

The Rule of Law implies that government agents should be subordinated to the same laws as applied to others. As a consequence, it seems hard to imagine an equality of treatment for VAT purposes of public bodies and private entities in a state that is not in essence a liberal country where the Rule of Law is an integrated part of the legal inheritance. That said it should be emphasised that the VAT is in its design fundamentally a liberal tax, its basis being neutrality – as little interference as possible with the efficient allocation of resources in society. In centrally planned economies, the role of indirect turnover taxes and their collection have been vastly different.[15] In the eastern European countries during communist rule, turnover taxes were a major source of income. They were however very different from liberal turnover taxes. Their function was not only to raise revenue, but also to regulate prices and profits. They usually operated with different rates. And since government set prices, the core feature of the VAT, its non-distortive character in relation to relative prices, was of course lost. Given the totally different objectives and character of turnover taxes in centrally planned economies, it seems irrelevant to discuss the treatment of public bodies in them – these are actually not really VATs in the sense of the word used in this research.[16]

In conclusion, as regards the VAT systems discussed in this research, the policy discussion and system design implications are relevant, viewed in a political philosophical perspective, independent of what level of government involvement etc. is preferred. Actually, the VAT is, in its very design features, a liberal tax.

§15.03 CONSIDERATIONS RELATING TO THE CHARACTER OF THE VAT

It was noted above in section §14.04, with the presence of deeming provisions in the New Zealand GST act, the issue arises of whether the character of the tax is also different. New Zealand GST has a very broad definition of the consideration. In addition, transfer payments (including subsidies) are deemed to be consideration. These transfers are however provided between taxpayers and the recipient of the deemed supply, which will always be a public body having a right to deduct input VAT.[17] The inclusion of the transfers will never, therefore, impact upon expenditure for

14. *Ibid.*
15. See Goode (1984), pp. 160–163.
16. Not surprisingly, the spread of the tax, and increased reliance upon it as a source of revenue for governments around the globe, is happening at the same time as the international trend towards trade liberalisation and market deregulation. See, for an analysis of the increased economic integration and implications for VAT design, Wallace (2007).
17. Millar (2012) notes this as well, see further below.

consumption that is taxed. However, it is different with rates (the local property taxes which are also subject to GST in New Zealand). Here, GST is added on rates payable by occupiers of property, which may be private individuals. Consequently, GST is imposed on 'collective consumption' as these rates are not consideration for specific services, but taxes to fund such activities as lightning, street cleaning etc.

The question therefore arises of whether a VAT ought to cover also this kind of 'collective consumption'. As noted in section §1.02, various explanations have been presented as to why public bodies are excluded from the field of application of VAT. The discussion here concerns the difficulties pointed out by several commentators of subsuming essentially tax-financed activities to the tax. The difficulties and their proper solution are dependent on how one looks at the character of the tax and whether economic activities resulting in collective consumption are properly falling within the field of application.

Aujean, Jenkins and Poddar state that 'perhaps the greatest conceptual difficulty impeding the development of a more rational system for applying VAT to public sector bodies is the insistence under existing models on identifying explicit consideration before a supply is seen to be made'.[18] They point to the fact that public bodies, even in situations where there is no specific consideration charged, are acting as intermediaries/producers of services and goods and not as consumers. The question then becomes, as pointed out by the authors, how wide the definition of the consideration should be in order to remove market distortions and non-neutralities.

Aujean, Jenkins and Poddar here take a practical and economic standpoint and make the point that it would simplify administration if subsidies also were subject to tax. However, the important point is that public sector bodies are seen as fully taxable persons with a right to full input tax deduction regardless of the stance on what nexus is required.[19] Poddar, in a later submission, seems to prefer that taxable consideration is defined broadly to minimise incentives for substitution of non-taxable consideration for taxable amounts.[20] He still keeps this issue open for discussion.

Englisch has noted:

> as regards government services that do not constitute taxable transactions because they do not convey individual benefits in exchange for an individual consideration, they should not be burdened with VAT/GST, notwithstanding their non-economic nature. Since no specific fees are charged, the tax cannot directly be shifted to the citizen as the final consumer, nor is there any expenditure on his or her behalf indicating ability to pay that could be attributed to the government services.[21]

He continues:

> it cannot be argued that the beneficiaries of public goods finance them by paying taxes... That would mean imposing VAT/GST as a tax on other taxes that are by

18. Aujean, Jenkins and Poddar, *IVM* (1999).
19. Aujean, Jenkins and Poddar, *IVM* (1999). See also Millar (2012).
20. Poddar (2005).
21. Englisch (2009), p. 32.

> definition unrelated to any funding of specific government activities, and which moreover do not indicate but rather presuppose ability to pay.[22]

Lastly, Millar has noted, *inter alia* in her detailed discussion on whether collective consumption should be a part of the tax base, that most, if not all, collective consumption should not form part of the tax base for VAT.[23] She considers this to be the logical approach as there is no real difference in outcome for the individual from simply increasing the rate of income tax. She continues:

> Such an approach would also raise more revenue than intended unless the imposition of VAT on income tax was accompanied by a decrease in the rate of one or other, or both, of the two taxes, accommodating the very different policy designs of the two taxes in the process. In the end, such moves would simply alter the balance between the two types of tax. There is no obvious logic to grossing up income tax for VAT to give the appearance that collective consumption is being taxed if all that happens is the rates of each tax are re-adjusted to achieve the same net tax effect on individuals. The difficulty of explaining the policy to voters might also be a powerful reason not to expand the notion of consideration this far.
>
> Where the government charging the VAT is not the government providing the collective consumption, different issues arise. As noted, Aujean et al allow for the possibility of applying VAT to local taxes in order to simplify administration, as is done in New Zealand. However, complex constitutional and political issues may arise in this respect, particularly in Federal nations. When different levels of government are involved, the full inclusion of government in a value added tax regime can result in the shifting of revenue between those governments.

Collective consumption is subject to GST in New Zealand as rates (local property taxes charged by local authorities) are subject to VAT. This is a fundamental difference from, as far as I know, all other VAT systems, except perhaps for the Australian GST system where the possibility exists by way of regulation, to charge VAT on taxes. The policy in Australia is however clearly not to tax collective consumption, as explained by Millar.[24]

Fundamental is how one views the requirement of a nexus between a payment and a supply, which has a direct impact on the concept of consideration and consumption.[25] For the purposes of the discussion, consumption defined as 'direct utility paid for directly', as in European VAT, could be termed 'a reduced scope' (where expenditure for consumption is not taxed if the level of payment is not determined based on the value of the supply, see Case C-246/08 *Commission v. Finland*). Consumption defined as 'any utility paid for directly' seems more in line with an economically neutral definition and could be termed 'economic scope'. It is arguably aimed at with the main definition of the consideration in New Zealand GST. A supply can be anything, but there does need to be some sort of supply – the payment has to be for something. Lastly, consumption defined as 'any utility received by anyone', i.e.,

22. *Ibid.* In his conclusions he suggests that VAT must be construed as a tax on expenditure for private consumption, as necessitated by the application of ability to pay.
23. Millar (2012).
24. Actually, the inclusion of subsidies in EU VAT could also be viewed as an extension to taxing collective consumption. It is therefore preferable, in my view, to interpret the extension narrowly.
25. On the traditional definition of the concept of consumption, see Henkow (2008), Chapter 3.

also covering collective consumption, could be termed 'increased economic scope'. The inclusion of grants and subsidies, and taxes such as rates in New Zealand, reflects a concept of consumption that is even wider than the traditional economic definition. Both the first and second concepts could be subsumed under the expression 'expenditure for consumption'. As argued by Englisch, the increased economic scope could not really be subsumed under the expression 'expenditure for consumption'.

I support the position that VAT, in its fundamental characteristics, is a tax on private expenditure.[26] The legal appraisal of the case law on the nexus required in New Zealand illustrates the strength of this characteristic – even with the broad definition of consideration in New Zealand GST, the courts have been reluctant to see an expenditure for consumption where there is no direct link between a payment and a supply. To include collective consumption is foreign to the character of the VAT. Even in cases where it is just a flow-through, as in New Zealand, the deeming of collective services and payments as falling within the scope deviates from the basic characteristics of the VAT.

This leads to the two important conclusions as regards the implications of the character of the tax, and the New Zealand experience, on the design features of a VAT and the treatment of public bodies. First, public bodies ought to be viewed as intermediaries in VAT, i.e., as taxable persons in EU terminology, as they are not private entities capable of making expenditure for private consumption. They should in principle have the right to deduct VAT charged on acquisitions.

Second, a nexus between the payment and a supply should be required in order for the payment to be subject to VAT. The distinction made in section §1.03[D] between various ways of funding would then be relevant to the application of VAT/GST. The 'economic scope' of the nexus ought to be considered. Taxes, subsidies and grants should not be subject to VAT. Consideration paid for services provided should be subject to VAT and fees and dues paid should also be taxed.

The first conclusion conforms to the view presented by Aujean, Jenkins and Poddar, and other commentators; that public bodies ought to be included fully within the scope of the VAT system. The right to deduct input VAT is inherent in the inclusion within the scope of VAT (whenever an input is not directly linked to an exempt output, i.e., the right to deduct exists when the input is linked to activities funded by taxes and other income falling outside the scope of VAT, see further below). Importantly, what nexus is required between a payment and a supply, and whether subsidies and taxes are covered or not, do not influence this conclusion. Public bodies are taxable persons and all their activities ought to be considered as, or deemed to be, economic activities. This conclusion also seems to conform to the present understanding among commentators on what the preferred system design ought to be.

26. For the reasons presented by Englisch as well as based on my previous assessment of the legal structure of the VAT and its inherent character, see Henkow (2008), Chapter 3.

§15.04 DESIGNING AN EXCLUSION SYSTEM

In Part II of this book, the EU exemption system was discussed. It was shown that in order to determine whether a public body is excluded or not, several issues need to be addressed. First, it needs to be determined whether the activity of the public body is an economic activity at all for VAT purposes. When the activity cannot be performed on the market, it does in principle not fall within the scope of VAT. Second, it needs to be determined whether the body is governed by public law or private law. Only the legal regime applicable under national law can determine which applies. Exclusions are not made in EU VAT for public administration tasks performed by private law entities. Third, it needs to be determined whether the activity in question is governed by public law or private law. Consequently, a public body is only excluded from the field of application of the EU VAT system when, either the activity as such is not economic in nature, or it is governed by public law, under the national law applicable.

Two limitations apply to the latter exclusion in order to ensure that distortions of competition will not arise – in order to respect the principle of fiscal neutrality in respect of VAT. First, a number of listed activities are not covered by the exclusion (and Member States may consider that this limitation is not applicable when activities are carried out on a negligible scale). Second, a test must always be made whether competition will be distorted if the public body is treated as such.

Member States have certain discretion to determine the scope of the exclusion due to the fact that the status of 'public body acting as such' is determined with reference to national law. Importantly, this discretion does not extend to determining when the exclusion does not apply due to the fact that distortions of competition arise. That question, which is a finding of facts subject to review of national courts, is not left to Member States' discretion.[27]

The reference to Member States' national law implies that differences exist between the Member States. This has also been confirmed by the Copenhagen Economics' study, there is unequal treatment between different Member States. This is an inevitable consequence of the reliance on national law and the differences in public administration practices between the Member States.

The exclusion has lead to a preference to self-supply and some Member States have enacted VAT compensation schemes for public bodies to deal with this distortion.

As pointed out already in the first chapter, exclusions from the VAT system lead to a number of economical distortions and problems. They violate the general applicability of the tax, they result in tax cascading, they create a preference to vertically integrate and self-supply and they lead to administrative and compliance burdens. The fact that the EU system entails an exclusion is thus in itself less desirable from a system design perspective.[28] There is also a wide consensus among commentators that a full taxation system is preferable. However, if an exclusion system is considered to be desirable, for some reason or another, or a radical change to the EU

27. See, for a somewhat different view, de la Feria, *Intertax* (2008).
28. The character of the VAT and implications on the system's design are discussed further below.

system is not an option for political reasons, the issue arises whether the EU system nevertheless should be kept intact or (substantially) reformed.

In order to answer this question, it ought to be kept in mind that the EU consists, at the time of writing, of 27 independent states with their own culture with regard to public administration and their own public laws. It would probably be very difficult to harmonise the regulations on public bodies completely within the EU. Any exclusion would thus have to accept a certain margin of discretion for the Member States to apply it to their national structure of public bodies. Nonetheless, there seems to me to be room for significant improvements.

In my view and from a systematic point of view, the basic structure and thinking behind the exclusion, as interpreted by the Court of Justice, is sound. If an exclusion is made from the general rule that all economic activities fall within the scope of the tax, that exclusion ought to be subject to guarantees as regards fiscal neutrality. The neutrality of a VAT system is inherent in the general characteristic of the tax. It would be a flagrant breach of this neutrality to treat differently, similar supplies which are, from the recipient's point of view, exchangeable and thus in competition with one another. It therefore makes sense to have an exclusion for public bodies which is limited to situations where there is a distortion of competition. In one aspect however, a fundamental change is needed. It has to be made clear that all activities of public bodies are in principle 'economic activities' for VAT purposes (unless they concern the redistribution of funds in which case they fall outside the field of application but should still entail the right to deduct input VAT).

The system with references to national law to determine the scope of the exclusion is problematic. Even provided that distortions of competition arising within a country are handled through the limitations of the exclusion (when distortions of competition arise), the fact remains that those acquiring goods and services from public bodies in one country will be charged VAT while in another country they will not. As a consequence, the basis of assessment will therefore vary between the Member States. In addition, competition may also be distorted between the Member States as those taxable persons that have no right to deduct and acquire goods or services from public bodies will either have to pay VAT on the price or not, depending on in which country they acquire the services. If the taxable persons' services are supplied internationally and in competition, distortions of competition arise.[29]

Best practice, if the exclusion for public bodies should be kept, must therefore be to reduce the scope of the exclusion as much as politically possible, to clarify that all the activities of public bodies are 'economic activities' for VAT purposes and to find a definition of public bodies not relying on national law. The latter may however, considering the diversity of Member States' public administration, be difficult.

29. Agreeably, these kinds of distortions also arise due to the fact that Member States apply different VAT rates. Consider a bank that competes on the EU market underwriting a share issue. In countries such as Sweden and Denmark, acquisitions liable to VAT normally carry a VAT element of 20% of the cost (VAT rate is 25%). This would only be 13% in a country with a VAT rate of 15%. The difference in VAT rate is in itself distortive in a VAT system where exemptions are applied.

Furthermore, the exclusion should be limited when distortions of competition arise. The structure of the provision can be improved. The fact that some listed activities are presumed to lead to distortions of competition, and therefore fall within the scope, should be clarified. This list should also be updated and include as many activities as politically possible. Provided the activity is not on the list, the public body should still be treated as a taxable person when distortions of competition arise. Whether there is a need to determine the factors relevant when the existence of a distortion of competition is present could be discussed. (It should be clarified that distortions of competition may also arise cross-border within the EU.) Guidelines issued by the European Commission on how to interpret the provisions would be welcome. Lastly, it may need to be clarified that all direct expenditure, including fees and charges legally payable, are covered by European VAT.

Even with the above improvements to the present exclusion, economic distortions will continue to arise, such as a preference to self-supply vis-à-vis contracting out. If an exclusion system is chosen, there is therefore a need to reflect upon whether a VAT compensation scheme ought to be enacted on a EU wide basis.

Where an exclusion system is used, VAT compensation schemes do have benefits. They mitigate the distortion created against contracting out and thus increase neutrality but they could also bring about new distortions if compensation is paid to public bodies engaged in exempt activities in competition with private sector entities.

At this juncture I note that the Australian system seems to be very similar to a VAT compensation scheme for public bodies – but with the inclusion of public sector bodies within the scope of the tax and an exemption with credit for public administration. There are technical differences between the Australian full taxation system and the VAT compensation schemes in the way that they seek to achieve neutrality between self-supplying and contracting out, and the manner in which they deal with other distortions arising due to the refunding of input VAT to public bodies. The end result is nonetheless very similar. The Canadian rebate system is also similar to the VAT compensation schemes, seemingly most similar to the Danish schemes.[30] There are two important differences between the full tax systems and the exclusion systems with compensation schemes. In a full taxation model, the default rule is that VAT is due on considerations for supplies and that VAT on acquisitions is deductible. In an exclusion system, the default rule is that a public body falls outside the field of application and VAT is refundable only when specifically stated. The full taxation system is therefore most consistent with the character of the VAT and is also potentially easier to administer.

The Swedish and Danish compensation schemes have been dealt with in detail in this book. As is clear from the discussion, these compensation schemes do not cover all public bodies. Neither are they especially easily grasped. They are also subject to frequent change. One aspect that has led to changes and discussion is the funding of the system. In some cases there has been a deliberate intention to create a self-contained system while in others the compensation systems have been integrated with central

30. Millar (2012) also notes this similarity.

government's budget. It was found in Chapter 8 that both types of VAT compensation systems are questionable from a state aid perspective - irrespective of how they are funded. In order to eliminate the risk of being prohibited as state aid, and presuming that a full taxation system is not introduced, VAT compensation schemes should be regulated as part of the EU VAT system.

It is advisable to extend the compensation scheme to non-deductible VAT incurred by non-profit making private entities involved in socially important activities, as in Norway. In my opinion, the general right to compensation should be subject to a general limitation (that may be explained by national authorities) to the effect that if the public body is involved in an activity in competition with entities that are not entitled to compensation, no compensation should be paid (as in Norway but as a general rule). In the VAT Directive, neutrality in competition is more important a goal than combating horizontal integration.

Compensation for indirect VAT costs on an EU wide basis would be preferable from a tax neutrality point of view, but the problems in calculating the right compensation levels, with different structures of public administration and rates of VAT in the Member States, must be insurmountable. It would therefore be advisable not to include such a feature in an EU wide compensation scheme. Since in addition, such compensation could be said to discriminate on grounds of nationality, the compensation scheme should generally and preferably also be applicable to all EU VAT, not only domestic VAT within the EU.

It seems not to be necessary to apply the approach to central government. Government agencies can simply calculate acquisitions without VAT (exclude it from their budget). VAT should be charged on all supplies made for consideration - in accordance with the ordinary rules.

Lastly, it ought to be remembered that the problems handled through a compensation scheme would not disappear were the exemptions to be abolished, but the pressure on the compensation schemes would definitely decrease. All changes that make the tax more general, increase the scope of taxable persons so that public bodies are also included and decrease the number and/or scope of exemptions, reduce the distortions and increase neutrality. Such a reform would also conform to the character of the tax as it would seek to restore its fundamental design features and characteristics. It should therefore always be the preferred choice, whenever possible.

§15.05 DESIGNING A FULL TAX SYSTEM

A full tax model is advocated by commentators and the conclusion reached here is also that inclusion of public bodies within the scope of VAT conforms (the best) to the character of the tax, also from a philosophical perspective. The EU exclusion system clearly entails difficulties and does not conform with the basic design of the VAT. Considering the research undertaken, a preferred treatment will now be presented in the following theorems.

> All public bodies are treated as taxable persons. Independently of whether they are performing economic activities or not they are deemed to be taxable persons.

There seem to be few conceptual or legal issues with incorporating public bodies as such in the VAT system. Article 13 of the VAT Directive merely needs to be abolished. The actual inclusion is also relatively simple in Australia and New Zealand. Public bodies are simply mentioned as one type of body which is deemed to be involved in economic activities. In European VAT, this would entail a shift in the legal position as an activity such as the issuing of licences to use the electromagnetic spectrum would be considered to constitute an economic activity per definition, and not to be a non-economic activity as is the case today. If for political reasons, VAT should not to be charged on consideration for public administration services supplied (such as the issue of the licences mentioned), an exemption (or rather zero-rating) for public administration needs to be enacted.[31] Conceptually there seem to be very few issues involved in such a shift. Rather, it would entail a move to a more conceptually sound situation if public bodies were to be included within the VAT system and effectively treated as non-consumers.

One consequence would be that all payments between public bodies would be zero-rated unless for specific services (see below). For simplification reasons, all payments could be deemed to be considered as falling outside the scope of VAT, where the seller and the acquirer are both public bodies. This would reduce the tension in the system but is not essential for the fundamentals in a system design perspective.

> All VAT on acquisitions by public bodies is deemed to be incurred for taxed activities unless the acquisitions relate to supplies made in competition with private undertakings which do not have a right to deduct VAT.

All input VAT incurred by a public body should be deductible, as VAT can never, in principle, be incurred for private consumption purposes.[32] The deductible input VAT on deemed economic activities is thus treated as ordinary deductible input VAT. The VAT system however provides for exemptions from VAT not entailing a right to deduct input VAT, such as Article 132 of the VAT Directive, and limitations when non-economic activities are performed. For reasons of eliminating distortions of competition between public sector bodies and private sector bodies, the same rules on deduction should be applicable for both kinds of entities. To minimise any disincentive to contracting out, this limitation ought only to be applied in situations where competition with private undertakings exists. Arguably, there may be an issue concerning neutrality with private sector entities depending on how the deductible proportion is calculated with regard to activities falling outside the scope of VAT funded by taxes or general subsidies not constituting consideration. Conceptually however, there are no difficulties; public bodies should be able to deduct input VAT incurred for all activities (including deemed deductible input VAT) unless linked to transactions not entailing such a right as suggested in the theorem.

31. The content, wording and scope of the exemption should of course be discussed. In principle it ought to be as limited as possible in order to adhere to the general characteristics of the tax.
32. Agreeably, anti-avoidance rules need to be present, where employees of a public body uses the body to acquire goods and services for their own consumption. However, mechanisms to deal with such a situation exist – the self-supply rules. These would be applicable to public bodies as well.

The self-supply bias inherent in the very existence of exemptions, and present also in situations where there is competition between private and public bodies, should preferably be dealt with by abolishing the exemptions and zero-rating activities which are performed also by private sector entities at least if they are non-profit making. An alternative would be to tax internal supplies (see further below).

> The definition of the nexus between the supply and payment is such that it includes any utility paid for directly.

The conclusion was reached in section §1.03[D] that a tension exists between the differentiation in VAT/GST treatment based on how activities are funded and the fact that the same type of activity could be funded in different ways. As it was found in the evaluation based on the character of the VAT in section §15.03 that the 'economic scope' of the nexus should be applied in VAT, the situation will occur that some activities performed by public bodies are funded through income not subject to VAT when private undertakings, engaged in exactly the same activity, will have to charge VAT on their fees/income. Whether the recommended nexus (based on an assessment in the light of the character of the tax) should be followed in practice is therefore not self-evident. Poddar seems to have a preference towards having a broader definition of the nexus, by also including general grants and possibly taxes, for reasons of simplicity and to minimise incentives for substitution of non-taxable consideration for taxable amounts. I would however consider such a broadening to be inadvisable for the reasons discussed above.

The present treatment in the EU, where the taxable amount is extended to include also subsidies 'almost directly linked' could be questioned on the basis that this is stretching the boundaries of the character of the tax. Reference to the economic scope is advisable. The problem of distortions of competition between tax-funded activities and those not funded by taxes or subsidies should be dealt with through other measures than changing the nature of the direct link.

In addition to broadening the direct link requirement, there are, in principle, three methods of dealing with the distortions. First, the open market value for VAT purposes could be applied whenever a taxed activity is funded by subsidies or taxes. Article 72 of the VAT Directive entails a definition of the open market value which could be made applicable. Second, internal supplies of services could be taxed when used for exempt supplies. Internal supply provisions are present in European VAT, Articles 18 and 27 of the VAT Directive which set out the method used to deal with the distortions emanating from the existence of exemptions and the preference to self-supply intrinsic in the very existence of exemptions. Lastly, exempt supplies, funded by subsidies or taxes, and made in competition with non-funded suppliers, could be zero-rated.

Generally, applying the open market value or taxing internal supplies will not result in complete neutrality in competition vis-à-vis private undertakings. The open market value does not take into consideration the fact that some service providers are more cost effective and are therefore able to charge a lower price. The price is the same no matter how efficient the producer is. Similarly, the taxation of internal supplies does not take into account production efficiencies, as the open market value is also applied to internal supplies according to Article 77 of the VAT Directive.

Consequently, the only absolute guarantee for equal treatment between public bodies and private undertakings is to zero-rate supplies that are funded through taxes and performed by public bodies in competition with private undertakings. In Australia, the distortions created by differences in funding are dealt with by zero-rating certain activities where there is both government and private involvement (health care and education). While this is the preferred solution from a neutrality point of view it may be ruled out for fiscal reasons (revenue will be reduced). In addition, it may be hard to list all activities where substitution would presumably be a problem since it would depend on what the activities actually are that the public bodies are carrying out in competition with private undertakings. Nonetheless, some activities, such as health care and education, are currently exempt 'in the public interest' in European VAT. As regards these activities, it is generally acknowledged that they should receive a beneficial treatment for VAT purposes. Zero-rating should therefore in my view be applied to these kinds of activities.

> When funds emanating from taxes or subsidies not falling within the scope of VAT are used to finance activities that are currently exempt in the public interest, zero-rating is applied.

If zero-rating public interest activities could not be achieved politically, an internal supply method should be used. VAT on acquisitions directly linked to exempt supplies (i.e., not to the internal supplies) needs to be turned into a cost so as to put public bodies on equal footing with private undertakings. Internally supplied services should be taxed - otherwise the self-supply bias incidental to exemptions would entail a bias against contracting out for public bodies. The internal supply method is however not without flaws. It requires that the internal supplies that should be taxed are listed. It would be difficult to do this in a comprehensive and neutral manner.[33] In addition, the internal supply method is administratively burdensome. Denmark, for example, applied such a method for its local governments prior to establishing the VAT compensation funds. The method was abolished because a system with refunds of VAT expenditure on purchases was perceived, as administratively simpler and more efficient, since the communes in the new system did not have to add VAT to their calculations. Be that as it may, the internal supply method should be made to apply as regards internally produced services by public bodies used for exempt outputs in order to ensure a more neutral treatment with private entities.

In situations when supplies are taxed with VAT distortions may also occur between a government entity funded by taxes and private undertakings. Here, the open market value should be applied. Applying the open market value is a departure from the fundamental principle in VAT systems according to which only the actual consideration is taxed and therefore also breaches the principle of neutrality. However, the fact that taxes are used to fund activities is, in itself a breach of the principle of neutrality, as the value added is not taxed in these situations. Applying the open market

33. The problems are discussed in Henkow (2008), Chapter 7.6.

value to remedy this distortion in competition and breach of the principle of neutrality can therefore be defended. Public bodies should therefore be required to charge VAT based on the open market value of their taxed supplies. Non-public bodies whose activities are funded, wholly or partially, through subsidies not subject to VAT should be required to charge VAT based on the open market value of their taxed supplies only when they are engaged in such activities in competition with entities not funded, wholly or partially, through subsidies.

> Public bodies are required to charge VAT calculated with reference to the open market value of their taxed supplies. Non-public bodies whose activities are funded through subsidies not subject to VAT should be required to charge VAT, based on the open market value of their taxed supplies, only when they are engaged in such activities in competition with entities not funded through subsidies.

Bibliography

Aldestam. EC Stat Aid Rules Applied to Taxes – An Analysis of the Selectivity Criterion. Iustus, 2005.

Aujean, M., P. Jenkins & S. Poddar. 'A New Approach to Public Sector Bodies'. International VAT Monitor July/August (1999): 144–149.

Alley et al. New Zealand Taxation 2010: Principles, Cases and Questions. Thomson Reuters, 2010.

Attanasio, Orazio P. & Guglielmo Weber. 'Consumption and Saving: Models of Intertemporal Allocation and Their Implications for Public Policy'. Journal of Economic Literature 48, no. 3 (2010): 693–751(59).

Barker. Public Services in Western Europe 1660–1930. Oxford University Press, 1994.

Barrand. The Taxation of Non-Profit Bodies and Government Entities under the New Zealand Goods and Services Tax. Paper for the International Conference on Administrative Aspects of a Value Added Tax, Washington DC, 11–12 October 1990.

Barrand. 'The Taxation of Non-profit Bodies and Government Entities under the New Zealand GST'. International VAT Monitor January (1991): 2.

Bird & Gendron. Sales Taxes in Canada: The GST-HST-QST-RST 'System', Final Draft: 29 May 2009, available at www.americantaxpolicyinstitute.org (visited on 22 August 2011).

Blanchard, P. 'Some Basic Concepts of New Zealand GST'. In GST in Retrospect and Prospect, ed. Krever & White. Brookers, 2007.

Bogdan. Komparativ rättskunskap. Norstedts, 1993.

Boston, J., et al. Public Management: The New Zealand Model. Oxford University Press, 1996.

Chang. 'An Institutionalist Perspective on the Role of the State – Towards an Institutionalist Political Economy'. In Institutions and the Role of the State, ed. Burlamaqui, Castro & Chang. Edward Elgar, 2000.

Copenhagen Economics and KPMG. VAT in the Public Sector and Exemptions in the Public Interest. Final report for TAXUD/2009/DE/316, 1 March 2011.

Cnossen. 'Global Trends and Issues in Value Added Taxation'. International Tax and Public Finance 5 (1998): 399–428.

van Dijk & Lubbers. 'The VAT Compensation Fun(d)?'. International VAT-Monitor 11 (2000): 6–9.

Dickson. 'The New Zealand GST Policy Choice: An Historical and Policy Perspective'. In GST in Retrospect and Prospect, ed. Krever & White. Wellington: Brookers, 2007.

Dijkgraaf & Gradus. 'Cost Savings of Contracting Out Refuse Collection', Empirica 30 (2003): 377–396.

Douglas, R. 'The New Zealand GST Policy Choice and Its Political Implications'. In GST in Retrospect and Prospect, ed. Krever & White. Wellington: Brookers, 2007.

Due, J. 'The New Zealand Goods & Services (Value-Added) Tax – A Model for Other Countries'. Canadian Tax Journal 36 (1988): 198.

Ebrill, Keen, Bodin & Summers. The Modern VAT. IMF, 2001.

Ernst & Young. A Study of the Methods of Taxation of Public Bodies, prepared for the European Commission, 30 April 1998.

De la Feria, R. 'VAT and Public Bodies in EC Member States'. Intertax 36, nos 6/7 (2008): 268.

De la Feria. The EU VAT System and the Internal Market. IBFD, 2009.

Englisch. 'VAT/GST and Direct Taxes: Different Purposes'. In Value Added Tax and Direct Taxation, Similarities and Differences, ed. Lang, Melz & Kristoffersson. IBFD, 2009.

Flinders. 'Distributed Public Governance in the European Union'. Journal of European Public Policy 11, no. 3 (2004): 520–544.

Gendron. 'Value Added Tax Treatment of Public Sector Bodies and Non-profit Organizations: A Developing Country Perspective'. Bulletin of International Taxation December (2005): 514.

Gendron. 'How Should the U.S. Treat Government Entities, Nonprofit Organizations, and Other Tax-Exempt Bodies under a VAT?'. Tax Law Review 63 (Winter 2010): 477.

Gjems-Onstad. Merverdiavgift – en innføring. 8th edn. Gyldendal, 2009.

Gjems-Onstad. 'Refund of Input VAT to Norwegian NPOs'. International VAT Monitor 4 (2004): 244.

Gill. 'New Zealand'. In Distributed Public Governance: Agencies, Authorities and Other Government Bodies, ed. OECD (OECD, 2002).

Goode. Government Finance in Developing Countries. Washington: Brookings Institute, 1984.

Gottfried & Wiegard. 'Exemption versus Zero Rating: A Hidden Problem of VAT'. Journal of Public Economics 46 (1991): 307–328.

Green. 'Consulting the Public in Developing a GST'. In GST in Retrospect and Prospect, ed. Krever & White. Wellington: Brookers, 2007.

Handler, et al. 'The Size and Performance of Public Sector Activities in Europe'. WIFO Working Papers 246, WIFO. Austrian Institute of Economic Research, 2005.

Harries et al. Income Tax in New Zealand. Wellington: Brookers, 2004.

Henkow. Financial Activities in European VAT: A Theoretical and Legal Research of the European VAT System and the Actual and Preferred Treatment of Financial Activities. Kluwer Law International, 2008.

Henkow. 'Neutrality of VAT for Taxable Persons; A New Approach in European VAT?'. EC Tax Review 17, no. 5 (2008): 233.

IMF. Where Does the Public Sector End and the Private Sector Begin?. IMF Working Paper, WP/09/122 (2009), by Lienert.

Jiménez. 'VAT and Public Bodies in EC Member States'. Intertax 36, nos 6/7 (2008): 268–281.

Karlsson. Statliga stöd till banksektorn. Institutionen för handelsrätt. Lund University, 2011.

Koul. Guide to the WTO and GATT: Economics, Law, and Politics. Kluwer Law International, 2005.

Lear, Mossialos & Karl. 'EU Competition law and Health Policy'. In Health Systems Governance in Europe: The Role of European Union Law and Policy, ed. Mossialos, Permanand, Baeten & Hervey. Cambridge University Press, 2010.

Luja. 'Tax-Related Difficulties of State Aid Rules'. In Accounting and Taxation & Assessment of ECJ Case Law, vol. 5, ed. Lang & Vanistendael, EATLP International Tax Series (Helsinki: EATLP Congress, 2007).

Luja. 'Investment Funds, Tax Planning and State Aid'. European Taxation, December 2006.

Mamut. 'The State Aid Provisions of the TFEU in Tax Matters'. In Introduction to European Tax Law on Direct Taxation, 2nd edn, ed. Lang, Pistone, Schuch & Staringer. Linde, 2010.

Martin. ADD. 2008.

McKenzie. GST – A Practical Guide. 8th edn. CCH, 2008.

Millar. 'Echoes of Source and Residence in VAT Jurisdictional Rules'. In Value Added Tax and Direct Taxation: Similarities and Differences, ed. Lang, Melz & Kristoffersson. IBFD, 2009.

Millar. 'Smoke and Mirrors: Applying the Full Taxation Model to Government under the Australian and New Zealand GST Laws'. In VAT Exemptions: Consequences and Design Alternatives, ed. de la Feria (The Hague: Kluwer Law International, 2012).

Morden. 'Fifteen Years of Value Added Tax in South Africa'. In GST in Retrospect and Prospect, ed. Krever & White. Thomson Brookers, 2007.

de Secondat & Montesquieu. Translated by Thomas Nugent 1752, Batoche Books, 2001 [1748] (Montesquieu).

Muir. 'The Goods and Services Tax: Reflections on the New Zealand Experience, Six Years On'. Revenue Law Journal 3 (1993).

Musgrave & Musgrave. Public Finance in Theory and Practice. 5th edn. McGraw-Hill, 1989.

OECD. Distributed Public Governance: Agencies, Authorities and Other Government Bodies. OECD, 2002.

Poddar. Application of VAT to Public Bodies. Presentation at the International Tax Dialogue VAT Conference, Rome, 15–16 March 2005, available at http://www.itdweb.org/Pages/Conferences.aspx (accessed on 21 July 2012).

Privattandläkarna. Hinder för konkurrens på lika villkor inom tandvården består - ett helhetsgrepp är nödvändigt. April 2006.

Prosser. 'EU Competition Law and Public Services'. In Health Systems Governance in Europe: The Role of European Union Law and Policy, ed. Mossialos, Permanand, Baeten & Hervey. Cambridge University Press, 2010.

PSIRU (Public Services International Research Unit), University of Greenwich. Public Services in Europe; Trends and Developments, available at www.psiru.org, 2004 (visited on 2011-09-27).

Schön. 'Taxation and State Aid Law in the European Union'. CMLR 36 (1999): 911–936.

Scott, Ball & Dale. 'New Zealand's Public Sector Management Reform: Implications for the United States'. Journal of Policy Analysis and Management 16, no. 3 (1997): 357–381.

Schenk & Oldman. Value Added Tax: A Comparative Approach. Cambridge University Press, 2007.

Stephens. 'The Economic and Equity Effects of GST in New Zealand'. In GST in Retrospect and Prospect, ed. Krever & White. Brookers, 2007.

Tait. Value Added Tax: International Practice and Problems. IMF, 1988.

Terra. Sales Taxation: The Case of Value Added Tax in the European Community. Kluwer, 1988.

Terra. 'Value Added Tax and State Aid Law in the EU'. In VAT in an EU and International Perspective: Essays in Honour of Han Kogels, ed. van Arendonk & van der Paardt. IBFD, 2011.

Terra & Kajus. European VAT Directives; Introduction to European VAT. IBFD, 2012.

Terra & Kajus. A Guide to the European VAT Directives [Online]. Amsterdam: IBFD, available from http://online 2.ibfd.org/evd/ (accessed on 21 July 2012).

Thuronyi. Comparative Tax Law. Kluwer Law International, 2003.

Tilly. Coercion, Capital and European States, AD 990–1992. Blackwell, 1992.

Todd. 'Implementing GST - Information, Education, Co-ordination'. In GST in Retrospect and Prospect, ed. Krever & White. Brookers, 2007.

Tridimas. The General Principles of EU Law. 2nd edn. Oxford University Press, 2006.

Verkuil. 'Public Law Limitations on Privatization of Government Functions'. N.C. Law. Rev. 397 (2006): 2005–2006.

Wallace. 'Increasing Economic Integration: Implications for GST/VAT in the Asia-Pacific Region'. In GST in Retrospect and Prospect, ed. Krever & White. Brookers, 2007.

Wassenaar & Gradus. 'Contracting Out: The Importance of a Solution for the VAT Distortion'. CESifo Economic Studies 50, no. 2 (2004): 377.

Wassenaar, Dijkgraaf & Gradus. 'Contracting Out: Dutch Municipalities Reject the Solution for the VAT-Distortion'. Local Government Studies 36, no. 5 (2010): 617–536.

White. 'Appelate Interpretation of New Zealand's GST Legislation; An Initial Survey: 1986–2005'. Australian GST Journal 5, no. 10 (2005): 205.

White. 'Twenty Years of GST: The Best Path Forward'. New Zealand Journal of Taxation Law and Policy 13, no. 3 (2007): 357.

Williams. 'Value Added Tax'. In Tax Law Design and Drafting, ed. Thuronyi. IMF, 1996, Chapter 6.

Yang. 'VAT Treatment of Government Procurement: A Comparative Analysis'. International VAT Monitor September/October (2005): 34.

Official Legal References

European Union Official Material

Council Regulation (EC) No 1777/2005 of 17 October 2005 laying down implementing measures for Directive 77/388/EEC on the common system of value added tax

First Council Directive (EEC) No 67/227 of 11 April 1967 on the harmonisation of legislation of Member States concerning turnover taxes

Second Council Directive (EEC) No 67/228 of 11 April 1967, on the harmonisation of legislation of Member States concerning turnover taxes - Structure and procedures for application of the common system of value added tax

Sixth Council Directive (EEC) No 77/388 of 17 May 1977 on the harmonisation of the laws of the Member States relating to turnover taxes - Common system of value added tax: uniform basis of assessment

Council Directive (EC) 2006/112 of 28 November 2006 on the common system of value added tax, OJ of 11.12.2006, L347, as amended latest by Council Directive 2010/88/EU of 7 December 2010

Amended proposal for a Directive for the harmonisation amongst Member States of turnover tax Legislation, submitted by the Commission to the Council on 12 June 1964. Available at Terra, B. & Kajus, J. 2007, A Guide to the European VAT Directives (Online) Amsterdam IBFD. Available from http://online 2.ibfd.org/evd/ (accessed on 15 February 2007), Part 5.3.1

Proposal for a second Council directive for the harmonisation among Member States of turnover tax legislation, concerning the form and the methods of application of the common system of taxation on value added, Brussels, 14 April 1965, available at Terra & Kajus (2007), A Guide to the European VAT Directives (Online) Amsterdam IBFD. Available from http://online 2.ibfd.org/evd/ (accessed on 15 February 2007), Part 5.3.1

Proposal for a Sixth Council Directive on the harmonisation of Member States concerning turnover taxes Common system of value added tax: Uniform basis of assessment (submitted to the Council by the Commission on 29 June 1973):

Bulletin of the European Communities Supplement 11/73 (Proposal for a Sixth Directive, 1973)

Amendments to the proposal for a sixth Council Directive on the harmonisation of legislation of Member States concerning turnover taxes - Common system of value added tax: uniform basis of assessment; OJ C 121, 34 of 11 October 1974

First Report from the Commission to the Council on the application of the common system of value added tax, submitted in accordance with Article 34 of the Sixth Council Directive (77/388/EEC) of 17 May 1977. COM(83) 426 final

Commission Regulation (EC) No 1998/2006 of 15 December 2006 on the application of Articles 87 and 88 of the Treaty to de minimis aid, OJ, L 379, 28 December 2006

Report on the implementation of the Commission notice on the application of the State aid rules to measures relating to direct business taxation, COM(2004) 434, 9 February 2004

Council Directive 2009/162/EU of 22 December 2009 amending various provisions of Directive 2006/112/EC on the common system of value added tax

European Commission Decision of 6 September 2005 on the aid scheme implemented by Italy for certain undertakings for collective investment in transferable securities specialised in shares of small- and medium-capitalisation companies listed on regulated markets, OJ L268/1, 27 September 2006

Commission Decision of 28 November 2005 on the application of Article 86(2) of the EC Treaty to State aid in the form of public service compensation granted to certain undertakings entrusted with the operation of services of general economic interest (2005/842/EC)

Commission notice on the application of the State aid rules to measures relating to business taxation, OJ C 384/3, 10 December 1998

COM(2000) 348 final, Communication from the Commission to the Council and the European Parliament a Strategy to Improve the Operation of the Vat System within the Context of the Internal Market

COM(2003) 614 final, Communication from the Commission to the Council, the European Parliament and the European Economic and Social Committee, Review and update of VAT strategy priorities

Proposal for a Council Directive on the common system of value added tax (Reast) COM(2004) 246 final

Proposal for a Council Directive amending VAT Directive 2006/112/EC of 28 November 2006 on the common system of value added tax, COM(2007) 677 final

Green paper On the future of VAT: Towards a simpler, more robust and efficient VAT system, COM(2010) 695 final

Commission staff working document, Accompanying document to the Green Paper on the future of VAT: Towards a simpler, more robust and efficient VAT system, SEC(2010) 1455

Study, commissioned by the European Parliament's Committee on Budgetary Control, in the framework of the discharge 2006: Agencies, rapporteur H.-P. Martin. 'Best practice in governance of agencies – A comparative study in view of identifying best practice for governing agencies carrying out activities on behalf of the European Union', published by the European Parliament, 2008 (EP Study)

Communication from the Commission to the European Parliament, the Council, the European Economic and Social Committee and the Committee of the regions: Reform of the EU State Aid Rules on Services of General Economic Interest, COM(2011) 146 final

European Parliament, Question to the EP, PWQ 2000, P-2861/99, OJ C225 E/211, 7 January 2000

EFTA Surveillance Authority

EFTA Surveillance Authority Decision, No 155/07/COL of 3 May 2007 on State aid granted in connection with Article 3 of the Norwegian Act on compensation for value added tax (VAT) (Norway), OJ L 18 September 2008, 249/35

National Official Material

Australia

Australian Government, Australian Taxation Office, Goods and Services Tax Ruling, Goods and services tax: grants of financial assistance, GSTR 2000/11

Denmark

Finansministeriet's Økonomisk Administrative Vejledning (ØAV), www.oes.dk/oeav

BEK nr 1168 af 08/12/2008 Bekendtgørelse om momskompensation til institutioner for erhvervsrettet uddannelse, institutioner for almengymnasiale uddannelser og almen voksenuddannelse, erhvervsakademier, professionshøjskoler m.fl

Forslag til Lov om udligning af visse kommunale og amtskommunale udgifter til merværdiafgift og om Det kommunale Momsfond, LFF 1983–1984.2.117.

Betænkning nr 1437 from the Indenrigs- og Sundhedsminsteriets Finansieringsudvalg 'Et nyt udligningssystem'

Forslag til Lov om konkurrencemæssig ligestilling mellem kommuners og regioners egenproduktion og køb af ydelser hos externe leverandører i relation til udgifter til merværdiafgift m.v. samt om momsfondet, from 29 March 2006 (from the minister of the Indenrigs- og Sundhedsministeriet), 2005/1 LSF 192

Skat, Momsvejledningen 2010-2 (Gældende fra den 20. juli 2010)

BEK nr 28 af 06/01/2011 Gældene, offentliggörelsedato 19-01-2011, Indenrigs- og Sundedsministeriet

Letter to Viborg Kommune, J.nr. 2008–4504 of the Sundhedsministeriet of 8 January 2009

Finland

Mervärdesskattelag 30.12.1993/1501 (accessed at www.finlex.fi on 21 July 2012)
Skatteförvaltningens Anvisning DNr 41/40/2002 10.01.2002 Avstående från att återkräva mervärdesskatt och kalkylerad återbäring av kommunernas skattefria anskaffningar i anslutning till hälso- och sjukvård

New Zealand

Constitution Act 1986 (Public Act 1986 No 114, Date of assent 13 December 1986)
Local Government Act 2002 (Public Act 2002 No 84, Date of assent 24 December 2002)
Local Government Rating Act 2002
The Treasury (2005), A Guide to the Public Finance Act
Goods & Services Tax; A booklet explaining measures announced in the 1984 budget, 8 November 1984
Budget Report No. 68 of the New Zealand Treasury of 24 September 1984 to the Minister of Finance, entitled 'Value Added Tax: Public Utilities and Government Departments'
Governmental Paper B 27 (1985), Proposals for the Administration of the Goods and Services Tax (White paper)
New Zealand Inland Revenue, Tax Information Bulletin, Volume 3, No. 1
Inland Revenue Department Tax Information Bulletin: Vol. 16, No 1 (February 2004)
Tax Information Bulletin volume 3, No. 1
Budget Report No. 68 of the New Zealand Treasury of 24 September 1984 to the Minister of Finance, entitled 'Value Added Tax: Public Utilities and Government Departments'
A Guide to the Public Finance Act, The Treasury, August 2005

Norway

2009-06-19-58 Lov om merverdiavgift (merverdiavgiftsloven) latest changed through Lov 2011-06-24–27
Lov 2003-12-12 nr 108: Lov om kompensasjon av merverdiavgift for kommuner, fylkeskommuner mv. As per 2011-01-01 (Kompensasjonsloven)

Sweden

Regeringsformen (SFS 1974:152), RF
Kommunallagen SFS 1991:900
Lagen (1993:387) om stöd och service till vissa funktionshindrade
Lagen (1994:1799 om kommuners och landstings hantering av mervärdesskatt för år 1995
Lag (1995:1518) om mervärdesskattekonton för kommuner och landsting

Lag (2005:807) om ersättning för viss mervärdesskatt för kommuner och landsting (usually called Ersättningslagen
Socialtjänstlagen (2001:453)
Mervärdesskattelagen, SFS 1994:200
Lag (1990:578) om särskilt bidrag till kommuner m.fl.
Lag (2005:807) om ersättning för viss mervärdesskatt för kommuner och landsting
Förordning (2005:811) om ersättning för viss mervärdesskatt för kommuner och landsting
Proposition 1968:100
Proposition 1995/96:64, Ett nytt utjämningssystem för kommuner och landsting, m.m.
Proposition 1997/98:153, Vissa kommunala frågor
Proposition 1989/90:111 om reformerad mervärdesskatt m.m.
Proposition 2001/02:112 Förändringar i kommunkontosystemet
Proposition 2008/09:50 Ett lyft för forskning och innovation
SOU 1999:133 Kommunkontosystemet och rättvisan - momsen kommunerna och konkurrensen
SOU 2001:50 Kontroll i kommunkontosystemet
Ds 1997:74 Ersättning för viss mervärdesskatt till kommuner och landsting
Ds 2001:30 Finansiering av kommunkontosystemet
Förordning om exportkreditgaranti (Export Credit Guarantee Ordinance), SFS 2007:656
RRV 2001:6 Kommunkontosystemet - en kartläggning
Riskdagen; www.riksdagen.se
Konkurrensverket, Konkurrens i tandvården, 1993
Konkurrensen i Sverige: Åtgärder för bättre konkurrens, Konkurrensverkets rapportserie 2009:4
Statskontoret. Om offentlig sektor: Färre men större - Statliga myndigheter åren 2007–2010. 2010
Ekonomistyrningsverket (The Swedish National Financial Management Authority), ESV 2001:12 Översyn av förordningen (1993:529) om myndigheters hantering av ingående mervärdesskatt
Ekonomistyrningsverket's webpage. www.esv.se (accessed on 21 October 2010)
Skatteverket (2010), Handledning för mervärdesskatt

United Kingdom

HM Revenue & Customs, Local Authorities and similar bodies, Notice 749 (April 2002)
Value Added Tax Act 1994, 5 July 1994

Table of Cases

European Union Case law

Cases (including pending cases) from the General Court

Cases (including pending cases) from the Court of Justice

National court cases

New Zealand

Sweden

Table of Conventions

Treaties

Conventions

Index

T

V

W

SERIES ON INTERNATIONAL TAXATION

1. Alberto Xavier, *The Taxation of Foreign Investment in Brazil,* 1980 (ISBN 90-200-0582-0).
2. Hugh J. Ault & Albert J. Rädler, *The German Corporation Tax Law with 1980 Amendments,* 1981 (ISBN 90-200-0642-8).
3. Paul R. McDaniel & Hugh J. Ault, *Introduction to United States International Taxation,* 1981 (ISBN 90-6544-004-6).
4. Albert J. Rädler, *German Transfer Pricing/Prix de Transfer en Allemagne,* 1984 (ISBN 90-6544-143-3).
5. Paul R. McDaniel & Stanley S. Surrey, *International Aspects of Tax Expenditures: A Comparative Study,* 1985 (ISBN 90-654-4163-8).
6. Kees van Raad, *Nondiscrimination in International Tax Law,* 1986 (ISBN 90-6544-266-9).
7. Sijbren Cnossen (ed.), *Tax Coordination in the European Community,* 1987 (ISBN 90-6544-272-3).
8. Ben Terra, *Sales Taxation. The Case of Value Added Tax in the European Community,* 1989 (ISBN 90-6544-381-9).
9. Rutsel S.J. Martha, *The Jurisdiction to Tax in International Law: Theory and Practice of Legislative Fiscal Jurisdiction,* 1989 (ISBN 90-654-4416-5).
10. Paul R. McDaniel & Hugh J. Ault, *Introduction to United States International Taxation* (3rd revised edition), 1989 (ISBN 90-6544-423-8).
11. Manuel Pires, *International Juridicial Double Taxation of Income,* 1989 (ISBN 90-6544-426-2).
12. A.H.M. Daniels, *Issues in International Partnership Taxation,* 1991 (ISBN 90-654-4577-3).
13. Arvid A. Skaar, *Permanent Establishment: Erosion of a Tax Treaty Principle,* 1992 (ISBN 90-6544-594-3).
14. Cyrille David & Geerten Michielse (eds), *Tax Treatment of Financial Instruments,* 1996 (ISBN 90-654-4666-4).
15. Herbert H. Alpert & Kees van Raad (eds), *Essays on International Taxation,* 1993 (ISBN 90-654-4781-4).
16. Wolfgang Gassner, Michael Lang & Eduard Lechner (eds), *Tax Treaties and EC Law,* 1997 (ISBN 90-411-0680-4).
17. Glória Teixeira, *Taxing Corporate Profits in the EU,* 1997 (ISBN 90-411-0703-7).
18. Michael Lang et al. (eds), *Multilateral Tax Treaties,* 1998 (ISBN 90-411-0704-5).
19. Stef van Weeghel, *The Improper Use of Tax Treaties,* 1998 (ISBN 90-411-0737-1).
20. Klaus Vogel (ed.), *Interpretation of Tax Law and Treaties and Transfer Pricing in Japan and Germany,* 1998 (ISBN 90-411-9655-2).
21. Bertil Wiman (ed.), *International Studies in Taxation: Law and Economics; Liber Amicorum Leif Mutén,* 1999 (ISBN 90-411-9692-7).

22. Alfonso J. Martín Jiménez, *Towards Corporate Tax Harmonization in the European Community,* 1999 (ISBN 90-411-9690-0).
23. Ramon J. Jeffery, *The Impact of State Sovereignty on Global Trade and International Taxation,* 1999 (ISBN 90-411-9703-6).
24. A.J. Easson, *Taxation of Foreign Direct Investment,* 1999 (ISBN 90-411-9741-9).
25. Marjaana Helminen, *The Dividend Concept in International Tax Law: Dividend Payments Between Corporate Entities,* 1999 (ISBN 90-411-9765-6).
26. Paul Kirchhof, Moris Lehner, Kees van Raad, Arndt Raupach & Michael-Rodi (eds), *International and Comparative Taxation: Essays in Honour of Klaus Vogel,* 2002 (ISBN 90-411-9841-5).
27. Krister Andersson, Peter Melz & Christer Silfverberg (eds), *Liber Amicorum Sven-Olof Lodin,* 2001 (ISBN 90-411-9850-4).
28. Juan Martín Jovanovich, *Customs Valuation and Transfer Pricing: Is It Possible to Harmonize Customs and Tax Rules?,* 2002 (ISBN 90-411-9888-1).
29. Stefano Simontacchi, *Taxation of Capital Gains under the OECD Model Convention: With Special Regard to Immovable Property,* 2007 (ISBN 97-890-411-2549-1).
30. Michael Lang, Josef Schuch, & Claus Staringer (eds), *Tax Treaty Law and EC Law,* 2007 (ISBN 978-90-411-2629-0).
31. Duncan Bentley, *Taxpayers' Rights: Theory Origin and Implementation,* 2007 (ISBN 978-90-411-2650-4).
32. Sergio André Rocha, *Interpretation of Double Taxation Conventions: General Theory and Brazilian Perspective,* 2008 (ISBN 978-90-411-2822-5).
33. Robert F. van Brederode, *Systems of General Sales Taxation: Theory, Policy and Practice,* 2009 (ISBN 978-90-411-2832-4).
34. John G. Head & Richard Krever (eds), *Tax Reform in the 21st Century: A Volume in Memory of Richard Musgrave,* 2009 (ISBN 978-90-411-2829-4).
35. Jens Wittendorff, *Transfer Pricing and the Arm's Length Principle in International Tax Law,* 2010 (ISBN 978-90-411-3270-3).
36. Marjaana Helminen, *The International Tax Law Concept of Dividend,* 2010 (ISBN 978-90-411-3206-2).
37. Robert F. van Brederode (ed.), *Immovable Property under VAT: A Comparative Global Analysis,* 2011 (ISBN 978-90-411-3126-3).
38. Dennis Weber & Stef van Weeghel, *The 2010 OECD Updates: Model Tax Convention & Transfer Pricing Guidelines – A Critical Review,* 2011 (ISBN 978-90-411-3812-5).
39. Yariv Brauner & Martin James Mcmahon, Jr. (eds), *The Proper Tax Base: Structural Fairness from an International and Comparative Perspective—Essays in Honour of Paul McDaniel,* 2012 (ISBN 978-90-411-3286-4).
40. Robert F. van Brederode (ed.), *Science, Technology and Taxation,* 2012 (ISBN 978-90-411-3125-6).
41. Oskar Henkow, *The VAT/GST Treatment of Public Bodies*, 2013 (ISBN 978-90-411-4663-2).